CHINA IN
XI JINPING'S NEW ERA

POLITICS, ECONOMY AND FOREIGN POLICY

CHINA IN XI JINPING'S NEW ERA

POLITICS, ECONOMY AND FOREIGN POLICY

B.R. DEEPAK

PENTAGON PRESS LLP

First published in 2024 by
PENTAGON PRESS LLP
206, Peacock Lane, Shahpur Jat
New Delhi-110049, India
Contact: 011-64706243

Typeset in Times Roman, 11.5 Point
Printed by Aegean Offset Printers, Greater Noida, U.P.

ISBN 978-81-971986-4-9 (HB)

www.pentagonpress.in

Contents

III
SOCIAL ISSUES

IV
RELATIONS WITH MAJOR POWERS

V
INDIA'S CHINA CHALLENGE

Introduction

Looking through the domestic political and socioeconomic decisions that have been made during the last 10 years of Xi Jinping's rule, especially in the last 6 years, we may conclude that Xi has emulated Mao to become a populist nationalist strong leader domestically, and announced the arrival of China as a global power internationally. The former is mirrored by his "people oriented" philosophy (以人为本) of development, the alleviation of poverty in China, the "internal circulation" and advocacy for the so called "common prosperity", for the sake of which he doesn't shy away from cracking down on China's big techs and bigwigs across various sectors including the entertainment industry. The "people oriented" approach also include the COVID-19 handling or mishandling in China and lashing out at countries like India, the US and others for not being able to control the pandemic. It was "a major test of China's system and governance" as put by Xi Jinping in 2020, however, after the initial successes, the three years of stringent COVID controls at the cost of China's economic growth resulted in spontaneous protests across China that forced the regime to loosen restrictions all of a sudden resulting in massive loss of life.

Yet, it would be oversimplification of Xi's domestic political and socioeconomic policies, for the decisions are multi layered and far too complex. For example, it is also about the ultimate control of the Party-State on economic entities, for the economic reforms and liberalisation has indeed breached Party's ultimate control over the Gun and the Yuan. I have witnessed during my China visits that how after taking over the reins of the Party, Xi ordered closure of the PLA businesses across China, but corruption is endemic in any system, especially in authoritarian regimes where power is absolute. This could be gauged from Xi Jinping's anti-corruption campaigns that have gathered steam recently. Recent investigations into the the members of the Central Military commission that include his hand-picked loyalists like Li Shangfu, Zhang Youxia, Liu Zhenli, He Weidong and Zhang Shengmin etc. high ranking officials. Since the PLA Rocket Force and the Equipment Development Department has come under security, Zhang Youxia and Li Shangfu were heading the department. Therefore, there is a huge trust deficit between Xi Jinping and his own lieutenants in the PLA. On the other hand, Xi is wary of how the mega companies in China successfully controlled wealth of the nation, including the sensitive information through big-data. Moreover, it's not just about the tycoons, but also about to whom they are loyal to, pointing fingers towards the "factional feud" within the Party, especially the Shanghai faction that is believed to be controlling the financial nerve of the country. Xi Jinping is apprehensive that these big-tech may get involve in executing the so-called "financial coups" (金融政变). No wonder, Wall Street that once cajoled China, has fallen with Xi Jinping and people like Jack Dorsey, co-founder of Twitter and the investment tycoon Warren Buffet are calling for the "End of CCP". We have witnessed the fate of the IPO of Ant Group and DiDi listing in the US stocks.

Xi Jinping's worries have been exacerbated by the domestic economic slump and shrinking exports and foreign direct investment. The dwindling economic output partially owing to the prolonged COVID-19 restrictions have resulted in the closure of 460,000 small and medium enterprises in 2022, resulting in massive unemployment reaching 23.1 per cent in August 2023. As I have argued in an occasional paper[1] written for the Institute of Chinese Studies that China wishes to swap the Reform Era massive investment growth with the consumption driven growth, however, as there are structural problems with the economic growth model, therefore, the replacement in the short term would be problematic. With the deepening real estate crisis, and unequal distribution of wealth in China, the replacement would be difficult. The magnitude of the investment in infrastructure and real estate could be gauged through official figures released in early February 2023 by Zheng Guoguang, Director of the Office of the Leading Group for the First National Natural Disaster Comprehensive Risk Survey of the State Council. According to the figures, China has around 600 million buildings in urban and rural areas; 5 million kilometres of road networks; 900,000 bridges and tunnels, as well as more than 6,000 berths in coastal areas.[2] This doesn't include around 40,000 kilometres of high speed railway. The consumption and the exports were two other pillars that drove Chinese economic growth, but the figures from the first half the year 2023 are not promising. Especially when over 700 million of Chinese people are in debt and unemployment rate for the age group of 16-24 is over 20 per cent.

In the face of China's economic retrenchment, Xi Jinping has called for the state owned enterprises to play a larger role in the national economy and Party's intervention in government through various reforms. Cutting the mammoth growth of some of the private enterprises is largely owing to Party losing the control and legitimacy on one hand and blunting the finances of the political rivals of Xi who have stakes in these entities on the other. Xi Jinping's response is best captivated in his pronouncements during a visit to the Liaoshen War memorial on 16th August 2022 after the conclusion of the Beidaihe meeting. At the memorial, Xi said that "we will not allow anyone to change the colour of our nation" (我们决不允许江山变色). Conversely, the then premier Li Keqiang going to Shenzhen, one of the first SEZs in China and paying tribute to Deng Xiaoping demonstrated certain disagreements over the question of opening up and reforms. In Shenzhen, Li had declared that "the water of Yangtze and Yellow rivers will not flow backward" (长江黄河不会倒流). No wonder, Li Keqiang was not retained and the entire Central Committee and the Politiburo were studded with Xi loyalists from Fujian, Zhejianag and Shanghai where Xi served for many years. This fundamentally signals whose banner the Party will hold and whose line the Party will follow. These undercurrents in Chinese domestic politics are indicative of widening ideological contradictions within the Party and obviously, it is going to have an adverse impact on China's global image, and further sharpen the debate between the authoritarian regimes and liberal democracies.

Consolidation of domestic power, has resulted into Xi's personality cult and "political correctness" as regards the domestic policies of China are concerned. The "strongman image" of Xi has been held responsible for the so-called "re-education camps" and genocide of the Uighurs, the demolition of "One Country Two Systems" in Hong Kong and now the "change of status quo" in the Taiwan straits and along the India-China border. All these issues have put China in a corner, as there is an increasingly harsh international response, which has been exacerbated by its support to Russia in the wake of Russia-Ukraine War. No wonder, the US scholars have pronounced China as a "coercive and revisionist power" that is seeking to establish a China centric world order, antithetical to the liberal values of the West and its interests. This has also been acknowledged by the Chinese scholarship though qualitatively differently in domestic discourse. For example, Renmin University professor, Di Dongsheng has said that it is China that wishes to decouple from the American bubble, and create a Chinese bubble where the people will follow Chinese system and values.[3] Chinese Rajya gurus such as Zhang Weiwei and Jin Canrong etc. people believe that the US has been on the decline; so much so that it has run out with ideas and are copying the Chinese connectivity initiatives and launching their own such as Build Back Better world, and the establishment of India-Middle East Economic Corridor announced on the sidelines of the 2023 G20 Summit held in Delhi.

In the view of these domestic and international churnings, I am organising some of my articles written for *Sunday Guardian* in this compilation and dedicate to readers. These have been arranged in six sections, namely: Party governance; economic governance; social issues; relations with major powers; India's China Challenge; the Belt and Road Initiative; and China and the Indo-Pacific. Relying on the Chinese sources, the articles peep into the party-state in China and attempt to decipher the direction in which China is heading in the days to come. The book could be useful to academicians, policy formulators, researchers and students who are interested in Chinese politics, economy, society and China's engagement with major powers.

NOTES

1. Deepak, B. R. "China in Xi's "New Era": Denouncing the Era of "Crossing the River by Feeling the Stones" Institute of Chinese Studies Occasional Papers, No. 99, May 2023. https://www.icsin.org/publications/china-in-xis-new-era-denouncing-the-era-of-crossing-the-river-by-feeling-the-stones
2. Zheng Guoguang. "官方披露全国共有 6 亿栋楼，意味着什么?" (Officials revealed that there are 600 million buildings in the country. What does it mean?) https://zhuanlan.zhihu.com/p/609528415
3. Di Dongsheng. "建设后疫情时代的"一带一路", 输出我们强政府的经验与能力" (Build the "Belt and Road" in the post-epidemic era and export our experience and capabilities of strong government) 2 March 2021. https://www.bilibili.com/video/BV1Mh411C7G5/?p=1&share_medium=android&share_plat=android&share_source=COPY&share_tag=s_i×tamp=1612357050&unique_k=KyFHGw

I

PARTY GOVERNANCE

1

Communist Party of China at 100

The establishment of the Communist Party of China (CPC) on 1 July 1921 wasn't an accidental phenomenon. As the old democratic revolution ended in failure, and the repressive warlords connived with the imperialists, New Cultural Movement and its disseminator the *New Youth* established in September 1919, infused new energy into the anti-imperialist and feudal forces, sowed the seeds of communism in China under the stewardship of writers such as Chen Duxiu, Li Dazhao, Mao Zedong and Lu Xun, and ultimately paved way for establishment of the CPC in July 1921 with the help of comintern agent Grigori Voitinsky. After its establishment, the CPC had a brief stint of cooperation with the Kuomintang (KMT) during the First United Front (1924-27) but was soon outlawed by Chiang Kai-shek in the wake of the formation of the nationalist government. The CPC led uprisings in Nanchang (August 1927) and Guangdong (December 1927) ended in failure, however, the Japanese invasion of China's northeast in 1931 provided it a breather and another opportunity to criticise the inability of the KMT to fight the Japanese aggression.

After failure of the Nanchang and Guangdong uprisings, there was a paradigm shift in the leadership as well as its strategy. Even as the pro-Moscow faction went into incognito, Mao Zedong took the centre stage to lead the movement. The goal of realising a workers' revolution changed to peasants' revolution. The tactic of guerrilla warfare against the government oppression was adopted and became the part and parcel of communist strategy. Land reforms were carried out in the communist controlled areas known as Jiangxi Soviets. The pro-Moscow faction tried to assert its control briefly, however, the Zunyi conference of 1935 that resulted in the Long March and finally making Yan'an as the base area, made Mao the ultimate leader of the communist movement in China. The Japanese invasion of China and Chiang's determination to wipe out the communist resistance rather than fighting the Japanese made him extremely unpopular and created fissures inside the KMT army. By the close of the War of Resistance Against Japanese Aggression (1937-1945), communists had established 19 base areas with over hundred million population and half a million-strong army. In such a situation, the show of strength between the CPC and the KMT was imminent resulting in the bloody civil war (1946-1949) and final victory of the CPC and retreat of Chiang to Taiwan in 1949.

When the CPC came to power, it inherited a war ravaged country that was 'poor and blank' (一穷二白) an euphemism for economic impoverishment and cultural backwardness. Therefore, in order to create a favourable external environment for China's political and economic stability, China made an immediate choice, "lean to one side." Since the world was divided into two camps, China's national security was determined by "war is inevitable" a typical Hobbesian concept of malevolent relationship between the states that was coupled with "class struggle" within the state. This was deemed important for laying foundations of the basic socialist system and socialist construction, ultimately resulting in the building socialism with Chinese characteristics or the Sinification of Marxist and Leninist ideology. Massive land reforms, public ownership of the all means of production was carried out, and by the end of 1956 the socialist transformation was almost complete. Mao Zedong envisaged building China into a rich and powerful socialist nation that would catch up and overtake the UK, the US and other developed capitalist countries in 50 to 100 years. But, as differences with the Soviet Union grew, the paradigm shifted to "to fight with two fists" i.e. confrontation with both the superpowers. Since "war is inevitable" and "class struggle" dominated the external and internal discourse, China witnessed various movements such as the "Three Antis", "Five Antis" the "Anti-Rightist", "Great Leap Forward" movements in the 1950s, and finally the "Cultural Revolution" (1966-1976), sometimes also referred as ten years of chaos in China. These inflicted untold miseries on Chinese people, especially the Chinese Great Famine (1959-1961) snatched millions of Chinese lives.

Mao's successor, Deng Xiaoping de-Maoised China, ended the self-imposed isolation by initiating a policy of reforms and open door during the 3rd Plenary Session of the 11th Central Committee of the Communist Party of China in 1978. This happened owing to the policy adjustment of both the US and China as the Soviet Union was perceive as a common enemy. Big plans for economic development such as the "three-stage modernisation formula" were drawn and implemented. The new vision of modernisation paid dividends as China showed its enthusiasm for merchandise and encouraged private enterprise and competition; made serious attempt to import advanced western technology and management skills. China's entry into the World Trade Organisation in 2001 brought in export boom, registering almost 30 per cent annual growth until 2007 capturing more than 10 per cent of the global market. Politically, China sought a stable and peaceful surrounding. The third and fourth generation of Chinese leaders pursued the growth model relentlessly. They not only legitimised the communist rule by adhering to growth model but also set new benchmarks for developments. Especially during Hu Jintao's tenure (2002-2013), China witnessed unprecedented level of economic growth. China's GDP touched $8.3 trillion from a meagre $1.20 trillion when he took over from Jiang Zemin, registering an impressive 10 per cent and above annual growth. Not only the financial crisis was effectively dealt with, but it also together with other Asian economies contributed almost 50 per cent to the world's economic growth during the slump. Rapid growth catapulted China to the second largest economy of the world leaving behind countries like UK, France, Germany and Japan. Urbanisation registered fastest ever growth anywhere in the world, and by the end of 2012 over 52 per cent Chinese were living in the urban areas.

With the ascendency of Xi Jinping and his consolidation of power, China, perhaps again owing to the necessity of power struggle and fissures in the Party line, is harking back to the Mao era, Marx and Marxism, red tradition, the countryside campaign, state dominated economic growth, hyper-nationalism, and the wolf warrior diplomacy. Xi Jinping has put forth his grandiose ideas like the "Chinese Dream" for national rejuvenation, community of shared future for mankind, and "Belt and Road" initiative (BRI) so as to meet new challenges emanating from the US and its allies. These concepts reflect the historical and present realities of China, demonstrate a strong sense of continuity and connectedness, be it Chinese society, the CPC, or China's relations with its neighbours and major powers, however, the same has made many smaller countries vulnerable to China's debt trap. If the interviews of Renmin University Professor Di Dongsheng are to be believed, China wishes to create a "Chinese bubble" where the people around the world will play by Chinese rules as far as the usage of currency, products and consumerism is concerned. This line of thinking will certainty have a backlash. Notwithstanding, the loss of life, China in the past 72 years did alleviate over 850 million people from poverty and made China into a 15.7 trillion-dollar economy. It would be a matter of time when China replaces the US as the largest economy of the world, nevertheless, the CPC leadership is also facing serious external and internal challenges. Externally, the US and its allies have turned heat on China as far as trade and investment, security across the indo-Pacific, and technological collaboration is concerned. Internally, she is faced with issues of dissent, factionalism, aging population and the phenomenon of "lying flat" by the young Chinese who are increasingly losing their faith in social security. Moreover, China returning to Maoism, is likely to turn its relationship with countries into an ideological contest.

2

China's Return to Maoism

The post 1949 internal and external dynamics in China were determined by "war is inevitable" and "class struggle" paradigms. Mao Zedong, the then supreme leader of China, made an immediate choice of "lean to one side", but as differences with the Soviet Union grew, the paradigm shifted to "to fight with two fists" (两个拳头打人), confrontation with both the superpowers. Internally, as the "class struggle" took center stage, various campaigns such as the "Three Antis" (corruption, waste and bureaucracy) of 1951, "Five Antis" (bribery, theft of state property, tax evasion, cheating on government contracts, and stealing state economic intelligence) of 1952, the "Anti-Rightist Campaign between 1957-59, and finally ten years of chaos in form of the "Cultural Revolution" (1966-76) were launched one after another for the need of political struggles that inflicted untold miseries on the Chinese people. The "Red Guards" holding Mao's "Little Red Book" went on rampage, attacked and killed the "imperialists", "bourgeoisie", "capitalist roaders", and intellectuals in those vicious "struggle sessions", even the Confucius and Buddhist statues and temples were vandalised. It has been estimated that during the "Cultural Revolution", also pronounced as "10 bad years of great disaster" (十年浩劫), between half a million to two million people were killed and millions left scarred. If the fatalities caused by the man-made famine of 1958-61 are counted, a study titled "The Demography of China's 1958-61 Famine: A Closer Examination" by Zhao Zhongwei and Anna Reimondos (2012) points to 30 million excess deaths.

Though the Communist Party of China (CPC) never carried out a serious appraisal of the "Cultural Revolution", however, after the demise of Mao, the CPC did hold Mao responsible for the "great proletarian revolution" that he spearheaded. The resolution passed by the Sixth Plenum of the 11th Central Committee on 27 June 1981 entitled "On questions of Party history" pronounced him as arrogant and remarked that he "divorced himself from practice and from the masses, acted more and more arbitrarily and subjectively, and increasingly put himself above the Central Committee of the Party." Nevertheless, the resolution also exonerated him of the crimes by noting that "his contributions to the Chinese revolution far outweigh his mistakes." The criticism was perhaps necessary as China opened to the outside world, dismantled the planned economy gradually and allowed criticism of the "Cultural Revolution" by intellectuals. Since then, many writings appeared on the bookstalls across China, depicting death and destruction. Some narrations of the scarred victims are too graphic and have been known as "scar literature" (伤痕文学) in China.

However, with the ascendency of Xi Jinping and his consolidation of power, China, perhaps again owing to the necessity of power struggle and fissures in the Party line, is harking back to the Mao era, Marx and Marxism, red tradition, the countryside campaign, state dominated economic growth, hyper-nationalism, and the wolf warrior diplomacy. Early in February 2022, the CPC officially released the new version of *A Brief History of the Communist Party of China*, a designated textbook for the study of Party history. The new edition doesn't list the "Cultural Revolution" as a chapter in the contents, but makes it a part of the chapter entitled "Exploration and tortuous development of socialist construction" (1949-1976) and downplays the deaths and miseries inflicted by the "Cultural Revolution" on people as well as the role and motive of Mao Zedong for launching the "Cultural Revolution". Most striking feature of the new Party history is that Xi Jinping and his New Era occupies one-fourth of a century of party history, thus outweighing the socialist construction and reform era of his predecessors. Undoubtedly, without the shock of the "Cultural Revolution", the CPC would not have experimented with the liberalisation. On the other hand, the kind of economic, cultural and political space created by the reforms and individual economy in the last four decades has come back to haunt the CPC of its dangers, especially distrust of the authority by the millennial population. It is for these reasons that people are increasingly witnessing the following phenomena of the so called "Red China" in Xi's new era.

One, literary inquisition/persecution or the so-called *wenziyu* (文字狱), which refers to official persecution of intellectuals for their writings. The literary inquisition starting from the "burning of Confucian classics and burying scholars alive" (焚书坑儒) during the Qin Dynasty (221BC – 206 BC) to present day has gone unabated. Surprisingly, some of these were due to the naming taboo, i.e. even a single Chinese character that is part of emperor's personal name was also forbidden in writings. In recent years, Chinese characters which are negatively associated with Xi Jinping's surname 'Xi' (习) have been proscribed from the Chinese internet. For example, Cui (翠) character (emerald green) has 'xixi' (习习) on top and 'Zu' (卒) at the bottom. If the disassembled characters are translated, it implies Xi or Xi twins are dead. The bottom of Cui (翠) character is also read as 'cu' (卒) which means a pawn, therefore one can imagine the sensitivities related to these characters. Another hilarious example is how the characters such as 'louxi' (陋习 bad habits) have been changed to 'louren' (陋刃 bad blades) in a slogan "Raise the standard of civilized hygiene, get rid of bad blades" (提高文明卫生水平 革除陋刃) owing to the naming taboo. Netizens drawing comparison between Winnie the Pooh and Chinese President have also been censored.

Two, censoring of former Premier Wen Jiabao's letter, a tribute to his late mother published by *Macao Herald* is another case of literary inquisition. The reasons behind the censure are attributed to Wen's veiled criticism of Xi Jinping's policies and the "Cultural Revolution". One, the former Premier said in his tribute, "I retired (我退休了), after having worked in the Zhongnanhai for 28 years, including 10 years as Premier." This is construed as his veiled attack on Xi Jinping changing the constitution and wanting to become president for life. Two, he castigated "Cultural Revolution" many a times in his letter contrary to idolizing the symbols of "cultural Revolution" in the new era. He wrote, "During the 'Cultural Revolution', his father was imprisoned in a school and often subjected to barbaric (野蛮的) 'interrogation', beatings and abuses ("审讯" 和打骂)". Third, he envisaged a China that is "full of fairness and justice" (公平正义) hinting that he has opinion about the direction in which the Chinese society is heading. In the same vein, when Chinese origin Chloe Zhao won the Best Director award for her film "Nomadland" at the Golden

Globes in February, the film was censored in China, only for one reason that a decade back she had described China as "a place where there are lies everywhere". The "witch hunt" and purges of the "virus carriers" is not limited to Hong Kong and Xinjiang, the mainland Chinese have also faced the brunt. For example, recently a 19 years old Wang Jingyu, a resident of Chongqing municipality in Sichuan was arrested by the UAE police for extradition to China according to Wang. Wang's only 'crime' is that early in February 2022, he questioned China's version of the PLA causalities in the Galwan border clash. Another netizen called Qiu Ziming who also doubted the Chinese version of Galwan fatalities was sentenced to 8 months in prison for "defaming heroes and martyrs" on 1 June 2021. Many such people have been pronounced as "bedbugs" (臭虫) for "criticizing and discrediting the heroes" by state media.

Three, elimination of political enemies and opponents through campaigns like "Killing tigers and swatting flies" (打虎拍蝇) (tiger and flies is a euphemism for corrupt high and low ranking officials) and "Sweep away black and eliminate evil" (扫黑除恶) are been persistently carried out. Right from 2012 until last year, around 4 million officials across military, judiciary, law enforcement agencies, finance sector have been investigated. These included top guns like Bo Xilai, Zhou Yongkang, Ling Jihua, Xu Caihou, Guo Boxiong and Sun Zhengcai. Xi Jinping's long-time confidant, Wang Qishan, Chairman of the Central Commission for Discipline Inspection (CCDI) was instrumental in these campaigns. The Supervisory Commission that replaced the CCDI has been given sweeping powers to supervise over the malpractices related to corruption and other misconduct not only within the Party but across the entire government machinery and enterprises. As it has happened during various political campaigns and movements including the "Cultural Revolution", the CPC is encouraging people to report each other for "black and evil" offences. No wonder in 2020, 16,000 people across the country voluntarily turned themselves in to the discipline and supervision organs, and 66,000 voluntarily held themselves accountable for the problems according to the official figures, strikingly synonymous to the "rectification" and "criticism and self-criticism" campaigns of yesteryears.

Four, crackdown on "tigers and flies" may have diminished the possibilities of potential "political coups" to some extent, but the factional feud has intensified and spilled over to the state as well as private enterprises. Xi Jinping has clipped the wings of Shanghai clique by way of striking hard on their investments in entities like Jack Ma's Ant Group. Anti-monopoly crackdown has forced entities like, Tencent, ByteDance to pay heavy fines and change the leadership at top. Entrepreneurs like Sun Dawu and Zhang Zhixiong have been imprisoned for building agriculture and mining empires. Real estate tycoon Ren Zhiqiang, a close friend of Wang Qishan has also been proved and jailed for his criticism of Xi Jinping. It is perhaps the Ren Zhiqiang issue and investigation of Wang's aide Dong Hong, a senior disciplinary inspector of the CCDI that are said to be responsible for a wedge between Xi Jinping and Wang Qishan. Though the people who have been investigated have been pronounced as "liberals" in China, however, the main reason is said to avoid potential "financial coups" by these tycoons. With state tightening its noose around the business empires created during the golden age of deep globalisation, the individual economy is expected to face a rough ride in the coming days.

Finally, the ghost of "victim's psychology" added to the narrative of a "century of humiliation" and newly found economic and military prowess, perhaps has resulted in China's assertiveness demonstrated by its military show offs and wolf warrior diplomacy. This certainly is the microcosm of domestic political environment but devoid of the intensity of fear, mutual suspicion, distrust and policy paralysis of the "Cultural Revolution" when senior officials were browbeaten by the young red guards. Nonetheless, the undisputed role of Xi Jinping in foreign policy like Mao Zedong has been institutionalised and monopolised since his ascendancy to power, particularly after his thought was enshrined in the CPC and state constitutions. If Mao Zedong wished to export communism to the world, Xi Jinping is selling the "Belt and Road Initiative" and the notions such as "building communities of shared future" etc. with an unprecedented economic muscle, and the perceived superiority of the "Beijing consensus." But don't forget that China's permanent membership to the United Nations Security Council was restored during the "Cultural Revolution", and ice was broken with the US as relations with the Soviet Union turned hostile, a decision that has come back to haunt the US.

3

Power Struggle within China

Ever since his ascendance to power, President Xi Jinping has eliminated political enemies across military, judiciary, law enforcement agencies and finance sector. Some of the bigwigs who have been investigated and penalized include Bo Xilai, Zhou Yongkang, Ling Jihua, Xu Caihou, Guo Boxiong and Sun Zhengcai. Investigations are conducted by the Central Commission for Discipline Inspection (CCDI), China's top anti-graft body under the sweeping anti-corruption campaigns like "Killing tigers and swatting flies" (打虎拍蝇), and "Sweep away black and eliminate evil" (扫黑除恶). The hammer has also fallen on those who ironically were associated with probing some of these cases. The recent penalisation of Sun Lijun, Vice Minister of the Ministry of Public Security, and Fu Zhenghua, former Minister of Justice is a pointer.

On 30 September 2021, in a 700-character denunciation published on the CCDI official website said that "Sun Lijun, former member of the Party Committee and Vice Minister of the Ministry of Public Security, has been expelled from the Party and public office for serious violations of discipline and law." Two days later, on 2 October 2021, the same website posted that "Fu Zhenghua, Deputy Director of the Social and Legal Committee of the CPPCC National Committee, is suspected of serious violations of discipline and law, and is currently undergoing disciplinary review and investigation by the CCDI." Both Sun and Fu have been associated with the notorious "610 Office" established during Jiang Zemin's reign for persecuting Falun Gong practitioners and followers. Fu tried to win over Xi by distancing himself from the "Jiang Faction" and bringing down titans like Zhou Yongkang and Hu Jintao's aide Ling Jihua. Both were given life sentences in 2014 and 2016 respectively. Sun who was instrumental in preparing the ground for new security law for Hong Kong since 2017 also failed to win the trust of their leader.

Most of the content of the 700-character denunciation of Sun, is pretty routine vocabulary used for almost all the convicts, however, what stands out are two things. First, Sun has been accused of wantonly forming gangs inside the Party (在党内大搞团团伙伙), and the second is abandoning his post from the front line of the fight against the COVID-19 pandemic (在抗击新冠肺炎疫情一线擅离职守) and secretly possessing a large amount of classified material (私藏私放大量涉密材料) pertaining to the pandemic.

As regard the first, it is linked to the cases of people like Meng Hongwei, the former Interpol president who also served as Vice Minister of the Ministry of Public Security, Wang Like, former member of the Standing Committee of the Jiangsu Provincial Party Committee, his subordinate Luo Wenjin, former police chief, Criminal Investigation Department of Jiangsu Public Security Department, and now Fu Zhenghua. It may be remembered that when Sun Lijun was investigated last year on 19 April, Fu Zhenghua was quickly removed from the post of Minister of Justice. This together with Fu 'accepting' investigations on 2 October 2021, two days after Sun's verdict, cannot be a mere coincidence. These are believed to be closely linked to Zhou Yongkang, even Wang Lijun, the Chongqing police officer, who sought refuge in the US consulate in Chengdu during Bo Xilai affair, is believed to have close connections with the above people. The second accusation demonstrates that rather than combating COVID-19 in Wuhan in early 2020, Sun left for some other place while in possession of a large amount of classified material pertaining to the pandemic. It is believed that since the wife and son of Sun live in Australia, he could have shared sensitive information about the pandemic and Wuhan Institute of Virology with his wife, which is likely to have been intercepted by the Australian intelligence. This could also be the reason as to why Australia became the first and rather vociferous about demanding investigations into the origin of the COVID-19, risking deterioration of its bilateral relations with China.

It appears that the factional feud is getting intensified before convening of the 20th Party Congress next year. Chinese official media, *Xinhua News Agency* has admitted to existence of factions within the Party.

On 3 January 2015, in a report it referred to factions such as "secretaries gang" (秘书帮), "petroleum gang" (石油帮) and "Shanxi gang" (山西帮), attributed to once powerful petroleum and security czar, Zhou Yongkang and Ling Jihua, former director of the Central Committee General Office. Another commentary on CPC website on 5 January 2015 had stated that "Beneath the old tigers, there are big tigers, and behind the big tigers there are foxes and rats. Where gangs form, there are also gang lords; where there are cliques, there are also 'mountain tops,' and these kinds of 'mountain tops' are very harmful to our Party." Now, who are these "big" and "old" tigers behind the fallen "tigers" of political and legal system of China? The fingers are pointed towards Meng Jianzhu, a former member of the Political Bureau of the Communist Party of China and secretary of the Central Political and Legal Affairs Commission. Behind Meng Jianzhu, it is believed is the hand of Jiang Zemin and Zeng Qinghong. It appears that after having cleansed the army, bigtech, finance sector of his detractors, Xi Jinping is gradually cleaning the sensitive political and legal system, which is supposedly infested with "remaining toxin' of the "petroleum" and "Jiangxi gang."

4

The Rise and Rise of Xi Jinping

The Sixth Plenary Session of the 19th Central Committee of the Communist Party of China (CPC) was held between 8 and 11 November 2021. Though not spelt out in the communiqué that was issued at the close of the session, but has silently endorsed the unprecedented 3rd term for Xi Jinping, thus breaking away from the 10 years and 7 up and 8 down (七上八下) succession rule set by Deng Xiaoping after the demise of Mao Zedong. Of the 7th plenary sessions held in a period of five years, the 6th is generally dedicated to ideology and party building. The 6th plenum passed a landmark document titled the "Resolution on the major achievements and historical experience of the CPC's 100 years of endeavours" that establishes Xi's paramountcy at par with Mao and Deng. The tone was set by Xinhua in a near 13,500 character long essay entitled "Xi Jinping leads a century-old party on a new journey" on 6 November 2021. The article, flagged out his grass root connections, right from a very young age, be it his assignment in Liangjiahe, Shaanxi or Zhengding in Hebei or in Fujian and Zhejiang, and the direction and leadership he has provided to the CPC and China ever since he took reins of power in 2012.

Why are people debating the 'resolution' of 6th plenum? Well, the answer lies in the fact that over the past 100 years, the CPC has adopted just two resolutions related to historical issues, in 1945 under Mao and in 1981 under Deng. The First Resolution, analysed and drew conclusions on important historical events and personalities, and established undisputed leadership of Mao and his thought within the CPC. Chiang Kai-shek and Wang Jingwei were labelled as betrayers of the First United Front between the communists and nationalists; Chen Duxiu was blamed for "right capitulationism" (右倾机会主义), Wang Ming for his "left adventurism" (左倾盲动主义), Zhang Guotao for splittism (分裂主义), and Wang Ming, who criticized Mao's tactics and ideology was declared as self-styled "imperial envoy" (钦差大臣) of the Communist International and publically humiliated during the Yan'an Rectification Movement (1942-45). People who criticized the core leadership, were subjected to struggle sessions, tortured and even executed. It is estimated that around 10,000 people died during the Yan'an Rectification Movement. But, China, in the process of struggle, "produced its own leader, Comrade Mao Zedong, who on behalf of the Chinese people and proletariat, creatively applied the highest wisdom of mankind, the scientific theory of Marxism-Leninism, to Chinese conditions," said the first paragraph of the Resolution.

The Second Resolution passed by the 6th Plenum of the 11th Central Committee on 27 June 1981 entitled "On questions of Party history" confirmed the historical role of Mao Zedong and his thought, however, also pronounced Mao as arrogant and remarked that he "divorced himself from practice and from the masses, acted more and more arbitrarily and subjectively, and increasingly put himself above the Central Committee of the Party." Nevertheless, the resolution also exonerated him of the crimes by noting that "his contributions to the Chinese revolution far outweigh his mistakes." The criticism was perhaps necessary as China opened to the outside world, dismantled planned economy of the Mao era gradually and allowed criticism of the "Cultural Revolution" by intellectuals. The second resolution established the paramountcy of Deng Xiaoping in the CPC, which continued during the entire reform era (1979-2012) and his theory was enshrined in the party constitution at par with Mao's thought. Chinese people broke the "spiritual shackles of the personality cult and the dogmatism" as specified by the resolution, and rose to become the world factory and second largest economy in the world. It is generally believed that the first two resolutions on historical issues, played an extremely important role in confirming the guiding ideology and achievements of the core leadership on the one hand, and building consensus within the party in order to fulfil new targets and deadlines set by the leadership.

The Third Resolution like the previous two, confirmed the role played by previous leadership, and catapulted Xi Jinping to the position of a paramount leader and his thought at par with Mao's thought and Deng's theory. The communiqué that was issued on 11 November, devoted maximum space to Xi Jinping and least to Jiang Zemin. No wonder, the document in a veiled criticism to Jiang Zemin and Hu Jintao rule, pronounced it as "lax and weak governance (宽松软状况) which has been fundamentally addressed since ascendance of Xi to power. It endorsed Xi Jinping at the core and called upon the party, military and Chinese people to unite more closely (更加紧密地团结) around the core. His people centred (以人民为中心) philosophy, anti-corruption campaign and poverty alleviation, governance (治国理政), Five-Sphere Integrated Plan (五位一体 coordinated economic, political, cultural, social, and ecological advancement), Four-Pronged Comprehensive Strategy (四个意识 building a moderately prosperous society in all respects, deepen reform, advance law-based governance, and strengthen Party self-governance), Four matters of confidence (四个自信 confidence in the path, theory, system, and culture of socialism with Chinese characteristics), Two upholds (两个维护 resolutely uphold General Secretary Xi Jinping's core position on the Party Central Committee and in the Party as a whole, and resolutely uphold the Party Central Committee's authority and its centralized, unified leadership), essentially parts of his thought, have been given prominence throughout the document, albeit some were left out in the English version of the communiqué. A few others, such as his "dual circulation" and the "third distribution" whereby Xi has asked the rich to pay back to society were enumerated by Xinhua article. The anti-corruption campaign has also been seen as a measure to consolidate Xi's power and purge his detractors. According to the above Xinhua article, in the last 9 years over 400 officials at ministerial level or above have been penalised or investigated, which included people from the Standing Committee of the Political Bureau and Central Military Commission.

With realising the first centenary in 2021 by building a moderately prosperous society in all respects after eradicating absolute poverty, Xi has been mandated to take China towards realising the socialist modernisation in 2035 and the second centenary goals of China by the middle of this century, thus realising the Chinese dream of national rejuvenation, and China taking the centre stage in global affairs. His role in handling the US-China trade war, security related issues in the neighborhood or other global challenges like the COVID-19 pandemic, climate change, as well as his advocacy for building a 'health silk road', an extension of the Belt and Road Initiative and "community of shared future for the mankind," are also highlighted by the communiqué and Xinhua alike. However, the communiqué is tight lipped on some of the more problematic issues such as Tian'anmen massacre, Mao's man-made famine, and the cultural revolution that saw unprecedented death and destruction in China. This not alone, Xi Jinping has refrained from listing the "Cultural Revolution" as a separate chapter in the newly revised party history entitled *A Brief History of the Communist Party of China* early 2021. It has been made a part of the socialist construction period (1949-1976). Most striking feature of the new Party history is that Xi Jinping and his new era occupies one-fourth of a century of party history, thus outweighing the socialist construction and reform era of his predecessors. This in other words has been regarded as the beginning of new literary inquisition in China, nonetheless, denying serious appraisal of the blunders of the party will continue to haunt the CPC and draw criticism for years to come.

Though not spelled in the communiqué, the resolution, besides granting Xi the third term, also gives him unprecedented powers to designate his successor, and perhaps also restoring the title of Chairman. Coinciding with Xinhua article on 6 November, Singapore's *Strait Times* quoting an insider revealed that Xi Jinping is "mulling over a new succession system" in the place of an "unreasonable" old one. He is unwilling to let Jiang Zemin or Hu Jintao decide his successor. The article hints that Xi is likely to incorporate a number of his lieutenants in the central committee, monitor their 'performance' and elevate them to the desired position whenever he deems it fit. People like Chen Miner, secretary of the Chongqing Municipal Committee of the CPC, Ding Xuexiang, director of the Central Office of the CPC, Hu Chunhua, vice premier of the State Council, Li Qiang, secretary of the Shanghai Municipal Committee of the CPC, and Li Xi, secretary of the Guangdong Provincial Party Committee etc. are likely to be incorporated. In a nutshell, the third resolution has brought down curtains on the reform era, the journey for Xi Jinping in the new era is not going to be easy given the internal and external challenges China is facing amidst the pandemic. It is going to be full of struggles, black swans and grey rhinos to quote Xi's own phraseology.

5

China's Faction Feud Extends to Wall Street

Imagine a company losing US$ 10 billion since its inception and filing for an initial public offering (IPO) on the New York Stock Exchange at a valuation of US$ 68 billion, the biggest by any Chinese company since Alibaba's in 2014. The company in question is DiDi Chuxing, China's top ride-hailing app founded in 2012 by Cheng Wei, a former employee of Alibaba Group's regional and Alipay's operations. The company is headquartered in Beijing with 377 million car-riders, 13 million drivers and has around 80 per cent of the market share in China. Japan's Softbank Group's Vision Fund is the biggest shareholder with 20.1 per cent, followed by Uber's 11.9 per cent, Cheng Wei's 7 per cent and Tencent Holding's 6.4 per cent shares.

However, two days after its listing on 30 June 2021, the Cyberspace Administration of China (CAC) launched an investigation citing issues related to national data security, and ordered for DiDi's apps to be removed from app stores in China. The investigation knocked off around US$ 25 billion within a week and the shareholders are so perturbed that they filed lawsuits accusing DiDi of not disclosing information about its compliance with cybersecurity laws and regulations of China. Why should China crack down on its tech giants in the first place? Is it because of the antitrust investigations? Or is it due to the so-called antimonopoly policies of China as was the case with other tech giants including Alibaba? Or is there something else brewing inside China?

One, it cannot be a case of antitrust and market monopoly alone, for the simple reason that state investors such as Bank of Communication, China Merchant Bank, Poly Capital, China Life, CICC Alpha, CITIC capital, Pingan Insurance, and a dozen more have offered massive credit lines to DiDi. No wonder DiDi raised billions of dollars and forced Uber, the market leader in the segment, to sell its China business to it for US$ 35 billion in 2016, albeit it was allowed to retain 5.8 per cent shares in DiDi. Though the US-based Uber was kicked out of China with the help of Chinese state and private capital, but it was also the time when antimonopoly investigations were initiated against DiDi. Owing to DiDi's strong ties with the state apparatus, these investigations made little headway. Moreover, had it been for market monopoly, other state-owned tech giants such as China Mobile, China Telecom, China Unicom and many others would have faced investigations long back.

Two, the faction feud within the Communist Party of China has spilled over onto Wall Street. Liu Qing, a Harvard graduate, CEO of DiDi, is the daughter of Liu Chuanzhi, founder of Lenovo, who is considered to be close to Alibaba's Jack Ma. The above-mentioned equity capitals that are run by sons and daughters of the princelings have major stakes in DiDi. Boyu Capital is run by Jiang Zemin's grandson Jiang Zhicheng; Zhu Yunlai, former CEO of the CICC Alpha, is son of Premier Zhu Rongji; Pingan Insurance is managed by the relatives of former Premier Wen Jiabao; Liu Lefei, present chairman of the CITIC capital is son of the former politburo standing committee member Liu Yunshan. Some like Boyu Capital has huge stakes in Alibaba's Ant Group too. It is believed that irrespective of Xi Jinping gaining control of the People's Liberation Army, it is the princelings of Jiang faction that hold sway in the big businesses across China, especially in Guangdong province, largest province by GDP in China in 2020 (US$ 1.7 trillion). It is perhaps owing to the fear of "financial coups" that Xi Jinping is tightening the noose around the Shanghai clique. This is likely to turn the heat on DiDi's investors, and we should not be surprised if some more "tigers and flies" come a cropper.

Three, wary of strong connections of the Chinese hi-tech companies with the "princelings" and bigwigs of Wall Street, the CPC has come to realise that organs like the Securities Regulatory Commission (SRC) have failed to stop Chinese companies from listing abroad. It has been revealed that China had asked DiDi to put its IPO on hold as the CPC was celebrating its centenary on 1 July, but it appears that the investors were in a hurry and brushed aside the request. The loss of face made Xi Jinping to direct organs such as General Office of the Central Committee of the Communist Party of China and the General Office of the State Council issue "Opinions on Strictly Cracking Down on Illegal Securities Activities in accordance with the Law" on 6 July 2021. Section 5, Article 19 particularly deals with strengthening judicial cooperation in cross-border supervision, supervision of China's concept stocks, and system of extraterritorial application of capital market laws. It talks about improving data security, cross-border data flow, confidential information management and other relevant laws and regulations. It appears that some of the powers of the SRC, the State Administration of Market Regulations (SAMR) will be taken over by the CAC. The likely repercussions will be conscious or unconscious decoupling of China's "private" enterprises from the US. This conforms to what Renmin University professor, Di Dongsheng has said that it is China that wishes to decouple from the American bubble.

Four, data security has been cited as one of the reasons for punishing DiDi. In 2020, a bill passed by the US Congress and signed into law by Donald Trump stipulates that the audit papers of US-listed Chinese companies must be open for US regulatory inspection; failing to comply with this law will invite delisting. China's above mentioned telecom giants were delisted earlier this year. According to the *Global Times*, "this highly unfriendly move, plus Trump's high-profile assault on Huawei, ZTE and approximately three dozen of Chinese high-tech companies, seriously damaged bilateral ties". China "hardening its regulations" according to the paper could be attributed to the US posturing. Besides the "Opinions" issues by the CPC Central Committee and the State Council, the Standing Committee of the National People's Congress has passed a Data Security Law that makes it mandatory for all Chinese companies and entities to acquire government approval before providing any China based data to foreign entities and agencies. China is also working on another law on the protection of personal information. China fears that DiDi could have compromised China's data security law including some of the very sensitive details about maps and military entities inside China, albeit this has been denied by DiDi.

Finally, it could be discerned that outlawing DiDi is not as simple as it appears. It is far more complex, revealing a power struggle within China, unholy alliances between the investors, officials and political elites, China's financial war with the US, market monopolies, and even national security issues, among others. In the coming weeks, DiDi's business operation will come under stricter scrutiny of China's main antitrust watchdogs, the CAC and the SAMR, as has been the case with China's other tech giants including Alibaba, Tencent, Baidu, Ant Group, ByteDance Ltd., JD.com Inc. and Pinduoduo Inc. Ant Group's IPO was blocked and Alibaba was fined US$ 2.8 billion by SAMR. DiDi's quantum of punishment is likely to be much harsher, for it will serve a warning to those who are circumventing and undermining the party's state control.

6

Xi Jinping's Third Term: Beidaihe and Beyond

At the close of the secretive Beidaihe meeting, Xi Jinping headed to the Liaoshen Campaign Memorial in Jinzhou on 16 August 2022. Xi also had a meeting with the representatives of veteran soldiers and relatives of revolutionary martyrs and expressed his sincere solicitude to them. Liaoshen Campaign, turned the tide of the Civil War (1946-1949) in favour of the Communist Party of China (CPC) and marked the beginning of the KMT's ultimate downfall in mainland China. Xi Jinping harped on about the sacrifices of the people of northeast to the Chinese revolution and emphasised that "we will never allow the country to change its colour" (我们决不允许江山变色). Besides, he also talked about his favourite common prosperity, self-reliance and the Chinese dream. On the same day, Premier Li Keqiang headed to Shenzhen, the cradle of China's reform and opening up, and paid tribute to Deng Xiaoping. Li Keqiang emphatically declared about reforms that "Yangtze and Yellow rivers will not flow backward" (长江黄河不会倒流).

This has put both the leaders poles apart as far as future direction China will take, but also has given rise to speculations that "Li is likely to be promoted and Xi will not step down" (李上习不下). This is to say that after the 20th National Congress of the CPC, Li Keqiang could take over the post of general secretary and be in charge of the Party and the government, while Xi Jinping will still hold the positions of President and Chairman of the Central Military Commission. It could also mean to replicate the decision of the First Plenary Session of the Eighth CPC

Central Committee, where Mao Zedong was elected as chairman of the Central Committee and Deng Xiaoping as general secretary. However, given Xi Jinping's clout over the Party and the PLA, it is a wishful thinking. Nonetheless, it does reveal about the differences as regards Party's "general line" (总路线) and the criticism Xi must have faced for economic misgovernance and the lingering dynamic COVID zero policy. The history of the CPC stands witness to the political struggles that resulted from differing perceptions on the "general line" of the Party – be it the Wang Ming-Mao Zedong showoff or that between Hua Guofeng and Deng Xiaoping.

In this backdrop, while the third-term for Xi Jinping is very certain, however, it appears that there would be two-three changes in the Standing Committee of the Political Bureau if the convention, excluding Xi (69) is followed. According to the rule of "seven up eight down" (七上八下) initiated since the 15th Party Congress, Li Zhanshu (72), and Han Zheng (68) should be stepping down at the 20th Party Congress. Li Keqiang (67), Wang Yang (67), Wang Huning (67), Zhao Leji (65) should continue. However, there is no age limit written down in any official Party document, therefore, would be the prerogative of the "core leader" whom to retain and whom to exclude. According to this proposition, only two positions are falling vacant. The likely contenders are, Hu Chunhua (59) and Ding Xuexiang (59). In this scenario, Li Keqiang could be delegated to lead the National People's Congress (NPC) or the Chinese People's Political Consultative Conference (CPPCC). His position is likely to be filled by Wang Yang or Hu Chunhua, however, from a two-term perspective for a premier, chances of Hu Chunhua looks more promising.

The above arrangement will still strike a balance between Xi Jinping's faction and the Communist Youth League (CYL). Or, will Li Keqiang take retirement, as was revealed during the "Two Sessions" early this year? Will Xi Jinping agree to this kind of balance between his own grouping and the CYL? Or will he incorporate more of his loyalists like Chen Miner (62), CPC secretary of Chongqing, Li Qiang (63), Shanghai Communist Party chief, Cai Qi (67), CPC secretary of Beijing, and Li Xi (66), CPC secretary of Guangdong. Here again, Chen Miner and Li Qiang could be catapulted to the standing committee, if more than three positions are vacated, which appears to be a remote possibility. Therefore, from a futuristic scenario, only Hu Chunhua and Ding Xuexiang could be prepared for taking the mantle of the government and Party in the future. In case the standing committee is enlarged to nine members, Xi Jinping will have better choice to incorporate his own loyalists.

As regards the government, it is perhaps too early to speculate. Liu He's job could be delegated to He Lifeng (67), current Minister in charge of the National Development and Reform Commission (NDRC). The void created by Yang Jiechi (72) could be filled by the seasoned Wang Yi (68) if the rule book is not followed, but latter's replacement is still anyone's guess. Former Vice Foreign Minister Le Yucheng (59) was once considered as a strong contender, however, his pro Russia credentials, perhaps became problematic, especially after the Russian invasion of Ukraine, and hence was shifted to the National Radio and Television Administration. Nonetheless, he could be recalled to take up the mantle, if not, others in the line such as Liu Haixing (59), Liu Jianchao (58), Liu Jieyi (64) or even Qin Gang (56) could be called to shoulder the responsibility.

Finally, anything is possible given China's political system and the absolute power exercised by the top political leaders. We won't be surprised if some more tigers and flies fall from grace before the 20th National Congress. Moreover, since Xi Jinping is highly unconventional and has made no secret of his disdain for conventions in the Party, there could be many surprises! As regards what "banner" to hold and what "line" to follow, in all probability it will be along the resolution of the 6th plenum passed in November 2021.

7

20th Party Congress and the New "Regulations" for Cadres

On 19 September 2022, the *People's Daily*, the mouthpiece of the Communist Party of China (CPC) published the newly revised "Regulations on the selection and appointment of leading cadres of the party and government" (hereafter, Regulations). The "Regulations" were issued by the General Office of the Central Committee of the CPC, after these were deliberated upon and revised by the Standing Committee of the Political Bureau of the CPC Central Committee in August this year. The revision has been carried out on the "Regulations" that were issued in 2015, is unprecedented and capable of rendering wrong all the predictions made by China hands in terms of promotion and retirement of the CPC stalwarts in the Party and government for the prospective 20th Party Congress to be held in October 2022. How are the new "Regulations" different from the old ones?

One, the Articles 4, 5 and 6 of the 2015 "Regulations" categorically use terms such as "retire upon attaining the age" (到龄免职), "retire at the end of their term" (任期届满离任), "retirement age limit" (任职年龄界限), "tenure system" (任期制度), "number of terms" (届数) and "the maximum term" (最高任职年限) etc., clearly demonstrating that these were sort of hard rules implemented in principle since the 1990s. Other stipulations such as the cadres shall adhere to the CPC ideals and beliefs, honesty, and whether they have a sense of responsibility, lack objectivity, flexibility etc., were secondary limits. The new version of the "Regulations", therefore, abolishes the term limit, as well as the convention of "seven up and eight down" not only for Xi Jinping himself but across the spectrum and gives the "core leader" absolute powers in the selection, appointment and removal of cadres from the Party and government alike.

Implying that my speculations about Politburo Standing Committee of the 20th Party Congress could go wrong. I had argued that there would be two-three changes in the Standing Committee of the Political Bureau if the age-limit convention, excluding for Xi (69), is followed. According to the rule of "seven up eight down" initiated since the 15th Party Congress, Li Zhanshu (72), and Han Zheng (68) should be stepping down at the 20th Party Congress. Li Keqiang (67), Wang Yang (67), Wang Huning (67), Zhao Leji (65) should continue. If the revised "Regulations" are implemented all Xi Jinping loyalists, irrespective of their age could be retained and those belonging to other factions could be asked to stepdown. At present in the Politburo, Xi Jinping and his loyalists account for around 50 per cent, the same may jump to 70-80 per cent if the revised "Regulations" prevail.

Two, absolute powers accorded to Xi Jinping in the selection of cadres is also demonstrated by the fact that the 2022 "Regulations" put "adherence to the guidance of Xi Jinping Thought on Socialism with Chinese Characteristics for a New Era to prominence"; implementing the spirit of Xi Jinping's speeches as was the case with the 2015 "Regulations" has been dropped. While responding to reporters' questions, an official from the General Office of the Central Committee of the CPC said that the revision was carried out in the view that "Party Central Committee with Comrade Xi Jinping as the core has stood at the strategic height (战略高度) of leading the great social revolution (引领伟大社会革命) with the Party's great self-revolution (党的伟大自我革命), and has made a series of measures to comprehensively and strictly govern the Party…and has made breakthroughs in solving issues related to cadres retirement."

Three, Article 4 of the new version stipulates the "key is to solve the problem of being able to step down" (重点是解决能下问题). In and around these Party congresses, it has been observed that in order to make a cadre "step down" the Party often slapped serious charges of corruption or misuse of power and position. Article 5 of the revised "Regulations" stipulates that a cadre who has one of the following fifteen deficiencies, is deemed unsuitable for his current position. These include, lacking political ability, shaken ideals and beliefs, lacking sense of responsibility and fighting spirit, deviation from political achievements, violation of party's principle of democratic centralism, lacking organisational concept, lacking sense of professionalism, lacking leadership quality, laxity in work, misconduct, foreign immigration related issues of cadres and their spouses, negative annual assessment, health issues, and other circumstances. It could be discerned that "absolute loyalty" is the sole benchmark, which is also reflected in the recent "death penalty commuted to life" for former justice minister, Fu Zhenghua, his associate former Jiangsu deputy governor Wang Li'ke, and the "leader of clique" Sun Lijun, the once powerful deputy minister of China's public security. All are accused of corruption and being disloyal to Xi Jinping.

Finally, the revised "Regulations" further confirm Xi Jinping's hold on the Party, the People's Liberation Army, and the government. This is also an indication that in years to come, China will hold the "banner and line" of Xi Jinping's thought, making him the most powerful leaders since Mao Zedong. Abolition of the articles 4, 5 and 6 of the 2015 "Regulations" is a pointer to the fact that these were the product of the "reform and opening up era" and are not in sync with Xi Jinping's new era. The former mirrors China's commitment to the liberal order, and the latter signals China taking the centre stage in the global affairs and wanting to establish a new order.

If this is the case, mutual decoupling by China and the West in the new era will intensify. The ideological divide, too is poised to become intense. China in the new era appears to be looking inward; no wonder, "closed door policy" (闭关锁国) of the Ming-Qing China has been reinterpreted as "self-imposed restrictions" (自主限关) by none other than academicians from the Chinese Academy of History, a think-tank under the prestigious Chinese Academy of Social Sciences. The scholars have argued in a recent article that "the central government of the Ming and Qing dynasties adopted a foreign policy of "self-imposed restrictions". In the hindsight, whether to open up, how to open up, and how wide must be the scope of opening up, falls within the ambit of national sovereignty. Some scholars at home and abroad simply denounce it as "backward", and "barbaric", so much so they think that it violates the so-called "international law", which is completely untenable."

8

The Second Decade of Xi Jinping

The 7th plenary session of the 19th Central Committee of the Communist Party of China (CPC) that concluded on 12 October 2022 issued a near 3000 characters communiqué, took stock of the achievements of the Party and the state in the past five years, discussed and adopted a report to be made by the 19th CPC Central Committee to the 20th CPC National Congress, a work report of the 19th CPC Central Commission for Discipline Inspection (CCDI) to the congress, and an amendment to the CPC Constitution. The communiqué mentioned Xi Jinping 14 times, Xi at the core (核心) eight times, and Xi Jinping Thought on Socialism with Chinese Characteristics for a New Era five times.

The plenary session summed up the work of the five years and agreed that the "major achievements" of the Party and the country in the five years are the result of the "strong leadership" (坚强领导) of the Party Central Committee with "Comrade Xi Jinping at its core" and the guidance of Xi Jinping Thought on Socialism with Chinese Characteristics for a New Era. Eradication of absolute poverty (2020), completion of the historical task of building a moderately prosperous society in all respects (2021) and achieving the first centenary goal (2021) figured prominently. It was also emphasized that from here on, the CPC will embark on a new journey of building a modern socialist country (2035), and march toward the second centenary goal (2049), an agenda set by Xi Jinping during the 19th Party Congress. The principle of "people's supremacy and the supremacy of life" (人民至上, 生命至上) has been reiterated. It appears that the "dynamic zero

COVID policy" will not be withdrawn immediately even if the same has adversely impacted on China's economic growth.

This has set the ball rolling for the 20th Party Congress to be convened from 16 October and an unprecedented third and more terms for Xi Jinping. Three major areas where China watchers would be looking for clues, are where the Party, economy and foreign policy will be heading towards. In an "Expert Scholars' Dialogue" on China's 20th CPC National Congress organized by the ORCA on 11 October 2022 at India International Centre, this author in a dialogue with Dr. Jagannath Panda of the International Security and Development Policy, Stockholm had argued that the outcomes of the Party congress watched for would be 1) The "people's leader" (人民领袖), "people's economy" (人民经济), and "great power diplomacy" (大国外交).

As regards the "people's leader", the communiqué issued on 12 October, makes it amply clear that it would be "banner and line" of Xi Jinping's Thought all the way. This has been reinforced by laying emphasis on the "Two Establishes" (两个确立) and Two Safeguards (两个维护) and many other political slogans Xi has given in the last two terms and are mostly incorporated in the "Third Resolution." "Two Establishes" refer to 1) "To establish the status of Comrade Xi Jinping as the core of the Party's Central Committee and of the whole Party", and 2) "To establish the guiding role of Xi Jinping Thought on Socialism with Chinese Characteristics for the New Era." "Two safeguards" are, "Safeguard the 'core' status of Xi Jinping within the CPC" and "To safeguard the centralized authority of the Party." The sporadic outbursts such as "Sitong Bridge Incident" of 13 October in Beijing by a lone wolf to resist Xi's third term may occur here and there, but Xi Jinping's second decade has already been commenced by the communiqué.

For the execution of the "banner and line", as could be gleaned from the recently revised regulations for cadres' selection, Xi's loyalists (习家军) from Fujian, Zhejiang, Shanghai, Party School, and Shanxi-Gansu-Ningxia where he served in different capacities would be selected to the Central Committee, Politburo and Standing Committee of the Politburo. From Fujian alone, 6-7 people could be promoted, including two in the Central Military Commission. Xi's emphasis that "no one would be allowed to change the color of China's mountain and rivers" is meant to warn his detractors, and that the "Tigers and flies" campaign would continue, and that China will continue to adhere to the path, theory, system and culture with Chinese characteristics.

On economic front, if the statistics are to be believed, China's economic strength was catapulted from around $8.5 trillion to around $18 trillion ever since Xi Jinping took over the reins of the CPC in 2012. Per capita income doubled and urbanisation reached to around 65 per cent in 2022. However, the widening social inequalities are on the rise. Statistics reveal that the top 0.14 per cent of households in China own around one-third of China's wealth. Therefore, the main contradiction of "unbalanced and inadequate development and the people's ever-growing needs for a better life" identified during the last congress will continue to dominate the discourse. Hence the emphasis on "common prosperity", "inner circulation" and the "third distribution" etc. will continue to dominate the economic discourse in place of "economic reforms and opening up" albeit the latter has figured once in the recently released communiqué of the 7th plenum.

Notwithstanding the cursory emphasis on "reform and opening up", the era of laissez-faire growth is long over in China; the state-owned enterprises will further be enlarged and individual economy expected to face a rough ride in the coming days. The situation is further exacerbated by the "Dynamic COVID Zero Policy", "Bad finances of the local governments", "China's real estate bubble bust", the RMB depreciation, as well as the West's gradual decoupling from China, at least in the hi-tech domain. This would rock the boat of economic growth and the targets identified by scholars like Lin Yifu towards fulfilling the socialist modernisation by 2035 could be an uphill task. It is perhaps after summing up the above political and economic undercurrents that scholars like Wen Tiejun have coined "people's economy" acronym that is oriented towards safeguarding sovereignty, independent development and patriotic nature of the Chinese economy.

As far as the "Great power diplomacy" is concerned, the larger framework of the "two central pillars", i.e. "to build a community with a shared future for mankind" and "a new type of international relations" will remain in place. While the former will further incorporate Xi Jinping's "Global Development Initiative" and "Global Security Initiative" as its two flanks, the latter will also have the "Major Country Relationship" and diplomacy with the BRI or developing countries as other flanks. Since the path, the theory, the system emphasised by the CPC has given rise to distrust between China and the West, the ideological confrontation demonstrated by reconfiguration of forces in the so called democratic and authoritarian camps will witness intensification. This has been clearly spelled out in a section entitled "The nature of the competition between democracies and autocracies" in a recently released "National Security Strategy" of the US, where the PRC, has been pronounced as "the only competitor with both the intent to reshape the international order and, increasingly, the economic, diplomatic, military, and technological power to advance that objective." Hong Kong, according to the communiqué "has achieved a major transition from chaos to governance", it has to be seen, how the "Fujian clique" in the CMC and Eastern Theatre Command will respond to the Taiwan question, which like the previous Party reports will figure prominently in the 20th Party Congress as well.

9

Decoding Xi Jinping's Work Report to the 20th Party Congress

On 16 October 2022, Xi Jinping, on behalf of the 19th Central Committee of the Communist Party of China (CPC), delivered a report to the 20th CPC National Congress. Unlike the 19th National Congress, Xi Jinping skipped certain sections in his speech and read the 72-page long report within less than two hours. The report enumerated achievements, the CPC made during the first decade of the New Era (2012-2022), and drew a blueprint for the future direction of the party and state. Most of the things in the report conformed to what this author had written on Xi Jinping's third term, the revised regulations and promotion of his loyalists, as well as the banner and line, the state of economy and great power diplomacy of Xi Jinping. Nevertheless, there are certain newly packaged concepts and terms that require further interpretation. The emphasis has been given to "security", "struggles" and winning "regional wars" etc. terms, thus setting the direction Xi Jinping would be heading in his "new era."

First and foremost, by way of inserting "Two Establishes" (两个确立) and "Two Safeguards" (两个维护), and amending the party constitution, Xi Jinping puts himself at par with China's helmsman Mao Zedong, and above all the political leaders of the reform era (1979-2012). By incorporating Xi Jinping's Thought on Socialism with Chinese Characteristics for the New Era in the party constitution during the 19th National Congress, had already put Xi above Hu Jintao, Jiang Zemin and Deng Xiaoping, for their theories were added to the party constitution at the end of their terms or after demise as was the case with Deng's theory.

By incorporating "Two Establishes" and "Two Safeguards" in party's theory, makes "Xi Jinping at the core" and his thought sacrosanct, and the CPC as Xi Jinping's party. This is further established by the fact that Li Keqiang and Wang Yang have been dropped thus paving way for Mr Xi loyalists in the Politburo Standing Committee.

This could be compared to the cleric's bond with his Holy Book, especially by the "princelings" who believe, it's them who have the flesh and blood relationship with the masses and are worthy inheritors of party's legacy, not the likes of Jiang Zemin, Zhu Rongji, Hu Jintao and Wen Jiabao having no revolutionary roots. The leaning to the "left" is understood better, if we interpret "deviational" tendencies of the reform era, largely held responsible for eroding party's control and prestige. Therefore, crackdown on China's bigtech companies is a necessary outcome of correcting the errors, restoring the party line and authority of the CPC, albeit there is an element of factional feud in it too. No wonder, Xi Jinping has been emphasizing on to "inherit the good red genes (红色基因) and pass them down from generation to generation. In the 20th National Congress report, Xi reiterated the rhetoric that "The country is its people (江山就是人民) and the people are the country (人民就是江山). The CPC has led the people to fight for the country (领导人民打江山) and safeguard the country." If the country is the people and vice versa, then who is fighting whom is really a big contradiction.

Two, the word "security" has appeared as many as 46 times and has been pronounced as the "bedrock of national rejuvenation" (民族复兴的根基). The people's security has been identified as the ultimate goal, political security as fundamental task, economic security as foundation, military, technological, cultural, and social security as important pillars, and international security as a support. Here again, the security of the "unified leadership", "leadership system" that is related to the "political security" has been emphasized alongwith various other traditional and non-traditional securities with an aim to enhance CPC's power of discourse internally as well externally. Though economic security has been identified as foundation, but the report attaches more importance to "politics in command" over "economy in command" of the reform period.

Three, the "struggle" (斗争), has been a continuous theme of Xi Jinping's discourse on party building, fighting corruption or on various other domestic and international challenges. Not surprising, "struggle" has appeared 14 times in the report. Xi Jinping desires to foster and strengthen the "spirit of struggle" (斗争精神) in the cadres, so as they could safeguard China's dignity and core interests amidst the struggle and firmly grasp the initiative of China's development and security. It is owing to these struggles, Xi believes that "severe hidden dangers in the army" (严重隐患) have been eliminated across the party, state and the army. It is only after these struggles that party has maintained "absolute leadership" (绝对领导) over the army, without which the command of "the great struggle" (伟大斗争), the great project (伟大工程), the great cause (伟大事业), and the great dream (伟大梦想) would be either lost or go haywire. The struggles may range from "dynamic zero COVID policy" to anti-corruption campaign, as well as to the so called "wolf warrior diplomacy."

Four, the "Chinese style modernisation" (中国式现代化), is a "new wine" in the old bottle, meant to differentiate Chinese model of modernisation from the Western model, thus making the model more appealing to the developing countries. Xi Jinping defines it as modernisation of a huge population, common prosperity, material and cultural-ethical advancement, harmony between humanity and nature, and peaceful development. Eradication of absolute poverty (2020), completion of the historical task of building a moderately prosperous society in all respects (2021) and achieving the first centenary goal (2021) have been enumerated as some of the achievements of such a development model. More importantly, the direction the CPC will embark on a new journey of building a modern socialist country (2035), and march toward the second centenary goal (2049). It is also to argue that even if the population of China is much larger than the combined population of the developed countries, China has promised not to seek hegemony unlike the US and believes in "true multilateralism", mutual respect and benefits.

Finally, Xi Jinping clearly defines the scale of war. While talking about the modernisation of the PLA under the absolute leadership of the Party, Xi, apart from asigning the PLA the task of defending China's sovereignty and developmental interests, also sanction the use of military power in "regional wars." In this context, his rhetoric on Taiwan is worth noting. Without setting any timelimit, Xi says in his report that "complete reunification of our country must be realized" (祖国 完全统一) and "it can, without doubt, be realized" (一定要实现). This has been corelated to the great struggle, cause, project and dream of national rejuvination, and the first five years are deemed crucial.

10

Xi's Old and Young Guns in the CMC

In early August 2022, when the General Office of the Central Committee of the Communist Party of China issued the revised "Regulations on the selection and appointment of leading cadres of the party and government", it was widely believed that Xi Jinping will fill the central committee, the politburo, and the standing committee of the politburo with his loyalists from Fujian, Shanghai, the party school, Shaanxi-Gansu-Ningxia etc. regions where he severed in various capacities. The Central Military Commission (CMC) of the CPC wasn't an exception. The dramatic removal of Hu Jintao's from the closing ceremony of the 20th CPC National Congress, in essence, proclaimed the end of the reform era, and arrival of the new era, in which Xi Jinping would assume the role of the supreme leader of China.

The composition of the seven-member CMC in order is: Xi Jinping (Chairman), Zhang Youxia (Vice Chairman), He Weidong (Vice Chairman), and Li Shangfu, Liu Zhenli, Miao Hua and Zhang Shengmin as members. Zhang Youxia was retained irrespective of attaining 72 years of age, and He Weidong was given out of turn promotions. Liu Zhenli is expected to take over as the chief of the Joint General Staff, while Li Shangfu who is under the Countering America's Adversaries Through Sanctions Act (CAATSA), is likely to take over as the Minister of Defence. Miao Hua who was retained as a member, will continue to look after the political work inside the commission in tandem with Zhang Shengmin. They are expected to continue to cleanse the PLA from the remnants of

Xu Caihou and Guo Boxiong, the two military "tigers" who were purged during the first term of Xi Jinping.

Zhang Youxia, has been retained owing to his "red genes" (红色基因), his relations with Xi Jinping and family connections. Like Xi, Zhang also hails from Shaanxi. His father Zhang Zongxun was a close comrade in arms of Xi's father, Xi Zhongxun during China's bloody civil war against the Kuomintang government. Besides, Zhang is one of the very few People's Liberation Army (PLA) generals having real combat experience. He has fought in the China-Vietnam war of 1979, and later served in the Beijing Military Region and the Shenyang Military Region before the establishment of theatre commands. While serving in the General Armaments Department (GAD) of the PLA since 2012, Zhang immensely contributed to improving the PLA's weaponry and technology.

On 18 October, during a panel discussion of the delegation of the PLA and the People's Armed Police Force, Zhang Youxia had all praises for Xi Jinping and his report presented to the 20th CPC National Congress. Zhang argued that in the past ten years, President Xi has led us to achieve a series of "pioneering and iconic achievements" (开创性标志性的重大成就). "It is the first priority to understand and implement Xi Jinping Thought on Socialism with Chinese Characteristics for a New Era…to "firmly support the 'two establishments' (两个确立) and ensure that the barrel of the gun always obeys the command of the party (确保枪杆子永远听党指挥). It is necessary to focus on the "central task of the party" (党的中心任务), do a good job in preparing for and fighting the war in the new era … and strive to achieve the centenary goal of the founding of the army."

He Weidong, on the hand, served as deputy chief of staff of the Nanjing Military Region and commander of the Shanghai garrison. Before moving to the Eastern Theatre Command (ETC) in 2019, He, served as commander of the Western Theatre Command (WTC 2016-2019), a period that culminated into the 73 day Doklam standoff between the Indian army and the PLA on the Bhutanese territory, a precursor to the June 2020 Galwan bloody clashes. Since January 2022, he has been transferred to the Joint Operations Command Centre of the CMC. Both He Weidong and Miao Hua have served in the 31st Group Army of the PLA in Fujian under Xi Jinping, the then political commissar of the Fujian Military Region.

Li Shangfu, who is poised to be the next defence minister of China, has served in the Science and Technology Commission of the CMC, especially in the aerospace field for several years, and has been the man behind manned space projects of China in recent years. In 2017, he succeeded Zhang Youxia to become head of the Equipment Development Department of the CMC. Liu Zhenli has also participated in the Sino-Vietnam border skirmishes in 1986. Liu had also served in the Joint Staff Department of the CMC.

Though two of the members of the CMC may have real combat experience, however, China has not fought a war since 1979. In the face of China's increasingly aggressive approach in the East China and South China Sea disputes, as well as in the Taiwan Strait, the composition of the CMC looks more like a posturing, as most of the members are from the ground forces and have served in the Eastern Theatre Command. It is believed that the live-fire military exercise to blockade Taiwan in the backdrop of Nancy Pelosi's visit was scripted by He Weidong. His out of turn promotions could be related to this as well. Without setting any time limit, Xi Jinping has reiterated in his report that "complete reunification of our country must be realized" (祖国 完全统一) and "it can, without doubt, be realized" (一定要实现). If General Zhang Youxia's resolve to accomplish the "central task", i.e. realising the second centenary in 2049 is taken into account, the unification will have to wait for a longer period. However, if achieving the centenary goal of founding of the PLA is any timeline, then it will happen before 2027.

Notwithstanding the current posturing and rhetoric, given the complexity of the Taiwan issue and the US and Japan factors, China, perhaps is wary about using force at this point in time. However, it would also depend on how Xi governs China, and also the outcome of next elections in Taiwan and the US. Since He Weidong has commanded the WTC, India must be cautious about China's posturing along its northern borders, for China will continue to deny India space in the region and beyond through the so called "competition continuum" in various realms including the borders.

11

China in Xi's "New Era": Domestic Politics and Foreign Policy

On 16 October 2022, Xi Jinping, on behalf of the 19th Central Committee of the Communist Party of China (CPC), delivered a report to the 20th CPC National Congress. The report enumerated achievements, the CPC made in the New Era (2012–), and drew a blueprint for the future direction of the party and state. As it was widely speculated, Xi got the third term brushing aside the regulations and promoted his loyalists so as the banner and line of Xi Jinping's thought could be held high in the second decade of his rule. In order to put his third term in perspective, we may formulate the following assumptions:

1. As China increasingly faces national and international challenges, the economy in command has paved way for politics in command in Xi Jinping's new era "A slide toward weak, hollow, and watered-down Party leadership" of the reform era, confirms the contradiction that those in the CPC who have not inherited the "good red genes" have eroded the legitimacy of the Party, hence the "banner and line" of Xi Jinping's Thought on Socialism with Chinese Characteristics for the New Era must be held high so as the "color of China's mountain and rivers is not changed" and the path, theory, system, and culture evolved by the Party is not weakened and compromised.
2. In the global context, where peace is elusive, conflicts raging across the continents, when the world is witnessing deficit in the areas of development and governance, the discourse of power

> emanating from China in the form of building communities with shared future and Chinese style modernisation certainly would add a new perspective, an alternative that essentially denounces the dominated western discourse on development.

As regards the first assumption, it is clear from the 20th National Congress of the CPC that in Xi's third term, the "banner and line" of his thought on socialism with Chinese characteristics would be held high by his loyalists from Fujian, Zhejiang, Shanghai, Party School, and Shanxi-Gansu-Ningxia where he served in different capacities. To uphold the "banner and line" of Xi Jinping's thought is deemed an absolute necessity, for the leadership has come to believe that the situation of "lax and loose" governance of the party during the reform era has been fundamentally reversed by way of "strict and hard" governance of the party. The "strict and hard" governance, is a pointer to the fact that Xi's own concept words such as "Two Upholds",[1] Two establishes,[2] people centred philosophy, and the "Four matters of confidence"[3] need to be strictly adhered to. Obviously, the people responsible for "lax and loose" governance are the people like Jiang Zemin, Zhu Rongji, Hu Jintao and Wen Jiabao who do not inherit the "good red genes", and cared little for the color of China's mountain and rivers. No wonder Xi Jinping has been reiterating that "no one would be allowed to change the color of China's mountain and rivers and that the red genes would be transferred from generation to generation" so as the path, ideology, system and culture China evolved over the period of time is not changed.

This is also one of the reasons as to why Xi Jinping should strike hard on the big tech companies of China, which are run by the relatives of bigwigs of the reform period, and are believed to be the white gloves of Shanghai clique. Boyu Capital is run by Jiang Zemin's grandson Jiang Zhicheng, CICC Alpha was run by Zhu Yunlai, son of Premier Zhu Rongji, Pingan Insurance is managed by the relatives of former Premier Wen Jiabao, the CITIC capital is run by Liu Lefei, son of the former politburo standing committee member Liu Yunshan. Many of these capitals have big stakes in Didi Chuxing and Alibaba's Ant Group. Therefore, it is also for the fear of political as well as financial coups by his detractors that Xi has taken ultimate control of party and government in China.

As regards the economy, Xi Jinping steered it well during his first term, the second term was marred by the disruption of supply chains owing to the COVID-19 pandemic and the US-China trade war. If statistics are to be believed, China's burgeoning economic strength has been catapulted to \$17.2 trillion from around \$8.5 trillion when Xi took over in 2012. Per capita income rose from around \$6000 to over \$12000 in recent times. Urbanisation registered fastest ever growth anywhere in the world. During ten years of his rule, urban population increased from 52 per cent to 64.7 per cent. More than 100 million people were alleviated from poverty. Nevertheless, the era of laissez-faire economy has come to an end, and could be gleaned from a number of factors.

One, if we look at the growth of reform era, it was driven by massive government investment accounting for around 45 per cent of the GDP, most of which went into the real estate as Chinese citizens invested almost 70 per cent of their savings in the real estate. However, with the real estate bubble bust, the investment is in jeopardy and the returns in doldrums. Two, bad finances of the local governments amounting to over \$4 trillion is another issue. Since land was a cash cow for the village collectives and realtors, with the real estate bust, this steady source of income has been lost. Three, the "Dynamic Zero COVID" policy of the government has had adverse effect on the Chinese economy. Companies like Foxcon are contemplating relocating to other destinations. Four, depreciation of RMB and China-US trade war is another worry for China. According to a study conducted by the Peterson Institute for International Economics, "China is now the source of only 18 per cent of total US goods imports, down from 22 per cent at the onset of the trade war." The decoupling is visible as regards the products that have been subjected to high tariffs, and those in the hi-tech sector such as semiconductors. Finally, Xi Jinping's third term and increasingly inward looking policies that talk of "common prosperity", "inner circulation", "third distribution" and "unified domestic market" etc. have shattered the hopes of SMEs that once acted as the backbone of China's reforms and youth employment. The Central Economic Work Conference of the party, held on 16 December 2022 does offer some course correction as far as the policy of reforms and opening up are concerned.

As regards the second assumption, the larger framework of China's diplomacy built on two pillars, i.e. "to build a community with a shared future for humanity" and "a new type of international relations" will continue. The former upholds that since interests, aspirations and destinies of mankind are intertwined, therefore, the challenges are common and require common solutions. It is for this reason that the Chinese Dream has been integrated with the desire of the people, particularly of the developing countries for building a peaceful, secure and prosperous world that is open inclusive and ecologically friendly. The latter takes a new yet differentiated approach for developing state-to-state relations with mutual respect, fairness, justice and win-win cooperation at its core. Forging a new type of international relations, will pave the way for a community with a shared future for humanity, such is the belief of China.

New ideas have been added to this larger framework, for example, Xi Jinping's advocacy for the Global Development Initiative (GDI) and Global Security Initiative (GDI). "A New Type of International Relation" also has two distinctive flanks in the forms of "major country diplomacy and China's relationship with the Belt and Road Initiative (BRI) countries with differentiated foreign policy approaches. These have been projected as "global goods" which keep on adding new concepts such as "a health silk road", a "Community with a Shared Future in Cyberspace" and the "Chinese style modernisation" to the basic framework of China's diplomacy.

In the "New Era" under Xi Jinping, the Chinese discourse on its brand of socialism and development is no different from what Mao Zedong said in 1937 that Chinese socialism will not take the "old historical road of the Western countries." In 1956, in a speech entitled "On the Ten Major Relationships", Mao presented an alternative mode of socialism away from the Soviet model that conformed to the Chinese conditions and avoided errors made by the former. Mao also denounced Soviet Union openly and drew a strategy to forge alliances with the like-minded forces, neutralise the neutral countries and split and make use of forces antagonistic to China. Therefore, denouncing "crossing the river by feeling the stones" paradigm, in other words is denouncing the path, one defined by the Western institutions of International order.

In conclusion, if Mao denounced the Soviet discourse on socialism and modernisation in 1956, Xi Jinping has denounced the western discourse on modernisation by proposing the Chinese style modernisation – modernisation of a huge population, common prosperity, material and cultural-ethical advancement, harmony between humanity and nature, and modernisation of peaceful development. The Chinese modernisation has been pitched against the capital centric, materialistic and expansionist western modernisation that leads to social disparities and ecological crises by some of China's leading scholars like Zhang Weiwei of Fudan University.

China believes that western discourses of power and the practices associated with them are inadequate for creating a peaceful, just, and sustainable social order, and hence the justification for providing alternate discourses, which may not necessarily find appeal in the West, but China is hopeful that these would be accepted by the wider sections of developing countries and find their legitimacy over a period of time. Notwithstanding these innovative discourses of power, given the nature of national and international challenges faced by China, Xi's new era is going to be full of black swans and grey rhinos.

NOTES

1. Resolutely uphold General Secretary Xi Jinping's core position on the Party Central Committee and in the Party as a whole, and resolutely uphold the Party Central Committee's authority and its centralized, unified leadership), and secondly uphold the position of Xi Jinping's thought.
2. To establish the status of Comrade Xi Jinping as the core of the Party's Central Committee and of the whole Party" and "To establish the guiding role of Xi Jinping Thought on Socialism with Chinese Characteristics for the New Era
3. Confidence in China's path, theory, system and socialist culture.

12

China's Political Challenges in 2023

In a new year address on 31 December, Chinese president Xi Jinping told Chinese people that they have all along "stood firmly on the right side of the history" (坚定站在历史正确的一边); he reiterated the principle of "people's supremacy" (人民至上) and the "supremacy of life" (生命至上) as regards the prevention and control of the epidemic, which he said has entered a "new phase" (新阶段). Perhaps responding to the defiance of the people towards the incessant lockdowns and the anti-government outburst such as the White Paper Revolution, he said, "It is absolutely normal (很正常) to have varied demands (不同诉求) and differing views (不同看法) by people on the same issue, and consensus must be built on these through communication and consultation.

The pandemic entering a "new phase" refers to a sudden U-turn by China on its "dynamic zero COVID" approach that in the past three years relied on mass testing, strict lockdowns and building of the "mobile cabin hospitals" (方舱医院) for quarantine. China's National Health Commission (NHC) stopped publishing its daily briefing on the COVID-19 since 24 December 2022 when it reported 4,128 new cases. Nonetheless, the Chinese Centre for Disease Control and Prevention Centre has continued (CDC) to publish similar data on its Chinese language website, albeit the big chasm between the Central and provincial government's statistics continue to exist. For example, the day the NHC and CDC reported 4,128 cases, Qingdao in Shandong reported a spurt of between 490,000-530,000 cases every day, and that from 25 and 26 December a growth of 10 per cent could be added on this figure.

As of 3 January 2023, the CDC has given the new numbers of the infected and deaths as 7689 and 5258 respectively. It is indeed the case of from "zero COVID to zero deaths" after China redefined the new variant as "new novel coronavirus infection" (新型冠状病毒感染), essentially dropping it from Class A of the coronavirus infections and lifting the related prevention and control measures through a notification issued by the NHC on 26 December 2022. Irrespective of statistics of the CDC and NHC, the ground reality at China's hospitals, crematoriums and pharmacy counters tells an unpleasant state of affairs, albeit for funeral companies like Fu Shou Yuan International Group, a mainland listed company in Hong Kong this is the good news, as its "stocks are expected to rise more than 80 per cent in the next 30 days". The report says that "the gradual relaxation of epidemic prevention restrictions will create conditions for a strong recovery in Fu Shou Yuan's business development next year". Why has China taken a U-turn on the pandemic?

One, the "White Paper Revolution" was just a spark but not the main reason behind China's U-turn on "dynamic zero COVID" policy. China was already mulling ways to optimize its zero COVID policy – on 11 November 2022, the State Council Joint Prevention and Control Mechanism rolled out 20 measures to optimize COVID-19 response, and on 7 December, the same organisation issued a "new 10 measures" response, further optimising stringent COVID-19 lockdowns and quarantine periods. Undoubtedly, the "one-size-fits-all approach or excessive measures" by the local governments were denounced, so as normal daily life of the people is restored. The main reason behind the U-turn was unsustainability of the zero-COVID policy. In one of my previous articles, I had quoted that "a single nucleic acid test costs China around 215 million yuan a day, amounting to nearly 50 billion yuan a month"! Rather than ameliorating the COVID-19 situation, the testing companies were making fortunes.

Two, if the proceedings of the Central Economic Work Conference (CEWC) held in Beijing between 15 and 16 December is any indication, China has come to believe that all is not well with its economy. The conference focussed on economic growth by way of domestic consumption, foreign direct investment, stabilisation of real estate sector, and support to private enterprises, including the big-tech companies that were once penalised by the party-state. The conference argues that "foundation of economic recovery is not yet stabilized, and China is still facing three-fold pressure on contracting demand, supply shocks and weak expectations." Expansion of the domestic consumption would be an uphill task, as the consumer confidence is at its lowest ebb. The confidence has been shattered by the pandemic, but more importantly it is owning to China's inability to keep on investing about 45 per cent of the GDP domestically for the fear of low or even negative return on the investment in the real estate or other infrastructure projects. Depreciation of RMB is serious challenge that will impact the overall GDP of China. This year alone the Yuan has depreciated by 12 per cent.

Three, bad finances of the local governments amounting to over $4 trillion is another issue. Since land was a cash cow for the village collectives, realtors and enterprises, with the real estate bubble bust, this steady source of income has been lost. No wonder, local governments competed for building "mobile cabin hospitals" at such a huge scale for getting financial support from the Central government. If the auditing of such "hospitals" is carried out these may run into billions of dollars.

Four, prolonged China-US trade war is another worry. According to a study conducted by the Peterson Institute for International Economics, "China is now the source of only 18 per cent of total US goods imports, down from 22 per cent at the onset of the trade war. The decoupling is visible as regards the products that have been subjected to high tariffs, and those in the hi-tech sector such as semiconductors. Nonetheless, these goods have been replaced by the import of other goods e.g. computer monitors, consoles, toys etc. not really affecting the total trade volume. It has though triggered shifting of the supply chains to Southeast Asia and India by companies from the US, Korea and Japan. No wonder, the South China Morning Post, reports that in the first 11 months of 2022 some 4.37 million of China's small businesses have permanently shut their businesses. The unemployment rate amongst the youth has reached 19.3 per cent.

Finally, there is a silver lining for China if we look at its exports to the developing or the Belt and Road Initiative (BRI) countries. According the BRI portal, as of now, the "friend circle" of the BRI countries has extended to 150 countries and 32 international organisations. China's total export and import with the BRI countries reached $1.82 trillion, registering 20 per cent growth over 2021. According to a report published by Christoph

Nedopil Wang of Shanghai-based Green Finance and Development Centre (GFDC), since 2013, China's cumulative BRI engagement amounts to $932 billion, about $561 billion in construction contracts, and $371 billion in non-financial investments. Undoubtedly, these massive projects have contributed to the local development and provided employment opportunities to thousands of people. However, these have also raised various concerns, some genuine and some geared towards demonising China. The fact that China's BRI footprints in Asia, Europe, Africa and Latin America has forced the United States and its allies to counter the BRI with their own projects like Indo-Pacific Infrastructure Forum (2018), Build Back Better World (2021), EU's Global Gateway strategy (2022) etc. show that the West is rattled by China's influence.

However, rather than fire-fighting the external challenges, China will face far more serious challenges from its domestic audience as have been witnessed during the "White Paper Revolution" and the recent "fireworks" in Henan's Yiba county and Nanjing where people defied the government ban on firecrackers and even toppled a police car on 2 January 2023 inviting anger and counter measures from the authorities. The Public Security Bureau of Yiba county in a notification issued on 3 January warned that "the authority of the law enforcement agencies cannot be challenged" after it arrested the eight suspects.

II
ECONOMIC GOVERNANCE

13

China's AI Dream

Chinese idiom 'the backward catches up with the advanced (后来者居上) rightly explains China's great leap forward in the Artificial Intelligence (AI) in just over a decade's time. China's desire to 'catch up with and surpass' (赶超) the Unites states since Mao Zedong's times, appears to be realised at least in AI if we believe in the number of research papers published and the AI firms established by China. A study conducted by AI data analysis researchers of China Academy of Information and Communications Technology (CAICT), reveals that as of March 2019, the number of Chinese AI firms has reached 1,189 against the US's 2169. India was shown at number 5 with 169 firms. China's global share of research papers in the AI stood at 27.7 per cent, surpassing the US (20.4%), while India ranked third at 5.8 per cent. This phenomenon has also been revealed by Lee Kai-Fu's bestseller AI Superpowers, in which he envisions China and the US forming a powerful duopoly in the AI. What is behind China's AI dream?

One, China anticipated the role new technologies will play in the fourth industrial revolution and devised strategies at central as well as provincial governments level. This could be gauged from the policy documents China released from time to time. Some of the most important ones are, "Made in China 2025" and New Generation Artificial Intelligence Development Plan released by the State Council in 2015 and 2017 respectively. The former sets a goal of achieving 40 per cent self-sufficiency in core components and critical materials in a wide range of industries, including aerospace equipment and telecommunications equipment and achieve international recognition for Chinese brands by 2020 and enhance the same to 70 per cent by 2025. It also identifies ten core areas that include the AI, robotics, quantum computing, aerospace, new energy vehicles etc. The aim is to make China a "manufacturing power" (制造强国) from the current status of "world's factory" (世界工厂). The second report is AI specific, and identifies China's approaches and goals to be achieved by 2030. It could be regarded as a blueprint to "lead the world" in AI. Recently, China has adopted the Data Security Law, that makes it mandatory for all Chinese companies and entities to acquire government approval before providing any China based data to foreign entities and agencies.

Two, the legitimacy of the Communist Party of China is closely linked to the economic growth. In fact, it was the liberalisation drive that buried the ghost of Tiananmen in China. China is perhaps the only country in the world that has universalized the AI across its industrial ecosystem, be it finance, health, military, power grids, hospitality or personal homes. The above mentioned 2017 report envisages that by 2025, the scale of AI's core industry and AI related industries will exceed 400 billion RMB (US$ 60.3 billion) and 5 trillion RMB (US$ 754.0 billion). The same in 2030 will be more than RMB 1 trillion (US$ 150.8 billion) and RMB 10 trillion (US$ 1.5 trillion) respectively. Global market is expected to reach US$ 15 trillion in the same year. It is expected that by this time, China's AI theories, technologies, and applications should achieve world-leading levels and establish China's primacy in AI.

Three, it is under such a futuristic strategy that China has directed its universities to offer degree courses in AI. According to the 2018 China's AI Development Report compiled by China Institute for Science and Technology Policy at Tsinghua University, 36 universities across China are offering bachelor's degree program in "Intelligence Science and Technology" and 79 offering AI-related programmes. Top Chinese universities have set up their AI labs. The state has also directed big-tech companies like Baidu, Tencent, Alibaba, JD etc. to spearhead research and development in core and related AI industries pertaining to computer vision, speech, hardware, algorithm, and natural language processing. According to data released by International Federation of Robotics in June 2018, the global robot market reached US$ 50 billion in 2017. The market posted 380,000 industrial robots sold in 2017, of these 138,000 were sold by China. Nevertheless, China is also apprehensive of its big-tech companies undermining the state controlled finance sector as well as breaching data security by filing IPOs abroad. Investigations against DiDi in the wake of its Nasdaq IPO could also be analysed in this context, albeit like Alibaba's IPO stalling, it is also indicative of factional feud in the Communist Party of China.

Four, China has used AI for the so-called social governance or maintenance of social stability in restive regions such as Xinjiang and Tibet. In 2019, leaked Chinese government documents detail how AI is being used against the Uighurs in Xinjiang. The 400 pages of documents were also examined and reported by the *New York Times*. Surveillance is not limited to the Uighurs, but to every Han Chinese too. According to a *BBC* report filed in December 2017, "China has been building what it calls 'the world's biggest camera surveillance network' albeit the reporter was told by the police officials that it is used to help the general public. Across the country, there would be around 570 million CCTV cameras by the end of 2020. It is believed that by 2030, China will possess 30 per cent of the global big data. Notwithstanding its benefits, AI like other technologies will remain a double-edged sword.

Finally, AI undoubtedly will enhance productivity and generate more wealth in society. According to the above cited Tsinghua report, in coming days, AI will be applied in more industries and bring substantial efficiency improvements – 82 per cent for education, 71 per cent for retail, 64 per cent for manufacturing and 58 per cent for finance. In long run, it may be instrumental in ameliorating the labour shortage faced by the aging China, however, the same has led to involution among the Chinese millennials owing to the 996-work culture and an increasingly uphill social mobility which has resulted in the lying flat syndrome. China issuing various policy documents may have created a favourable environment for the investors and enabled China to leapfrog in such a short time. Nevertheless, China's weak privacy regulations, data sharing among government agencies and companies, big-tech companies Tsinghua Unigroup (Ziguanag) going bankrupt owing to bad debt, ongoing cold war with the US, China's decoupling from the West, especially in the hi-tech sectors will pose serious challenges for China's AI dream.

14

China's "Common Prosperity" and Leadership "Succession"

On 17 August 2021, General Secretary of the Central Committee of the Communist Party of China (CPC), Xi Jinping who is also head of the Central Committee for Financial and Economic Affairs chaired the proceedings of the tenth meeting of the Committee. The Committee deliberated on the issues related to promotion of "common prosperity" (共同富裕) and prevention and mitigation of major financial risks (金融风险). Xi's remarks that appeared on the Chinese editions of *People's Daily* and Xinhua emphasized that "Common prosperity is the essential requirement of socialism and an important feature of Chinese style modernisation. It is necessary to adhere to the concept of people-centered development and promote common prosperity in the pursuit of high-quality development." He further said that "It is necessary to strengthen the regulation and adjustment of high incomes, protect legal incomes in accordance with the law, reasonably regulate excessive high incomes (合理调节过高收入), and encourage high-income groups and enterprises to return more to the society (更多回报社会)." Below the headlines, it reported Li Keqiang, Wang Yang, Wang Huning, Han Zheng also attended the meeting. Why is Xi Jinping advocating "common prosperity" and what are the ways he wishes to achieve it? Why Wang Yang's name jumped the seniority list?

The excerpts of Xi Jinping's remarks demonstrate that the CPC desires to achieve the goals of "common prosperity" by way of building basic institutional arrangements for the coordination of primary distribution (初次分配), redistribution (再分配), and the third distribution (第三次分

配).The concept was proposed in the 1990s by Li Yining, an economist and honorary Dean of Guanghua School of Management, Peking University. Li proposed that the primary distribution is based on efficiency function of the factors in production; redistribution refers to the use of taxation and fiscal expenditure by the government to redistribute wealth between different income entities through social security, public services and subsidies; and the third distribution is all about philanthropy by the wealthiest through charitable public welfare methods. Li has also been advocating that markets should play a greater role in educational resource allocation.

The "Three distributions" have gained traction at least since 2019, for there is a general belief in China that allowing a few people to get rich first, has created huge social inequalities in the last four decades of reforms. According to the 2020 Credit Suisse report, richest 1 per cent of Chinese now hold 31 per cent of the country's wealth, up from 21 per cent in the year 2000. The same report says that 11 per cent of the world millionaires are produced by China. Immediately after Xi's remarks, Tencent announced that it will invest US$ 7.7 billion in China's common prosperity special project. Early in April, Tencent committed the same amount towards "sustainable social value innovation strategy." According to a report published by Bloomberg, "seven Chinese billionaires have directed a record US$ 5 billion to charity so far this year." These include Chen Dongsheng of Taikang Life Insurance Co. ($154.3M), Lei Jun of Xiaomi ($2.2B), Zhang Yiming of ByteDance ($77.3M), Wang Xing of Meituan ($2.3B), Yang Yuanqing of Lenovo Group ($15.4M), Li Yongxin of Offcn Education ($154.3M), and Colin Huang of Starry Night Foundation ($100M). After Xi's remarks, many more are likely to follow the suit. China cracking down on its tech giants and slapping hefty fines has also been seen in the context of China's "common prosperity" push, however, more serious issues of factional feud and feared "financial coups" are also cited as reasons behind their suppression.

Moreover, since some of the main drivers of China's growth such as exports and real estate have hit the roadblocks, China is striving hard to avoid the "middle income trap." China desires to expand its middle class from the current 400 million to 800 million between 2021-2035. This is considered important for realising the goals of "dual circulation", especially the "internal circulation" i.e. the domestic cycle of production, distribution, and consumption for sustainable economic development. Professor Li Shi, a well-known scholar on income distribution in China, has pointed out that in 2019, the annual per capita disposable income of the 40 per cent households was only 965 yuan per month, demonstrating that currently there are more than 560 million low-income people in China. Majority of these people reside in the countryside, and to raise the income levels of such a huge population is not going to be easy given the signs of involution in Chinese economy.

Besides, since the "common prosperity" is directly linked to the "Community with shared future for mankind" a dwindling growth at home may impact on China's "Belt and Road Initiative" and "China's dream of national rejuvenation." The period between 2020-2035 is crucial when China wants to realise its "socialist modernisation" by raising the per capita income of its citizens to around US$ 30000. In the words of Zhang Yongjun, deputy chief economist with the China Centre for International Economic Exchanges, "China will achieve the goal of becoming a medium-level developed country in per capita GDP terms by 2035 even if China's average annual growth rate is 4.5 per cent between 2025 and 2030 and about 4.0 per cent between 2030 and 2035." That may be the case, but questions are being asked when the Party-state owns everything and exercise ultimate control, why there is so much noise about the "third distribution"? Is it because the government's coffers are empty owing to the overstretched BRI funding and doles or that the state is re-enacting the slogan "overthrow the local despots and distribute land" (打土豪分田地) of the Mao era?

Finally, another takeaway from the 17 August meeting was the sudden promotion of Wang Yang in the Standing Committee of the politburo. Wang's name unusually appeared immediately after Li Keqiang leading to speculation and rife that he is either likely to replace Li Keqiang as Premier or Xi Jinping as the General Secretary. Interestingly, as has been a custom for a successor, Wang led a delegation to Lhasa to attend the 70th anniversary of the "peaceful liberation" of Tibet. Hu Jintao and Xi Jinping as designated successors of the CPC had also participated in the 50th and 60th anniversary of China's takeover of Tibet in 2001 and 2011 respectively. Wang succeeding Xi is very unlikely as 66 years old Wang, will hardly ensure Xi's political longevity and preserve his legacy. Li Zhanshu is believed to be his only close ally in the seven-member politburo. Though Wang has a close working relationship with Xi, however, to designate him as successor is a mere speculation, and perhaps meant to send false signals to the international community that succession is on the cards before the 20th Party Congress in 2022.

15

China's Factional Feud and the Policy of Reform and Opening Up

Factions in China have all along used ideological institutions to settle scores in somewhat zero-sum game. The institutionalisation of the leadership succession had struck a certain balance amongst the factions, however, by rewriting of the Party and State constitutions, amassing unprecedentedly huge power across the instruments of state power, and leaning to the side of the conservatives or radicals, General Secretary of the Communist Party of China (CPC), Xi Jinping has rocked this balance. This was observable before and after the proceedings of the 19th Party Congress, however, has become more conspicuous during the recently concluded 6th Plenary Session of the Nineteenth Central Committee of the Party. Recent publication of two articles supposedly by different camps in the "two newspapers and one journal" (两报一刊) demonstrates that the feud is getting intensified in the face of slow economic growth, stringent anti-monopoly laws and in the run up to the 20th Party Congress in 2022.

"Two newspapers and one journal "refer to the *People's Daily* (人民日报), the *People's Liberation Army Daily* (解放日报) and the *Red Flag* (红旗). The *Red Flag* has been renamed as Qiushi (求是) or Seeking Truth since initiation of the reform and opening up policy. News and editorials published in these are considered as authoritative statements of official government policy or that representing authoritative voice of the CPC. On 9 December 2021, the *People's Daily* published a 3985-character long article entitled "Reform and opening up is a great awakening of the Party" by Qu Qingshan, director of the Institute of Party History and Literature of the Central Committee of the CPC and also a member of the present powerful Central Committee. Though there is nothing special about an article that vehemently defends the Reform Era, but the timing and context pitches it against another article that could be regarded as written in defence of the New Era. Qu's article mentions Deng Xiaoping 9 times and Jiang Zemin and Hu Jintao each once for initiating and carrying forward the legacy of reforms, but there is no mention of Xi Jinping at all. Rather Qu argues that the CPC by way of correcting the "grave mistakes (严重错误) of the Cultural Revolution, "re-established the ideological line of seeking truth from facts, and liberated people's thinking from the long-term 'Left' confinement (长期"左"的禁锢) and the shackles of dogmatism." Qu argues that it was the reform and opening up that avoided the "old closed ossified road" (封闭僵化的老路) and the one which would have forced us to change our banner.

Interestingly, on 13 December 2021, Jiang Jinquan, director of the Policy Research Office of the Communist Party of China (CPC) Central Committee, the post that was headed by Wang Huning before, also wrote a 4332-character long article in the theory edition of the *People's Daily* entitled "Adhere to the overall leadership of the Party." The article makes mention of Mao Zedong twice and that of Xi Jinping six times. It recounts Party's struggle through revolution, construction and reform periods, and argues that the leadership of the party is the "fundamental and lifeblood" (根本所在、命脉所在) of the party and the country. Had it not been for the "strong leadership core" (坚强领导核心) it would have been impossible to make such great achievements. The same has been regarded as crucial for realising the great rejuvenation of the Chinese nation. Contrary to Qu's article, Jiang's article deems the Cultural Revolution as the "most serious setback" since the establishment of the People's Republic. Jiang, acknowledges the fact that after the Third Plenary Session of the Eleventh Central Committee of the Party, the CPC "restored and re-established the correct ideological, political, and organisational line," however, also argues that there was also a "deviation" (出现偏差) in the content and methods of the party's leadership, which was eliminated only after the 18th National Congress of the CPC." The article argues in favour of upholding Party's overall leadership; denounces individualism (个人主义), decentralism (分散主义), liberalism (自由主义), parochialism (本位主义) and nice-guyism (好人主义), and recommends elimination of 'double-faced people' (清除"两面人") for sabotaging the centralized and unified leadership of the Party. It concludes that General Secretary Xi Jinping and the Party Central Committee enjoys high degree of trust and sincere support of the entire Party, army and people.

If these two articles are read in tandem with the 4,700-word mission communiqué issued after China's latest Central Economic Work Conference, between 8 and 10 December 2021, it becomes clear that "economic construction as the centre" (以经济建设为中心) of the Deng Xiaoping era will return to the mainstream discourse in 2022 or at least until the situation stabilises. Owing to this, "seek progress while maintaining stability" (稳中求进) has been emphasized in the communiqué. No wonder the word "stability" (稳) was cited 25 times. The communiqué requires "all regions and departments to take the responsibility of stabilizing the macro economy and actively introduce policies conducive to economic stability." It appears that there will be some course correction as far as anti-monopoly laws, crackdown on hi-tech and edu-tech sector, and real estate financial supervision etc. recent policy measures are concerned, for the communiqué stresses on "first making the cake bigger." It could also be seen as a half step forward from the conservatives so as to reach a middle ground with the reformers as regards the "One central task" but there seems no commitment on one of the components of the "Two basic points" i.e. "Reform and opening up." It may be recollected that in 1987 when the then Premier of the State Council, Zhao Ziyang put forth a three-stage development strategy for China's modernisation in the next 62 years in a speech entitled "Advance Along the Road of Socialism with Chinese Characteristics" and proposed the concept of "one central task and two basic points" (一个中心两个基本点). "One central task" refers to economic development as the central task of the government, while "Two basic points" refer to the "Four cardinal principles" (the socialist road, the people's democratic dictatorship, the leading role of the Party, and Marxism-Leninism-Mao Zedong Thought), and the "Reform and opening up." These were reiterated by Deng Xiaoping on 9 June 1989 Tiananmen speech when he authorised the use of force against the protesting students.

There are no differences amongst the two camps as far as the issue of "Four cardinal principles" is concerned, however, the policy of "Reforms and opening up" has drawn flak of late, as it was missing from the "Ten upholds" in the Resolution of the CPC Central Committee on the Major Achievements and Historical Experience of the Party over the Past

Century passed during the 6th plenary session of the 19th CPC Central Committee in November 2021. Compromising on the "One central task," however, doesn't mean to say that Xi Jinping's position in the Party has been weakened, but certainly demonstrates the fact the reformers are upset with the state of the economy in China and would like to have a bigger say in economic matters.

16

China's Blueprint for the Year 2022

China's "Two sessions" or the back to back meetings of the Chinese People's Political Consultative Conference (CPPCC) and the National People's Congress (NPC) between 4 and 11 March 2022, were largely overshadowed by the ongoing Ukrainian crisis. It is in these sessions that the past year's performance is spelled out, a policy blueprint for the new financial year is drawn, and government strive hard to meet the stated targets. Some of the takeaways from this year's Government Work Report (GWR) presented by Premier Li Keqiang on 5 March are analysed as following.

First and foremost, since the Communist Party of China (CPC) is gearing up for the 20th Party Congress, later this year, therefore, the "Two sessions" have set the tone for China's political, economic and foreign policy trajectory, not only for this year, but also beyond the prospective third stint of the Communist Party of China (CPC) General Secretary, Xi Jinping. In the middle of deteriorating US-China relations, technology denials by the West, and domestic power struggle, Xi Jinping by way of launching "wolf warrior diplomacy", "anti-corruption campaigns", "common prosperity", "anti-monopoly laws", poverty eradication programmes etc., seems to have steered himself out of these predicaments, The ongoing Ukrainian crisis has certainly provided a breathing space, perhaps a role that calls for China's mediation in the crisis by the US and the EU alike. The GWR emphasis on the "strong leadership" of the CPC Central Committee with Comrade Xi Jinping at the core", Xi Jinping's thought, realising the "first centenary", "poverty alleviation", formulation of the "third historic resolution" and China starting "a new journey to build a modern socialist country in an all-round way, "marching toward the second centenary goal", and "government and military building" under his leadership, suggests that Xi will remain China's undisputed leader under present circumstances without any credible opposition. Russia-Ukraine crisis will further amplify the calls for a strong leadership core in China.

Two, since stabilising economic growth is directly proportional to legitimacy of the CPC, a moderately high growth of 5.5 per cent has been set for the year 2022, which is expected to create 11 million new urban jobs this year. According to GWR, China's gross domestic product (GDP) reached 114 trillion yuan ($18 trillion), registering 8.1 per cent growth in 2021. It is certainly impressive given the desired target of 6 per cent, however, if the data of all the four quarters is analysed, China's growth declined from 18.3 per cent in Q1 to 7.9 per cent in Q2, to 4.9 in Q3 to 4 per cent in Q4 according to China's National Bureau of Statistics (NBS). Nevertheless, given China's trade war with the US, declining real estate, global slump and pandemic, the growth could be considered impressive, in fact, fastest in a decade according to the NBS. Given the slump in the last two quarters, China is poised to spend and disburse more money to the provincial governments. According to statistics, central government's expenditure will increase by 3.9 per cent and transfers to provincial governments are projected at 9.8 trillion yuan ($1.5 trillion). The domestic consumption and exports could be worrying, as could be seen in the Q3 and Q4, moreover, relocation of the supply chains and countries finding alternate sources could impact negatively on China's foreign trade in 2022.

Third, as regards the foreign policy, the GWR lay emphasis on adhering to "an independent foreign policy" of peace. It talks about peaceful development, the building of a new type of international relations, and "a community with a shared future for mankind." Taiwan as usual has been clubbed together with Hong Kong and Macao, so as to portray the issue as an internal affair. While the GWR calls for "One-China principle" and the "1992 Consensus", "peaceful development of cross-strait relations" and the "reunification of the motherland", it denounces "Taiwan independence" and "interference by external forces." The document calls upon the people on both sides of the straits to work together for the "glorious cause of national rejuvenation." Since the reunification is crucial for realising national rejuvenation, the confrontationist approaches are likely to continue, not only in the Taiwan strait but internationally too. Therefore, to expect China to retreat to pre 19th Party Congress era is impossible. With an ever expanding economy and defence allocation, China wanting to take a "centre stage" in international affairs, will bring it into confrontation with the liberal order. Xi Jinping's project of the century will continue as mentioned by the GWR, however, the focus would be on "high quality", "steadily expanding" new areas of cooperation, and continued emphasis on the construction of new land-sea passages in the west. China's defense budget is set to grow at 7.1 per cent in 2022 "amidst complex global situation" according to China's *Global Times*. US$ 230 billion spending besides a matching internal security budget, second largest after the US is geared towards achieving "centennial goal" in 2027 when the People's Liberation Army (PLA) will celebrate the 100th anniversary. These goals and "military struggles" certainly include the unification of Taiwan. The Quad and AUKUS have been described by China as US strategy to encircle China.

Finally, the GWR continues to adhere to the COVID-19 zero-tolerance policy, even as the cases throughout the world are on the decline. Recently, China has seen a spurt in cases in Hong Kong, Shenzhen, Jilin, Fujian and Liaoning etc. places. Increasingly people have been debating if the "zero clearing out" and "mass testing" policy of the government is the only answer or not? Whether "co-existence" is an option or not. A gradual exist strategy is being debated and worked out, however, with the sharp rise in cases across China, this approach may be stalled. It is however, established that the "zero clearing" has enabled testing companies in China to reap huge profits ranging between 228 per cent and 6500 per cent according a report by Bloomberg. The Chinese model to fight COVID-19 that gained currency in the initial phase of the pandemic is no longer been debated.

17

Evergrande Crisis: End of laissez-faire Growth in China

In my last column, while analyzing Li Guangman's highly publicized article entitled "Everyone can feel that a profound transformation is underway", I had argued that "the real estate sector, which was one of the pillars to place China's economic growth on a solid trajectory is riddled with problems. Though the sector accounts for around 29 per cent of the national GDP, however, also has maximum bad debts amounting to US$ 7.7 trillion. The nonperforming loans have reached a whopping 30 per cent across the five largest banks of China." The Evergrande (恒大) crisis is just a tip of the iceberg. The real Estate giant owes US$ 305 billion in debts, more than US$ 6 billion in insolvent investment portfolios collected from it's over 200,000 employees, and has 1,300 project sites in 280 cities across China, of which 800 are under construction residential projects. Besides, the conglomerate also owes money to around 1.5 million customers, some of whom have been protesting against the giant across China. There are speculations that Evergrande crisis is China's Lehman Brothers moment. Will the Chinese government save the conglomerate or let it go bust? Is China heading and also leading the world towards an economic crisis?

China's real estate bubble has been around for quite some time. With the massive urbanisation drive in the reform period, property prices rocketed in big cities. No wonder, more than 70 per cent of urban China's wealth is parked in real estate. However, the 'real estate bubble' (房地产泡沫), according to He Keng, deputy director of the Finance and

Economics Committee of the 11th National People's Congress, "in no way is less than 30 per cent, therefore, average housing prices should drop by 30 per cent." He is not very optimistic about China's economic prospects in the second half of 2021, what he fears most is a "hard landing" (硬着陆) by the real estate sector, resulting in a financial crisis. Therefore, He hopes for a "soft landing" (软着陆) in order to avoid the implosion. Evergrande's problems just demonstrates that. If the Chinese government let it fail, Chinese economy will be paralysed, millions of migrant workers employed in the construction sites will be unemployed, steel, cement, glass and various other ancillary industries will be affected and even go bankrupt, least to talk about the bad debts of the banks.

One may argue that a country having US$ 3.9 trillion in foreign exchange reserves may easily tide over the crisis of this magnitude. But, is there enough cash? China's foreign debt, according to the State Administration of Foreign Exchange, reached US$ 2.52 trillion by March 2021. It was also reported that fiscal debt in 2020 crossed US$ 1 trillion. Added to this, the finances of the provincial governments are pegged at around US$ 4 trillion. Now, Xu Jiayin, the owner of Evergrande is alleged to be close to Shanghai clique. It was during Jiang Zemin's reign that Xu rose to glory as a realtor. *Red Roulette: An Insider's Story of Wealth, Power, Corruption and Vengeance in Today's China* (2021) by Desmond Shum, also writes about the ways Xu bribed the big and powerful in China. "Xu's preferred method was through giving outrageously expensive gifts" (p. 165). Shanghai clique, allegedly controls financial sector in mainland and Hong Kong, of which Xi has been very wary of. Therefore, why should Xi Jinping bail out his detractors? And what about other developers such as Soho, Fantasia, Sunac, Ludi, Fuli, Rongchuan, Baolide, Wanda, Country Garden and many other who have also taken a plunge. Evergrande's share fell by around 80 per cent in this year alone.

Given the threat of contagion spreading to others areas, one of the possibilities is the Chinese government managing the crisis by taking over Evergrande and nationalizing its assets and subsidiaries. If the reports are to be believed, Anqing city administration has already announced that it will take back all the landholding it had sold to Evergrande. On 22 September, China's Central Bank injected a total of 120 billion yuan (about US$ 18.5 billion) of reverse repos to maintain liquidity in the banking system. This could also be interpreted as China taking measures to calm the nervousness amidst Evergrande crisis and falling Chinese equities across the globe. Meanwhile, Evergrande's onshore property unit revealed on 22 September that it has negotiated a plan with bondholders to repay interest on local yuan bonds due on 23 September. In another story filed by Asiamarkets.com on the same day, it has been revealed that the Chinese Government is planning to restructure Evergrande into three separate entities. This may also be the reason for a little rise in Evergrande's share prices. Or, will the prophecy of the *Wall Street Journal* prove right when it claimed that China has made preparations for Evergrande's demise. Whatever may be the outcome, the crisis, nonetheless, marks the end of laissez-faire growth in China.

18

China's Crippling Debt Crisis and the Property Bubble

In the reform era, China witnessed unprecedented economic growth and saw the emergence of a "middle class" (中产阶级), estimated to be over 400 million according to the 2019 White Paper on China's "New Middle Class" (新中产阶级). The "New Middle Class", projected to be 200 million strong, has a decent annual income of more than 100,000 Yuan, and mostly lives in the tier one and tier two cities of China. The middle class has been instrumental in driving consumption in China, and interestingly holds around 70 per cent of collective wealth in real estate. For the "New Middle Class" the ratio is given at 56 per cent by the White Paper. In recent years, owing to the bad debts of the real estate developers, stringent COVID-19 lockdowns, domestic and global economic slump, the risk of relying on real estate investment is getting dangerous. The sector has increasingly come under the scanner of the party-state for irregularities, corruption, delivery defaults and a serious debt crisis.

It all started with the Evergrande (恒大) fiasco in late 2021, but got snowballed in June 2022, when the same company issued a notice that Evergrande Longting Project in Jingdezhen City, Jiangxi Province has been completely suspended owing to unavailability of the funds. The crisis engulfed the banks too; many froze the deposits of their clients, as was witnessed in Henan and Nanjing, resulting in protests and sloganeering in front of the banks. Worse, the customers of "forward housing delivery system" (期房制) have suspended mortgage loan payments (停贷) and some have taken to the legal course. China's *21st Century Business Herald*

《21 世纪经济报》reported that as of 14 July, more than 230 property owners across the country have collectively suspended mortgage loan payments for unfinished projects (烂尾楼) in Beijing, Shanghai, Henan, Hebei, Hubei, Hunan, Jiangxi, Guangxi, Shanxi, Liaoning, Anhui, Fujian, Jiangsu, Yunnan etc. cities and provinces, a clear indication that the trend is spreading from tier one to tier two and three cities. Shares of the 40 banks fell by 2 per cent [in some cases by 3 per cent], sending shockwaves across China, especially at a time when provincial governments are deep in debt amounting to over US$ 4 trillion. Nearly half of the unfinished buildings belongs to the Evergrande, which alone has a debt of over US$ 300 billion. Other developers such as Aoyuan, Xinyuan, Xinli, Sunshine City, Shimao, Greenland etc., have also suspended their projects.

The real estate sector accounts for 29 per cent of China's GDP, the sector contributed to unprecedented infrastructure growth, urbanisation as well as growth of the related ancillary industries like glass, cement, steel, household appliances etc., albeit there have been cases of the so-called ghost cities too. The last decade (2011-2020) saw exponential growth in the sector, the prices doubled, sales tripled and total area sold increased by 60 per cent. According to a report by Yicai, new home sales totaled 15.5 trillion yuan (about $2.2 trillion) in 2020, which is seven times the sales of new homes in the US in the same year. The real estate bubble gave rise to speculation, as China's middle class borrowed heavily to buy houses. According to George Magnus, household debt rose from about $2 trillion in 2010 to more than $10 trillion in 2021, with the ratio of debt to disposable income surging to about 130 per cent. Furthermore, in order to limit borrowing of real estate developers, Chinese government issued "three red lines" (三条红线) – a debt-to-asset ratio of 70 per cent or lower, a 100 per cent cap on net debt to equity, and enough cash on hand to satisfy short-term borrowing, debts, and liabilities, adding insult to the injury. Besides, the "dynamic zero" COVID policy, global economic slump, the Ukraine-Russia conflict etc., dampened the interest of real estate companies, for they were starved of cash and were unable to finish the ongoing projects, least to talk about their enthusiasm for new projects. This has raised global concerns, as China's real estate market is closely linked to the global market through raw material imports and development financing.

Undoubtedly, the stressed-out mortgage owners are the biggest victims, however, the systemic financial risks faced by the banks are real, for undelivered projects can only become bad debt, which in turn is likely to shake the domestic financial system of China. Will this be China's Lehman Brothers moment, perhaps not. The banks in China are owned by the state and so is the land. On 14 July, more than 10 banks, including the six major state-owned banks, issued statements in response to the suspension of mortgage loan payments. Industrial and Commercial Bank of China and the Agricultural Bank of China disclosed that the current suspended projects involve non-performing loans of 637 million yuan and 660 million yuan respectively, accounting for 0.01 per cent and 0.012 per cent of their mortgage loans. The Bank of Communications disclosed it as 99.8 million yuan, accounting for 0.0067 per cent of its domestic housing mortgage loans. Others like the Bank of China and China Construction Bank did not disclose the specific data of their mortgage business, but both stated that the scale involved was limited and the overall risk controllable. Most of the banks stated that they have established an overall coordination mechanism and across the board investigations of the "guaranteed handover" (保交楼) of housing projects. People perhaps have not forgotten the case of Baoshang Bank in Inner Mongolia, whose ratio of non-performing loans was 1.68 per cent in 2016, but surged to 98 per cent in 2020, the year when it was dissolved by the Chinese government.

Additionally, it has been reported that "area of suspended work" (停工面积) accounts for about 5 per cent (about 500 million square meters) of the industry's construction area of 9.7 billion square meters. The report posits that even if the mortgage assets due to unfinished projects reach a high level of 2 per cent, the absolute number will still be not very large. Nonetheless, there is a counter argument that goes that even if the proportion involved is less than 1 in 10,000, the owners involved are tens of thousands. Under such circumstances, the collateral damage by suspension of mortgage loans will obviously be terrifying. However, since the banks are government owned entities, they have nothing to worry; the developers have made enough money and are lying-flat (躺平) in the times of slowdown; it is the middle class, the weakest link in the banks-developer and customer ecosystem, who have lost faith in the banking system of China, and not to forget the cities that have been dotted with the scars of unfinished projects! Whether the planned launch of a 300 billion yuan ($44 billion) real estate fund will help property developers to emerge from the debt crisis or not and restore the faith of the middle class in the property market, only the time will tell.

19

Chinese Diplomacy and the Discourse of Power

The basic premise of discourse theory is that humans use communication whether verbal or written to construct knowledge and truth. Michel Foucault argues that the knowledge and truth that shape our lives is created through discourse by people in power. The western discourse of power in the 20th century was so powerful that the marginalised world found it difficult to counter it with an alternative discourse. It is only in recent years that emerging economies have been able to find some space in the western discourse. Of these, China appears to be more innovative in offering an alternative discourse of power, be it the multilateralism of the BRICS, AIIB, SCO or the pillars of its foreign policy or a more recent construct of Chinese style modernisation (中国式现代化).

The larger framework of China's diplomacy is based on the so-called two central pillars – "to build a community with a shared future for humanity" (人类命运共同体) and "a new type of international relations" (新型国际关系). The former was advocated by China on a number of occasions since 2013, elaborated in a keynote speech by Xi Jinping at the General Debate of the 70th Session of the United Nations General Assembly (UNGA) in 2015. The idea is rooted in Chinese traditional philosophy of "the world is one family" (天下一家).The concept upholds that since interests, aspirations and destinies of mankind are intertwined, therefore, the challenges are common and require common solutions. It is for this reason that the Chinese Dream has been integrated with the desire of the people, particularly of the developing countries for building a peaceful, secure and prosperous world that is open inclusive and ecologically friendly. The latter takes a new approach for developing state-to-state relations with mutual respect, fairness, justice and win-win cooperation at its core. Forging a new type of international relations, will pave the way for a community with a shared future for humanity, such is the belief of China.

Other discourses such as the Global Development Initiative (GDI) and Global Security Initiative (GDI) have been fed to the basic framework; it is the second pillar that has two distinctive flanks – major country diplomacy and China's relationship with the Belt and Road Initiative (BRI) countries. The GDI was proposed by Xi Jinping in September 2021 while addressing the 76th Session of the UNGA aimed at helping the UN to achieve its 2030 sustainable development goals. Some of the stated objectives are poverty alleviation, food security, COVID-19 response and vaccines, financing for development, climate change and green development, industrialisation, digital economy, and connectivity. Building a health silk road and a "Community with a Shared Future in Cyberspace" rolled out on 7 November could be part of the GDI as well as GSI. The GSI is a precondition of the former and castigates the Cold War mentality, formation of blocs, small cliques, and the old thinking of zero-sum game. On its part, China pledges not to seek hegemony.

As regards the "major country relationship", China has argued that major countries must co-exist in harmony and cooperate with each other on the basis of mutual respect, equality and mutual benefits. By way of "mutual respect" China has demanded that the US respect its chosen path, ideology and system, believed to be the root cause of ideological confrontation between the two. "Working together, we both win; fighting each other, we both lose" phrase has been repeatedly used. On the question of Taiwan, China has asked the US to observe the three joint communiqués and the one-China principle, and respect each other's core interests and major concerns. As regards China's relations with Russia, the same has been pronounced as an anchor of international balance and strategic stability However, in the backdrop of Russia's prolonged war with Ukraine and reverses in the war, China has found itself in a difficult situation, and the position it has taken may be difficult to defend in the coming days. China's relationship with the BRI countries doesn't carry the element of "mutual respect", nonetheless is based on the principle of amity, sincerity, mutual benefit and inclusiveness. Whether the new discourse – the Chinese style modernisation, rolled out during the recently concluded 20th National Congress of the Communist Party of China will make China model more attractive in these countries or not, only the time will tell.

The Chinese style modernisation, can be traced back to the "Self Strengthening Movement" (1861-1894) when Qing officials gave the slogan – "Chinese learning as essence, Western learning as application." After the collapse of the dynasty, the leading intellectuals of China including Hu Shi called for "total westernisation," and the "science and democracy" shaped the discourse during the May Fourth Movement of 1919. In 1937, when Mao Zedong wrote "On Contradiction", he was clear that Chinese socialism will not take the "old historical road of the Western countries." In 1956, in a speech entitled "On the Ten Major Relationships", Mao presented an alternative mode of socialism away from the Soviet model that conformed to the Chinese conditions and avoided errors made by the former. Mao also denounced Soviet Union openly and drew a strategy to forge alliances with the like-minded forces, neutralise the neutral countries and split and make use of forces antagonistic to China.

These discourses are no different from socialism with Chinese characteristics practiced by China during the reform period. However, it appears that in order to build a "socialist market economy", China attempted "crossing the river by feeling the stones." These "stones", according to Wen Tiejun, a top agriculture economist of China, were "symbolic norms defined by the West," in other words treading the path, one defined by the Western institutions of International order. Therefore, if Mao denounced the Soviet discourse on socialism and modernisation in 1956, Xi Jinping has denounced the western discourse on modernisation by proposing the Chinese style modernisation. Xi Jinping defines Chinese Style modernisation as modernisation of a huge population (人口规模巨大), common prosperity (共同富裕), material and cultural-ethical advancement (物质文明和精神文明相协调), harmony between humanity and nature (人与自然和谐共生), and modernisation of peaceful development (和平发展道路). These have been pitched against the capital centric, materialistic and expansionist western modernisation that leads to social disparities and ecological crises by some of China's leading scholars like Zhang Weiwei of Fudan University.

These discourses at the same time are presented as important public goods provided by China for the benefit of humanity. China opines that western discourses of power and the practices associated with them are inadequate for creating a peaceful, just, and sustainable social order, and hence the justification for providing alternate discourses, which may not necessarily find appeal in the West, but China is hopeful that these discourses would be accepted by the wider sections of developing countries and find their legitimacy over a period of time.

20

"Rural Management" Back in China

Recently, the word "rural management" or the so called "nongguan" (农管) has set the Chinese social media ablaze. Slogans such as "Growing melons and vegetables in front and back of houses are prohibited", "Fine of over 100 million yuan for burning stubble", "Certificate required for farming", "Farmers are not allowed to dry their quilts in their courtyards" .... etc., appearing across China's countryside have once again brought back focus on the "Three Rurals" (三农), i.e. agriculture, countryside and peasantry in China.

The so called "rural management" is an acronym for "Agricultural Comprehensive Administrative Law Enforcement Personnel" belonging to the Ministry of Agriculture and Rural Affairs. It has been reported by the netizens that the "rural management" has not only confiscated the chickens, ducks and geese raised by the villagers, but also intervened in how to farm the land, requiring the villagers to take an agricultural certificate, evoking public criticism and despise. Netizens have argued that the personnel will end up making money, but this time they have targeted the poor! By the end of 2022, the agricultural comprehensive administrative law enforcement agencies at the city and county levels were established. According to Chinese government, there are already 2,564 Rural Management organs established across the country, with over 82,000 agricultural law enforcement officers on duty.

The establishment of the Agricultural Comprehensive Administrative Law Enforcement Personnel finds it origin in the "Deepening Party and State Institutional Reform Plan" issued by the Central Committee of the

Communist Party of China in 2018. On 28 May 2020, the Ministry of Agriculture and Rural Affairs issued a notice on the "Guiding Catalogue of Agricultural Comprehensive Administrative Law Enforcement Measures (2020 Edition)" listing 251 administrative penalties running into 99 pages imposed by the "agricultural management" personnel. Some of these require approval for sales and promotion of livestock and poultry including silkworms. The "Agricultural Comprehensive Administrative Law Enforcement Management Measures" was reviewed and approved by the Ministry of Agriculture and Rural Affairs in November 2022, and came into effect on 1 January this year. The "rural management" is not a newly established institution, but integrates the administrative law enforcement functions of the internal institutions and subordinate units scattered in the local agricultural and rural departments. However, the question that has been asked is, if the original intention of the establishment of the "rural management" is to protect the rights and interests of farmers, then why there is an opposition?

The "nongguan" has been compared to the notorious "chengguan" (城管) or the The Urban Administrative and Law Enforcement Bureau that has been established in every city in China. Since the "urban management" officials are known for unleashing terror on the illegal urban vendors, the establishment of the "rural management" has also aroused similar anxieties. Some of the videos of the "rural management" have invited fury of the netizens. In one video that is still available on weibo, a rural management officer is heard saying: "Who do you think we the rural management officials are? What the traffic police cannot handle, we can handle. Empowered by special powers, we take action first and report the matter later." Bad days ahead for farmers, comments a netizen on weibo, the Chinese twitter. Certainly, since everything under heaven falls under the jurisdiction of the "rural management" there are apprehensions that farmers' rights and freedom would be compromised and their choice to grow agricultural products would be scuttled.

The "rural management" have been provided with new uniforms and professional equipment, including walkie-talkies, cameras, recorders protective gears such as first aid kits, signal jammers, and stab-resistant vests etc., from which it could be gleaned that the authorities are aware of the intensity of conflict between the "rural management" and farmers on the one hand and instil fear in the minds of farmers about the rural law enforcement agencies on the other. Going by the development history of their counterpart the "urban management" in urban areas of China, the confrontation, especially during the initial stages of its establishment was the norm. There have been cases of "urban management" personnel being stabbed to death by the "illegal vendors" and vice-versa. On 21 April, a video circulated on the Internet showed a farm supervisor pushing down a tall tree planted in the courtyard of a villager's house. While pushing the second tree, the farmer rushed out with a long stick and knocked down the supervisor.

In its defence, the Department of Laws and Regulations of the Ministry of Agriculture and Rural Affairs on 18 April, stated that the law enforcement boundary of "agricultural management" is limited to "seeds, pesticides, veterinary drugs, feed, agricultural machinery, animal and plant quarantine and epidemic prevention, quality and safety of agricultural products, fishery administration and other fields." It is to enforce the rule of law and to improve the level of professionalisation and standardisation of law enforcement in the countryside. According to statistics, from 2020 to 2022, comprehensive agricultural law enforcement agencies at all levels across the country have investigated and dealt with a total of 304,700 illegal cases of various types, mediated in 18,900 disputes, and recovered economic losses of 1.496 billion yuan. There are concern that each of the above administrative penalties could be a stepping stone for power expansion of the "rural management" personnel, therefore, "it is necessary to organize special training sessions so that law enforcement officers must thoroughly understand the spirit of the document, and do not exceed or abuse their powers during the law enforcement process, argues Xu Daofa in Dongchu net.

Zhihu or the Chinese Quora has argued that since the growth in the cities has saturated; people's wallets are empty and are struggling with the unpaid mortgages, the farmers have no problem with food and clothing, and they don't have much debt. No matter how poor they are, they still have a pumpkin field in the backyard of their homes, therefore, the countryside is a blue ocean that everyone envies. The key is to collect money, which has far-reaching consequences. For example, the "agricultural management" has discovered a new economic growth point called rural property tax, which at 18 yuan per year is not at all unreasonable. The 800 million farmers generate an income of 1.815 billion yuan! This is precisely why they want to take over the "Three Rurals" space.

Though the government has stated that comprehensive administrative law enforcement in agriculture will not interfere with the normal production and life of farmers, and that "agriculture management" personnel are not in charge of everything, its responsibilities are stipulated by law, and the specific scope is in the law enforcement "guidance catalogue" published by the agricultural and rural departments. However, their comparison with the "urban management" personnel as revealed by the videos on social media, do ring alarm bells in the countryside. The above guidelines and measures do give an impression that China may be gradually slipping back to the days of greater state intervention and towing the "grain as the guiding line" and the "war is imminent" theory of the Mao era. Nonetheless, the violent enforcement is likely to intensify the latent contradictions and give birth to the likes of Chen Sheng and Wu Guang, who revolted against the Qin dynasty following the death of Qin Shihuang.

21

Clamour about China's Economic Collapse

In the wake of China's plummeting economic indicators, the economists have been debating the 'economic collapse' of China. Paul Krugman in an opinion column in the *New York Times* posits that China's economic stumble is systemic and holds China's weirdly resistance to reforms responsible for it. However, he argues that even if the "Chinese leadership seems to be growing more autocratic and more erratic with each passing year", it will push through those reforms and "put more income in the hands of families, so that rising consumption can take the place of unsustainable investment." This argument has been trashed by John Ross, a senior fellow at Chongyang Institute for Financial Studies, Renmin University of China. Ian Johnson in a recent article in *Foreign Affairs* prefers to call it Xi's Age of Stagnation or "new national stasis", or *involution (内卷)*. Unlike Krugman, he sees the root cause for China's economic troubles in "political ossification and ideological hardening."

This perspective matches that of Liu Mengxiong, former member of China's CPPCC, who in a wield yet scathing attack on Chinese leadership said that the reason for China's recent "downward economic spiral" lies in economy, but the root cause is the politics." He argued that the three engines – investment, consumption and exports of China's growth story have run out of steam (动力不足) and even could come to a grinding halt (死火). Citing the figures of National Bureau of Statistics (NBS) for July 2023, he said these showed deflationary trends. According to Liu, in the second quarter, the amount of foreign investment in China touched only

4.9 billion USD, down 87 per cent compared to the previous year! Now, "new three engines of growth" according to him are the NBS, the Central Publicity Department of the CPC and the *Xinhua News Agency*! Adam Posen, in an article in the *Foreign Affairs* also argued that it was the "end of China's economic miracle."

Now, what are the economic indicators revealing? According to the NBS, the economy continued to recover and improve in the first half of the year, achieving continuous quarter-on-quarter growth. It says that in the first half of the year, China's GDP registered year-on-year increase of 5.5 per cent at constant prices. Primary, secondary and tertiary industries grew by 3.7 per cent, 4.3 per cent and 6.4 per cent respectively. The data also reveals that the investment in real estate fell by 8.5 per cent. The sales area of commercial housing nationwide was 665.63 million square meters, a year-on-year decrease of 6.5 per cent; the sales volume of commercial housing was 7,045 billion yuan, a decrease of 1.5 per cent. In July, the national consumer price (CPI) fell by 0.3 per cent year-on-year; the total retail sale of social consumer goods was 3,676.1 billion yuan, a year-on-year increase of 2.5 per cent, and a month-on-month decrease of 0.06 per cent. Nonetheless, the biggest cause of concern has been the unemployment rate, which for the age group of 16-24 was 21.3 per cent in June, and the NBS stopped issuing the figures since then. In the words of Fu Linghui, spokesperson of the NBS, the overall employment pressure is caused by the structural problems, as a result, the "young people find it difficult to get jobs (求职难) and certain sectors find it difficult to recruit employees (招工难)." As regards the foreign trade, in July the exports fell by 9.2 per cent; and imports by 6.9 per cent. From January to July, the import and export of general trade increased by 2.1 per cent year-on-year basis.

Going by these figures, except for the unemployment rate, the Chinese economy is not doing bad, but why there is so much clamor about its collapse? The "difficulties and challenges" faced by China according to an opinion piece in Huanqiu Shibao are: insufficient domestic demand (内需求不足), some enterprises have difficulties in running their business (经营困难), key areas (重点领域) are fraught with many risks and hidden dangers (风险隐患), and the external environment is complicated and grave (复杂严峻). These challenges have been affirmed by the meeting of the Political Bureau of the Central Committee of the Communist Party of

China on 24 July 2023. In fact, all these problems are interconnected and are structural as pronounced by some of the experts above. Let's visit the three pillars of China's economic resilience and the problems they are encountering.

As I have argued in an occasional paper written for the Institute of Chinese Studies recently that the economic growth during the Reform Era was driven by massive government investment accounting for around 45 per cent of the GDP, most of which went into infrastructure and real estate as Chinese citizens invested almost 70 per cent of their savings in the latter. The magnitude of the investment could be gauged through official figures released early February this year by Zheng Guoguang, Director of the Office of the Leading Group for the First National Natural Disaster Comprehensive Risk Survey of the State Council. According to the figures, China has around 600 million buildings in urban and rural areas; 5 million kilometres of road networks; 900,000 bridges and tunnels, as well as more than 6,000 berths in coastal areas. This doesn't include around 40,000 kilometres of high speed railway.

This is the kind of construction frenzy that went on during the reform period. However, currently investments in infrastructure and real estate have turned non-productive which led to a spurt in debt to GDP ratio, bad debts and mortgage crisis. With the real estate bubble burst, investments remain in jeopardy and returns are bleak. Real estate giants like Evergrande and Country Garden are unable to service their debts, so is the case with 50 odd other real estate companies in China. According to Sohu.com, there are more than 400 million people with mortgages in China, and the total amount of mortgage loans exceeds 50 trillion yuan. This shows that speculation in the real estate had been the norm.

As regards the foreign investment in China, the official figures reveal that from January to July 2023, the actual use of foreign capital in China was 766.71 billion yuan, a year-on-year decrease of 4 per cent, equivalent to 111.8 billion US dollars, a decrease of 9.8 per cent. Statistics from China's State Administration of Foreign Exchange show that foreign companies' inward direct investment in building factories etc. in China from April to June was US$ 4.9 billion. The decrease compared with the same period last year reached 87 per cent, setting a new high. An article in Nikkei has argued that it has resulted from the US policy of promoting "friend-shoring" so as to build supply chains with friendly countries. It may be recalled that the US has put investment restrictions on China in the fields of semiconductors and artificial intelligence. Therefore, if the "decoupling" or the "de-risking" continues, the FDI in China is bound to face further hurdles.

The second pillar that drove Chinese economy was consumption. In fact, the issue is related to the investment, both public and private. As the returns in the real estate are diminishing, this has dealt a heavy blow to household appliances and other ancillary industries. Moreover, the vicious cycle of the debt is a bigger problem. According to data released by the Central Bank of China, as of the end of 2022, 780 million people across China were in debt, with an average per capita debt of 133,400 yuan. Not to mention of credit cards, the overdue amount exceeded 200 billion yuan. According to the Toutiao news, of the above 780 million people, the overdue rate was 42 per cent, implying that almost 300 million people had defaulted on servicing the debt.

The third pillar of China's economic miracle has been the exports. Undoubtedly, China has emerged as the largest trading partner of more than 120 countries in the world. The US economic dominance has long been over. Nevertheless, the recent statistics published by the National Development and Reform Commission reveal that in the first half of 2023, China's total import and export volume was US$ 2.92 trillion, a decrease of 4.7 per cent. Among them, exports were US$ 1.66 trillion, down 3.2 per cent; imports were US$ 1.25 trillion, down 6.7 per cent; the trade surplus was US$ 408.69 billion, an increase of 6 per cent. However, if we look at the July figures alone, a *BBC* report reveals that China's exports to the US fell by 23.1 per cent year-on-year, and the EU fell by 20.6 per cent. Obviously, sluggish global growth has reduced demand for Chinese goods; the US-China hi-tech war; geopolitical tensions between the two largest economies, and the de-risking from China by the West has also resulted in plummeting figures in trade and investment.

In conclusion, the figures released by Chinese government sources portrays both a resilient as well as alarming picture of the state of China's economy, especially the systemic problems are challenging and could be ameliorated only by the government intervention. The deepening of the reforms in sectors such as telecom, energy, insurance, information technology where government has denied market access to foreign investors could be an option. The rejuvenation of private enterprises that according to Shi Jinchuan, Professor at Zhejiang University, has faced "twofold challenge of obstructed vertical advancement and heightened horizontal competition" and the over steps such as "administration superseding law" remains problematic. The stimulus is another option but the Chinese government has been hesitant so far. More importantly, as long as the lot of troubled real estate sector as well as provincial governments' debt crisis is not handled properly, the vicious cycle will persist. Added to this, as long as the sluggish external demand and China's geopolitical and security environment remains in disarray, the sustainable recovery of the Chinese economy, and consumption replacing the investment calculus would not be easy.

III
SOCIAL ISSUES

22

Tracing the Origin of COVID-19

COVID-19 first appeared in Wuhan, China, and has subsequently spread to 220 countries and territories around the world. To date, the virus infected more than 173 million people and taken lives of 3.72 million people. Of these, almost 38 per cent fatalities took place in the US, Brazil and India, India alone accounted for almost 10 per cent of all global deaths. People's lives have been disrupted, economic activities have come to a grinding halt, and trillions of dollars have been lost as economies registered negative growth as high as 7.3 per cent in case of India, millions of jobs have been lost and millions have been pushed below the poverty line. Even after 18 months since its outbreak, the world is clueless about its origin as well as its end. As regards the origin of the virus, the zoonotic and lab accident theories are making rounds. The former, gained currency during the first wave of the virus, however, as the variants became deadlier in subsequent waves killing people of all age groups, the latter has gained traction and the US president Joe Biden has even directed his intelligence agencies to submit a report within 3 months. Why have events taken such a sharp turn? What are the plausible scenarios emerging out of the COVID-19 origin investigations?

First of all, if the lab-accident hypothesis is true, the credibility of the some of the leading virologists, science journals, and the World Health Organisation (WHO) will take a beating. This will also demonstrate that China's penetration in the US goes beyond Wall Street and Washington, and perhaps Xi Jinping was right when he told Joe Biden in 2015 that "China will own America" by 2035, albeit in a light hearted mood.

Nevertheless, US's heavy reliance on Chinese supply chains in some sectors including pharmaceuticals has been exposed amidst the pandemic. In the same vein, a quantum jump in China's farmland purchases, real estate investments, and business stakes of the owners of mainstream US media at minimum vindicate the China buying America view. Now examine this: when Dr. Shi Zhengli, the "bat women" of China published a paper in *Nature* on 3 February 2020 advocating the zoonotic origin theory of the Wuhan Coronavirus spread, she was supported by 27 public health scientists in a statement published by *Lancet* on 19 February 2020. The scientists said they were in "solidarity with all scientists and health professionals in China who continue to save lives and protect global health during the challenge of the COVID-19 outbreak." The WHO also took this line and ruled out that the virus originated from lab-accident in its *Report* issued in February 2021 after their investigations in Wuhan. This line of thinking was projected in the mainstream media globally, especially in the US and any attempt to circulate news related to the lab accident hypothesis was completely blocked, including from social media's like Facebook, so much so the accounts of the "spreaders" of such a "conspiracy theory" were also closed temporarily.

Two, an article by Nicholas Wade, a science writer associated with the *Nature, Lancet* and *New York Times* on 5 May 2021 in the *Bulletin of the Atomic Scientists* weighs the zoonotic as well as lab-leak hypotheses and inclines towards the latter. The argument is supported vehemently by the British Professor Angus Dalgleish and Norwegian scientist Dr. Birger Sørensen, in a paper accessed by the *Daily Mail* of the U.K. The duo argue that they have had "prima facie evidence of retro-engineering in China for a year." The scientists also concluded that the "SARS-Coronavirus-2 has no credible natural ancestor." Indian researchers in a paper titled "Uncanny similarity of unique inserts in the 2019-nCoV spike protein to HIV-1 gp120 and Gag" had argued that they have "found that the 2019 – nCoV spike glycoprotein contains 4 insertions," but the paper had to be withdrawn. Dr. Luc Montagnier, a 2008 Nobel Prize winner for Medicine has supported this argument by pointing to "molecular tinkering" with the spike proteins and that the virus is "manipulated and accidentally released from a laboratory in Wuhan."

This has created a storm in China and the rest of the world. China published a series of editorials blaming the US of "politicisation" of the virus. As for the US virologists, who hereunto were adhering to the zoonotic hypotheses, now argued that there could be a possibility of lab-leak, therefore further investigations were required. Even the Biden administration that issued an executive order banning the use of terms such as "China virus" and "Wuhan virus" when referring to COVID-19 in January 2021, has now ordered an investigation into the origin of the virus. The US Secretary of State, Antony Blinken vowed to hold China accountable to origin of the virus in an interview given to the Axion HBO on 7 June 2021.

If this is the case, why did Dr. Anthony Fauci, the director of the National Institute of Allergy and Infectious Diseases, and Dr. Peter Daszak, of the EcoHealth Alliance, US and many other scientists give in to the zoonotic theory so quickly? Why is the US mainstream media doing a volte-face now? If the Fox News anchor, Tucker Carlson's story is to be believed, the US has gathered credible information from a "highest-level Chinese defector" to the US, who is believed to be cooperating with the National Defense Intelligence Agency (DIA). If this is a credible piece of information, the Biden Administration has been forced to take a tougher stand, who hitherto appeared to be giving a respectful burial to the virus origin. This was in contrast to the Trump administration's investigations and calling the virus a "China virus." It was perceived that President Biden didn't want to rock the troubled boat of the US-China relationship beyond castigating China's assertiveness in the Taiwan Strait and human right issues in Xinjiang, Tibet and Hong Kong. Remember his son, Hunter Biden still holds 10 per cent stakes in a Chinese equity firm named Bohai Harvest RST Equity Investment Fund Management Co. Notwithstanding Biden's intentions, things don't look good given the geopolitical rivalry between the established hegemon and the challenger.

Three, the investigations will also implicate the US, for it points fingers towards the US virologists and state organs that funded dangerous "gain of function" research in China's Wuhan Institute of Virology (WIV), which is banned in the US. US top virologists like Dr. Ralph Baric have been collaborating with Dr. Shi Zhengli for many years. In late May, in a Senate hearing, Dr. Fauci told lawmakers that the US granted US$ 600,000 in funding to the WIV for coronavirus research through Peter Daszak's non-profit EcoHealth Alliance. The *Daily Mail* also reveals that between 2013 and 2019, the Pentagon gave US$ 39 million to EcoHealth

Alliance. Dr. Fauci's emails from last year reveal that he didn't entertain the idea that the novel coronavirus could've leaked from a lab, contrary to the views of a fellow scientist Kristian Andersen, a virologist at the Scripps Research Institute in California who did point out that "some of the features (potentially) look engineered." Furthermore, emails also establish Dr. Fauci's cordial relations with Chinese government officials such as George Gao Fu, director of the Chinese Centre of Disease Control and Prevention. Given this nexus between the US Virologists, government entities and organisations with their counterparts in Wuhan, and also as to why the US was encouraging and conducting hazardous "gain of function" research when the same is banned in the US, it could be deduced why US virologists tried to put a lid on the lab-accident theory.

Four, so even if both the zoonotic and lab-leak hypotheses have not been proved right to date, nevertheless, public opinion at this point in time is right in demanding free and fair investigations. However, even if the origin of the virus is established, at maximum voices asking for trillions of dollars in compensation, as Donald Trump has been asking recently, will become louder. But who has paid compensation for the origin of pandemics? In the history of epidemics, no country has ever been blamed and asked to pay indemnities. AIDS originated in the US, did the US compensate people who were infected or killed by it across the globe? H1N1 or the swine flu that originated in Mexico and killed millions worldwide, did countries sue Mexico for compensation? Similar is the case with Ebola and Mers and the list continues. Even if the political slug is dragged to the International Court of Justice, who abides by the ruling nowadays? This may be followed by sanctions, but the same have been imposed on Russia for other reasons obviously. These may have hurt Russia economically to some extent, but did they diminish Russia's role or influence? What the likely scenario is therefore, is that it may hasten China's economic decoupling from the West, which in certain hi-tech sectors is already happening. It will also intensify the cold war between the US and China and turn the Indo-Pacific more volatile and fraught with dangers of armed conflict.

Finally, the lab-accidents do happen, however, whether they are part of other conspiracy theories, including the one that COVID-19 is an outcome of the "biological weapon program of China" which so far has not gained credence, needs to be investigated. Nevertheless, the US and its allies cornering China on the virus origin and human rights issue, has certainly mellowed down the "wolf-warrior" approach of China, and Present Xi Jinping has called on the Communist Party leaders to project a "trustworthy, loveable and admirable" image of China in a speech on 31 May 2021. The unfolding of events in the US recently establishes the fact that conflicts of interest are certainly at the centre of all narratives. It is owing to these conflicts of interests that a certain narrative is created and sold. So much so that social media and some reputed science journals have blocked information or forced scholars to withdraw their findings that are antithetical to the mainstream narrative.

23

Chinese Millennials and the Philosophy of "Lying flat-ism"

In recent times, "lying flat" philosophy of the Chinese millennials has taken the cyberspace by storm. The storm was triggered by a post entitled "Lying flat is justice" on Chinese search engine, Baidu in April 2021. The user named "Kind-Hearted Traveller" identified as Luo Huazhong, wrote, "I have not been working for two years, just having fun and don't see anything wrong in it. Pressure mainly comes from people around you who position and compete with you, it also comes from the values of the older generation. All sorts of pressures keep popping up before you all the time. Every time you search for a popular news, it is all about romances and pregnancies etc. of celebrities in "procreative surrounding" (生育周边), as if some 'invisible creatures' (看不见的生物) are creating a kind of thinking and pressure on you. But, we don't have to be like this. I can just sleep in the sun in my wooden bucket like Diogenes, or I can live in a cave like Heraclitus and think about "logos", since this land has never had a school of thought that exalts human subjectivity, I can develop one of my own. Lying flat is my wise movement. Only through lying flat, can humans measure up to things."

The post attracted millions of responses and Luo was pronounced as the "lying flat master" and his philosophy as "lying flat-ism" (躺平主义) by netizens. The storm of "lying flat-ism" and the mass it is gathering has taken the government by surprise, and the post was soon taken off the Chinese cyberspace. The *South China Morning Post* has defined "lying flat-ism" as "to represent a silent protest to unfairness, often the result of structural and institutional factors that can no longer be altered by personal efforts." It is an antithesis to "ants in the pants"(热锅上的蚂蚁) phenomenon of the socialist construction and reform period that culminated into a hustle culture of "996" or working from 9am to 9pm, 6 days a week. It is the reaction to "involution" (内卷) in Chinese society as reflected in Luo Huazhong's above post. As a response to this, Chinese millennials have refused to become money making machines for the ruling class and are resorting to not getting married, not having children, not having a job, not owning property, consuming as little as possible, and not communicating to the outside world. In other words, it is a kind of Gandhian passive resistance or non-cooperation movement that is non-violent. An article on Sohu.com has pronounced it as a "new cultural movement of the new youth in a hundred years." So, what has triggered "lying flat-ism" in the new era?

One, Chinese millennials are finding upward social mobility extremely difficult, unlike the older generation of the reform era, when China witnessed unprecedented economic growth by attracting foreign investment and capital. China's biggest disruptive brands such as Huawei, ZTE, Alibaba, Tencent, Baidu etc. are the by-products of that economic boom. The export growth which China witnessed in the last two decades is the thing of a bygone era. Though President Xi Jinping has stated that China will rely mainly on "internal circulation" i.e. the domestic cycle of production, distribution, and consumption for its development, but unemployment has reached unprecedented levels in recent years. The unemployment rate for those aged 16 to 24 was 13.1 per cent as of February 2021, far above the national urban jobless rate of 5.5 per cent according to China's National Bureau of Statistics. According to the 2021 census, 218.36 million people in China are university graduates, a 73 per cent increase from 2010. Imagine the pressure on government and young people when between 8 to 9 million students enter the workforce every year.

Two, it reveals a serious demographic crisis in China. Once in a decade census (2020) conducted by China reveals that China's population rose 5.38 per cent between 2010 and 2020 to reach 1.41billion, slowest since census began in 1953. Data revealed a fertility rate of 1.3 children per woman for 2020, which is at par with many developed societies. Demographic deterioration has forced China to replace its 2016 two-child policy with a new three-child policy in 2021. But will it help if the former didn't bear any fruit. An editorial in the Chinese edition of the *Global Times* seems to suggest that China can do it. It says, "We should have confidence that China is a country with strong macro-control capabilities, and we will certainly be able to do more effectively than Western countries in adjusting the population structure." Remember Mao once said that "the failure to solve the food problem was entirely the result of the cruel and ruthless oppression and exploitation of imperialism, feudalism, bureaucratic capitalism, and the Kuomintang reactionary government, rather than overpopulation." China knows that the loss of demographic dividend will have a huge impact on the overall outlook of economy, but the Chinese millennials unlike their counterparts of the construction and reform periods have refused to dance on the tunes of their leaders, rather have found refuge in "lying flat-ism" and have resisted to be leeks that are harvested by the ruling class (割韭菜) at will.

Three, it is also a struggle against the increasing social inequalities. Though the state capitalism has made tremendous achievements in the last four decades, millions of people have been alleviated from the abject poverty, however, the widening social inequalities arising out of the nexus between political and economic powers within the party state has become a new Achilles' heel for the Party. Statistics reveal that the top 0.14 per cent of households in China own around one-third of China's wealth. Last year, Premier Li Keqiang contradicted President Xi Jinping on poverty alleviation issue when he said during a press briefing that "China has over 600 million people whose monthly income is barely 1,000 yuan ($140) and their lives have further been affected by the coronavirus pandemic." On 11 March, 2021 during a press briefing Li Keqiang dropped yet another bombshell by declaring that there are over 200 million Chinese people doing 'flexijobs' (灵活就业), implying that these many people are doing more than one or two jobs at a time in order to secure their livelihood. Premier Li Keqiang advocated that these people should be brought under the social security net and offered state subsidies.

In a nutshell, China's aging population, weak domestic demand, and shrinking exports, and "lying flat-ism" may exacerbate China's economic and social issues. No wonder, the official media has criticised the "lying flat" philosophy. Xinhua, in a commentary entitled "'Lying flat' is shameful, where is the sense of justice?" published on 20 May 2021 said, "choosing to "lie flat" in the face of pressure is not only unjust, but also shameful. Such a "poisonous chicken soup" has no value. On 28 May, Chinese edition of the *Global Times* in its editorial wrote, "China is at the most crucial stage of the long road to national rejuvenation. Young people are the hope of this country. Neither their personal circumstances nor the circumstances of this country will allow them to 'lie flat' collectively. No matter whether they are active or passive, they will become the most diligent and spiritually strongest group in the world." Sohu.com even tried to convince the Chinese millennials as to how 'lying flat-ism' or "demotivation culture" (丧文化) has been destroying young Japanese for the last 30 years! The article says that "the proportion of the singles in Japanese population has reached as high as 30 per cent. Among them, the proportion of men who have never married before the age of 50 is 23 per cent, and the proportion of women is 14 per cent. It is predicted that by 2035, half of Japanese people will be singles." Quoting a survey conducted by the National Institute of Population and Social Security Research, Japan, the article says that "the male and female 'virginity rate' for 18-34 years old in Japan stood at 42 per cent and 44.2 per cent respectively, and the rate is still on the rise." Some academicians from reputed universities have also defended the official condemnation of 'lying flat' people. In the words of professor Li Fengliang from Tsinghua University, "involution plays the role of screening function in education." Obviously, it didn't go well with the 'lying flat' community who retorted back by saying that that "Tsinghua professors should be subjected to a termination system, so that they know what involution means."

Notwithstanding the criticism and pitfalls of 'lying flat-ism', Chinese millennials are of the view that no matter how hard they work under the present 996 system, how hard they try to save money, buy a house or car with a loan, get married and have children, they cannot satisfy people or make themselves happy. The question they are asking is: is there a better resistance than "lying flat"?

24

China's Crackdown on its Entertainment Industry

On 29 August 2021, more than 30 official media outlets at the central, provincial and municipal government levels reposted a 2798-character long article entitled "Everyone can feel that a profound transformation is underway!" from Li Guangman's official WeChat account. Li, a columnist and former editor of the *Central China Electric Power* has justified China's crackdown on entertainment industry. In Li's words, government's actions from "suspension of Ant Group's IPO, to the central government's rectification of the economic order, anti-monopoly, to 18.2 billion yuan fine imposed on the Alibaba and the investigation of Didi Chuxing, to central government's solemn commemoration of the 100th anniversary of the founding of the Communist Party of China (CPC), the proposed path of common prosperity, and a series of recent actions to rectify chaos in the entertainment industry (娱乐圈乱象) tell us that mega changes are taking place in China and that spheres such as economic, financial, cultural, and political are undergoing a profound transformation (深刻的变革) or a profound revolution (深刻的革命). It marks a return from capitalist cliques (资本集团) to the masses (人民群众), a transformation from capital-centred (资本为中心) to people-centred (人民为中心). Hence, it is a political transformation (政治变革) with people as the mainstay, and all those who obstruct this people-centred transformation will be rendered useless. This profound transformation is also a return to the original intent of the CPC (中国共产党的初心), a return to a people-centred (以人民为中心) approach, and a return to the essence of socialism (社会主义本质)."

Surprisingly, the politically charged essay drew Hu Xijin's criticism. Hu, the editor in chief of the jingoistic *Global Times*, opined that "the article made an inaccurate description of the situation, made use of some exaggerated language, deviated from the country's major policies, and caused misleading." Rather than pronouncing the measures to clean the entertainment industry as a "revolution", Hu maintains that all is aimed to "further improve social governance" (社会治理). Hu sees the "profound transformation" as a continuous process of the reforms, rather than China "bidding farewell to the reforms." These contradictory messages have given rise to the speculation that there are factions within the CPC supportive of each such views. Why has Li Guangman's essay created such a storm in China? Was it intentional? Or must it be interpreted as "Bombard the headquarters" big-character poster of the Cultural Revolution-2? What are the plausible scenarios that the essay hints at?

One, the reasons behind the crackdown on the big-tech, edtech and now the entertainment industry range from curtailing the financial clout of Shangai clique, cost of schooling and tutoring by the millennial Chinese in the aging society, and China's scandalous entertainment industry. According to Li Guangman, "scandals involving Wu Yifan, Huo Zun, Zhang Zhehan's devil worship at Japan's Yasukuni Shrine, and recent rape allegation against Hunan TV host Qian Feng have made people feel that the Chinese entertainment industry has already rotten to the core (烂透了)." Tax evasion by celebrities is cited as another reason. The Cyberspace Administration of China (CAC) has dealt a heavy blow to the celebrity "fan clubs" (饭圈). The State Taxation Administration (STA) on its part fined actress Zheng Shuang 299 million RMB (US$ 46 million) for tax evasion, and Zhao Wei and Gao Xiaosong were banned and their content taken off from various platforms. If Zheng Shuang and Zhang Zhehan invited the ire of netizens for visiting Yasukuni Shrine, Zhao Wei wearing a dress made of Japanese military flag two decades back has also been subjected to condemnation by the xenophobic netizens. She is believed to be close to bigwigs like Jack Ma and Wang Lin, associated to the Shanghai clique. It is also believed that Zhao Wei's censorship is also linked to investigations of Zhejiang party secretary, Zhou Jiangyong, for the celebrities, business tycoons and party bosses are in hand and globe and form a strong alliance. The clean-up of the entertainment industry, in the words of Li Guangman "will wash all the dirt, capital markets will no longer be paradise for capitalists to get rich overnight, cultural markets will no longer be heaven for sissy-boy stars (娘炮明星), and news and public opinion will no longer be in the position of worshipping western culture. It is a return to the revolutionary spirit (红色回归), a return to heroism (英雄回归), a return to courage and righteousness (血性回归)."

Two, it is also related to the promotion of "common prosperity" (共同富裕) and prevention and mitigation of major financial risks (金融风险) as could be discerned from Chinese president Xi Jinping's remarks made on 17 August 2021. Xi had remarked that "It is necessary to strengthen the regulation and adjustment of high incomes, protect legal incomes in accordance with the law, reasonably regulate excessive high, and encourage high-income groups and enterprises to return more to the society." This is the so called "third distribution" the CPC has imposed on its billionaires and wealthy people, perhaps selectively. According to a new ruling, an individual holding deposits more than 500, 000 RMB will be subjected to investigation. China's bigtech companies like Tencent, Bytedance, Xiaomi, Meituan, Lenevo etc. groups have already "returned" more than US$ 5 billion to the society.

Three, Li Guangman's essay also hints at levelling the "three great mountains" of education, medical care, and housing. Edtech has already come under scanner and billions of dollars have been eroded from the market with China bringing these companies under the antimonopoly and data security protection laws. Children access to online gaming has been restricted to three hours a day, and that also during the weekends. Medical sector, where there is an unholy nexus between big pharmaceutical companies, hospitals and doctors could be the next for cleaning up. Hainan has already placed a new procurement system that has reduced the prices of drugs by 31.91 per cent. The real estate sector, which was one of the pillars to place China's economic growth on a solid trajectory is riddled with problems. Though the sector accounts for around 30 per cent of the national GDP, however, also has maximum bad debts amounting to US$ 7.7 trillion. The nonperforming loans have reached a whopping 30 per cent across the five largest banks to US$ 15 billion.

Finally, Li Guangman cautions China about the US military threats, economic and technological embargo, financial attacks and political and diplomatic siege (政治及外交围剿). Li accuses the US of "waging biological warfare, cyber warfare, space warfare and public opinion war against China." According to him, "In this hour, if we still rely on those big capitalists to fight the forces of imperialism and hegemonism, and if we continue bow before US's tittytainment strategy (奶头乐战略) and if we allow our young generation lose their virility and masculinity, then we don't need an enemy – we will have brought destruction upon ourselves." No wonder, the hammer has also fallen on a fan club of popular South Korean K-pop band BTS for raising illegal funds. On 2 September, China's National Radio and Television Administration issued a notice that puts a lid on reality shows like Produce 101. The article may not have "Bombard the Headquarters" essay effect, however, it raises many questions about various social, political and economic contradictions brought into play amidst an intense power struggle within the rank and file of the CPC just before the 20th Party Congress next year. Until then, cleaning up of the "chaos" across various sectors is likely to go unhindered.

25

A Storm in China's CHIP Industry

Until very recently the US maintained asymmetric advantage in global technological innovations. However, since the last two decades, the leadership has been increasingly challenged by China's "great leap forward" in developing digital infrastructure architecture with deep pockets. In 2014, China set up the National Integrated Circuit Industry Investment Fund, known as the "Big Fund" (大基金) aimed at leapfrogging China's semiconductor industry. The next year, China rolled out an ambitious Made in China 2025 with an objective of achieving 70 per cent "self-sufficiency" by 2025 in core components and critical materials, jolting the US and other players from their slumber. If these were not good enough reasons for US-China cold war, heavy disruption by the COVID-19 pandemic across industries such as telecommunication, electronics and automobile forced countries to build new supply chains away from China.

As the US tightened it noose around hi-tech exports, the Chinese semiconductor industry faced the heat. In a push to raise more money, it has been reported by the Chinese media that in the first phase of its funds, the Big Fund raised 138.7 billion yuan ($20.5 billion), and for the second phase between 2019 and 2021, more than 200 billion yuan ($30 billion) were raised. Given the proportion of 3-4 times, it is expected to leverage the scale of social financing of nearly one trillion yuan (around $148 billion). Such a huge funding with not so spectacular result raised many eyebrows in China's power corridors, and the anticorruption watchdog of the Party, the CCDI started investigations into the corruption running amok in the industry. In November 2021, Gao Songtao, the former vice president of Huaxin Investment Management Co. Ltd., also known as Sino IC Capital was investigated. The arrest of Xiao Yaqing, China's minister of industry and information technology in July 2022 was followed by the fall of eight industry leaders across China's Big Fund and Tsinghua UniGroup.

Bigwigs like Ding Wenwu, president of China's Big Fund, Du Yang, Yang Zhengfan, and Liu Yang all associated with Sino IC Capital have fallen from grace. It may be noted that Sino IC Capital manages assets belonging to the Big Fund. Some others who have come under the scanner of the CCDI are Wang Wenzhong, a partner of Shenzhen Hongtai Fund Investment Management Co. Ltd., and Lu Jun, the former deputy director of China Development Bank. Besides, Zhao Weiguo, the former chairman of Tsinghua UniGroup, and Diao Shijing, the former president of the same company, were also investigated in July. The Tsinghua UniGroup is believed to be closely related to the Big Fund. In the words of Pan Helin, co-director and researcher of the Digital Economy and Financial Innovation Research Centre of Zhejiang University International Business School, "Anti-corruption campaign must go on, and unmask the hypocrisy, [real] face, and formalism (虚伪，面子，形式主义) of the semiconductor industry." According to statistics, there are 142,900 chip-related companies in China. In the first half of 2022 alone, China added 30,800 chip-related companies.

These investigations in China coincided with the CHIPS and Science Act passed by the US Congress on 28 July and its enactment into a law by President Biden on 9 August. The bill allocates US$ 52.7 billion over five years to fund and incentivize semiconductor manufacturing in the United States with 25 per cent tax credit, and authorizes nearly US$ 170 billion in funding over five years for research and development. The bill includes provisions that generally prohibit beneficiaries of the CHIPS funding and investment tax credit from expanding semiconductor manufacturing in China for a period of ten years. According to a statement from the US Department of the State, the bill will "prepare our economy for the 21st century and strengthen our regional supply chain diplomacy, including through the US-EU Trade and Technology Council, the Indo-Pacific Economic Framework, and the Americas Partnership for Economic Prosperity."

As expected, the bill drew China's ire and government officials levelled it as "violation of the WTO's non-discrimination principle." Some others called it a "major shift of the US crackdown on China" and US' "arbitrary push for supply chains to be removed and decoupled from China." This is understandable as "China's dependence on global semiconductors still exceeds 90 per cent, and the localisation rate of chips in some fields is less than 10 per cent" according to a report. In the 13th Five Year Plan, China has envisaged to design and develop 32/28nm, 15/14nm, and accelerate the R&D on 10/7nm chips, however, it appears that these fell short of their objectives.

Yet China remains confident that the US' "economic coercion" is doomed to fail, for China imported about US$ 440 billion worth of chips in 2021, far exceeding the number of subsidies the US is going to provide under the new Act. China is confident that the semiconductor investment in China is on an upward trajectory as "China consumes up to 40 per cent of global output of semiconductor microchips." Presently, majority of the world's semiconductor companies are located in the East Asia-Pacific region. In 2020, Taiwan controlled 63 per cent of the market share, with South Korea at 18 per cent and China at 6 per cent. According to a recent industry report (2022), the self-sufficiency rate of China's integrated circuit industry is relatively low, especially in the field of mid-to-high-end chips, and the phenomenon of dependence on imports is serious. According to analysts, the localisation is bound to accelerate with SMIC's Shenzhen factory production since 2022, but the chips produced would be mostly of 28nm.The reports reveal that the SMIC has achieved breakthrough in developing a quasi 7nm process irrespective of the US sanctions.

Since the 4.0 industrial revolution is being fueled by the big data, the CHIPS and Science Act and the Chip4 Alliance of the US, Taiwan, South Korea and Japan has forced China to crackdown on its semiconductor industry that is believed to be highly corrupt, and partially controlled by the Shanghai clique. Given the importance of the industry and the US decoupling, China will continue to pump money in the sector albeit in a more regulated and cautious way and strive for self-sufficiency especially in 10nm and lower chips segment that are crucial for quantum computing, AI, hypersonic, and 5G etc., technologies. The realisation of the same, will further accelerate China's economic dominance and military assertiveness in the region and beyond.

The Global Players

One has to understand that in the initial period, behind the success of the Taiwan Semiconductor Manufacturing Co. (TSMC), it was the US R&D and design, only the manufacturing was outsourced to the TSMC. As a result of this model, the US absolute advantage of the 1990s in this sector fell from around 40 per cent market share to 12 per cent in the year 2020. Conversely, in 2020, Taiwan controlled 63 per cent of the market share, with South Korea at 18 per cent and China at 6 per cent. Presently we can say that around 90 per cent chips of the US bigtechs like Apple, Amazon, Google, Nvidia, and Qualcomm are imported from Taiwan. Since, China has entered the scene and invested heavily in semiconductor industry and have hired people from TSMC, the US is wary of this development; added to this the geopolitical competition with China for the leadership in Chip industry, the US has enacted its own Chip Act recently, inviting investment including from the TSMC in this sector with incentives. The US even banned all the companies having US components to do business with China, the US citizens including the green card holders have also been banned from assisting China or having had their businesses in China.

The US going back to manufacturing in semiconductors wont impact adversely on the Taiwan, rather it will open up investment opportunities for TSMC in the US, in a similar way the TSMC has enlarged its cake by investing in South Korea and Japan. Moreover, the US still remains one of the leading global player in R&D in semiconductors having the capability of producing 5nanometer and lower chips that are crucial for having massive capacities in AI and various other new technologies related to quantum computing. If we look at the worth of the US bigtechs like Intel, Broadcom, Micron technologies, Qualcomm, Texas Instruments, Nvidia, NMD etc. it is still bigger than the combined strength of their rivals in Taiwan, Japan and South Korea. Based on this absolute completive advantage, the US is wanting to push China out from this competition.

26

China's Response to the "White Paper Revolution"

Holding high an A4 white paper in her hands, a young lady protester tells the crowd with teary eyes, choked yet indignant voice:

> After so many days of lockdown, a man-made disaster (人祸) happened. People witnessed that fire brigades were not able to enter [the premises], water barely reached the windows [of the building]! And the government proclaimed that the gate [of the building] was open, it was the residents who didn't escape on their own! A day after the Korean stampede, there were so many reports in each and every media. But, is there any official report (官方报道) in our media about the deaths of our people and citizens in this disaster? Has it been reported? Not at all! All are lies! All are silent (全都是沉默)! All are quiet (全都是静默)! Therefore, we started a white paper mourning movement. *Did we say anything on it? Nothing! All the resentment is in our heart! All the condolences are in our heart!*

This emotional outburst of a protester, is perhaps the best depiction of the whole sequence of events leading to the "White Paper Revolution" and the intent behind it. The protester was referring to fatalities caused by a fire incident in a high-rise building in Urumqi, Xinjiang that has been under strict COVID lockdown since August 2022. The seething anger of the people against the draconian COVID restrictions and their economic woes have been sporadically exploding in various regions of China.

The first salvo of defiance was fired by the residents of Guangdong's Haizhu district on 15 November, when they took to streets, smashed lockdown barriers and clashed with the police. A few days later a video of a Chongqing resident, dubbed as "superman brother" (超人哥) called on the local government to admit its mistakes and not to make a fuss over the "little influenza" (小感冒). In defiance, he shouted "take my liberty, give me death" (不自由毋宁死). In Henan's Zhengzhou, since mid-October, Foxconn's iPhone assembly employees have been at loggerheads with their employer on the question of wages and lockdown restrictions. Many jumped off the walls and travelled long distances on foot to their respective hometowns, only to be blocked by the "big whites" (大白) at various check points. On 23 November, they clashed with the "big whites" once again and both sides sustained injuries.

Urumqi incident acted as a catalyst and people in various cities, especially university students in Chengdu, Shanghai, Beijing, Guangzhou, Xi'an, and Qingdao displayed defiance rarely seen in China. Demonstrators reiterated the slogans put by Peng Zaizhou (real name Peng Lifa) on the two large white banners he hung from the Sitong Bridge in the heart of Beijing, just three days before inauguration of the 20th National Congress of the Communist Party of China (CPC). The slogans read: "*No to PCR testing, yes to subsistence. No to lockdown, yes to freedom. No to lies, yes to dignity. No to Cultural Revolution, yes to reform. No to great leader, yes to voting. Don't be a slave, be a citizen*!" Peng's bold and defiant move emboldened the protestors to an extent demanding "Xi Jinping step down! CPC step down!" on 24 November, at Middle Urumqi Road in Shanghai. In Tsinghua university, the alma mater of Xi Jinping, students shouted "Democracy! (民主) Rule of law! (法制) Freedom of expression! (表达自由)" etc., slogans. Notwithstanding the tightly controlled censorship, the movement managed to spread on the Internet and was widely covered by foreign media.

Though the protests were spontaneous, but, their scope and scale was limited to big cities. Though they were in opposition to the tough "dynamic COVID zero" policy of the party-state, however, their roots run deeper, and demonstrate a certain political appeal. Obviously, the economic slump, real estate bubble bust, mortgage crisis, closure of small businesses, growing social inequalities, unemployment amongst the youth, and increasingly inward looking policies in the new era are some other triggers.

As regards China's response, there is no mention of the protests in official media. Nonetheless, it could be discerned from the plenary session of the Central Political and Legal Affairs Commission (CPLAC) of the CPC, held on 28 November that there has been extensive discussion on the issue and the party is contemplating a way out from its present predicament. The CPLAC has squarely blamed it on the "infiltration and destructive activities of hostile forces" (敌对势力渗透破坏活动) and declared that the political and legal organs of the CPC "should resolutely crack down on illegal and criminal acts that disrupt social order (打击扰乱社会秩序的违法犯罪行为) in accordance with the law. The statement pledged to take strong measures to implement the spirit of the 20th National Congress of the CPC and resolutely safeguard national security and social stability. The crackdown and rounding up of the protesters have been initiated, and the police has been checking mobile phones of passengers for any VPN and foreign apps or any objectionable content on their devices.

Two, in order to "prevent and control the pandemic" (防控疫情), all regions have "adjusted" (调整) the winter vacation time and have notified holidays in advance. In some cases, special arrangements have been made to transport students to their homes. The CPC is wary of university students who have been at the forefront of movements such as the May Fourth of 1919 and Tian'anmen of 1989.

Three, stringent lockdowns have been eased up starting with some areas in Urumqi, followed by Guangzhou, Kunming and Beijing's Chaoyang district. On 30 November, during a symposium held at the National Health and Medical Commission, Vice Premier Sun Chunlan avoided mentioning "dynamic COVID zero" (动态清零), often reiterated in official documents and speeches, rather she talked about "low pathogenicity" (致病性的减弱) and "low lethality" (低致命性) of the Omicron virus. This could be considered as a course correction and a face saving move, especially when you have a wolf by its ears. It was in this context that Sun proposed "taking small steps without coming to a halt" (走小步不停步), albeit she still harped about "major positive results China have achieved" in epidemic prevention and control in the last three years.

Sun Chunlan has become synonymous with China's stringent epidemic prevention and control. She talked tough when she was sent to Wuhan in 2020, and to Shanghai and Hainan in 2022. Xinhua in a commentary on 1 December also called for "swift lockdowns and swift lifting of lockdowns" (快封快解) as a new model for dealing with the pandemic.

Four, the residential committees (居委会) who at the behest of "higher authorities" imposed stringent lockdowns and posed as "big whites" are increasingly being blamed for the fiasco. These are the people, largely held responsible for creating barriers and welding main gates of apartment buildings much to the despise of common people. Furthermore, on many occasions, these have acted like the notorious "red guards" of the "Cultural Revolution" era forcefully entering houses of the quarantined people and damaging their personal belongings. Nonetheless, the "big whites" have their own story to tell. Many complain that they have not been paid for months by the testing and labour companies. Worse, they have been subjected to all kinds of abuses by everyone, and have sought justice in the court of law. Insatiable desire of the COVID testing companies for exacting super profit, and low self-sufficiency of many provinces are part of the problem.

According to reports from Strait.com, China has invested nearly 14.7 trillion yuan in health expenses in the prevention and control of the epidemic in 2021 and 2022. A single nucleic acid test cost China around 215 million yuan a day, amounting to nearly 50 billion yuan a month! In other words, mass testing could be regarded as a mean to sustain the COVID zero policy. However, in the wake of protests, the government has started to prove testing companies. Zhang Shanshan, the daughter of Zhang Hezi, the major shareholders of Shenzhen Nuclear Gene Technology Co. Ltd., has 35 nucleic acid companies registered under her name. Netizens have started to expose the unholy nexus between the local government, testing companies and the "big whites." Recently many "big whites" have been rounded up and imprisoned by the police.

Finally, though Xi Jinping emerged as the helmsman of China after conclusion of the 20th National Congress, however, the dynamic COVID zero, and the protests have diminished his image. Since the CPC commands the barrel of the gun, the protests are likely to be nipped in the bud, albeit use of force resulting in bloodshed will further tarnish the image of party-state amongst the masses. Nonetheless, seeds of the dissidence have been sown and they may continue to sprout intermittently, for the protesters appeared fearless, demonstrated definite political consciousness with clear goals and adopted simple yet powerful ways to convey their message.

IV
RELATIONS WITH MAJOR POWERS

27

China and the "Middle East War"

In the wake of Hamas's carnage inside Israel on 7 October 2023, the spokesperson of the Ministry of Foreign Affairs, Mao Ning said that China calls for "immediate ceasefire" (尽快停火) "resumption of peace talks" (恢复和谈), "two-state formula" (两国方案) but didn't mention Hamas by name at all, albeit in some briefings the official media addressed them as "armed groups" (武装组织) from the Gaza strip. It is no secret that Hamas and Hezbollah are supported by Iran, and China has been aiding the heavily sanctioned Iran. The world knows how Huawei and ZTE, two of China's telecom giants circumvented sanctions and sold US origin products to Iran during Donald Trump's presidency. ZTE was forced to pay almost US$ 2 billion.

Undoubtedly, the Arab world has emerged as a new strategic pillar of China. China's economic penetration has deepened in the region and has clear strategic goals. In order to understand these goals, and how China sees the raging wars in Europe, Middle East and possible war in East Asia, Long Kaifeng's four articles expounding "three major wars" paradigm have been briefly discussed below. The first was written in 2018 and the other three between April and June 2023. The articles reveal how China is playing or will play its role in these wars that aim to destroy the US hegemony and replace American centrism with Eurasian centrism.

Long Kaifeng, a retired military officer and strategist argues in the first article written in 2018 that at present the "Fourth World War" is going on, where three major wars are unfolding; the outcome of these will destroy the unipolarity of the US and establish a new world order dominated by Eurasia (欧亚主导的) centrism. He believes that the US has reached the pinnacle of its hegemonic expansion and is on the decline, which is in uniformity with the "rise of the East and decline of the West" indicating China's global ascent. Long posits that during the Korean war, the US almost lost its hegemonic advantage to the USSR, had it not been forced to compromise with China (不得不对中国妥协) during the Vietnam War, the advantage would have been lost. Therefore, these wars together with the Iraq and Afghan wars led by NATO demonstrated that the US would not be able to withstand an expended protracted war. Long argues that the unipolar hegemonic order established by the US since its withdrawl from Afghanistan has collapsed, and the US centric order would be replaced by a Eurasian centric order after the following three inevitable wars.

According to the Chinese strategist, the US will fight three inevitable wars in Europe, the Middle East and East Asia for protecting its hegemony in these regions. Long lists these war campaigns as the Mediterranean campaign dominated by the US and Russia where China and Europe will play a supporting role, the Middle East war campaign where China, Russia, Europe and the United States would be natural players (自然主要玩家), and the East Asian campaign to redefine the Asia-Pacific order. The key to the East Asian war campaign where China and the US are the major players with Russia playing a marginal role, and the Southern Kuril Islands, the Korean Peninsula, the Diaoyu Islands, and Taiwan as the major flashpoints. Long estimates that it will take 10 to 30 years, or even longer for these wars to change the US dominated world order, therefore, China must be prepared for a protracted war and seize the historical opportunity of the changing world. This is perhaps the logic behind "Right now there are changes – the likes of which we haven't seen for 100 years (百年未有之大变局) – and we are the ones driving these changes together," President Xi Jinping told President Putin during his Russia visit in March 2023, to which Putin said "I agree".

Long argues that China is not afraid of fighting a war with the US, for unlike the erstwhile USSR China has it all – a perfect industrial structure and strong industrial production capacity, and the market in the 'Belt and Road' countries in Europe, Asia and Africa. With these two things alone, it would be meaningless for the US to engage with major powers even in a new cold war, least to talk about the hot war owing to nuclear deterrence, hypersonic missiles and capabilities to launch virus, genetic, cyber etc., warfare. He rules out a direct confrontation with the major powers, however, states that the possibility of a direct war on the territory of a third country, similar to the Korean and Vietnam War, is very likely.

Three more articles that were written between April and June 2023 are essentially expanding the scope of his 2018 article. Long Kaifeng argues in the article written on 1 May 2023 that the only way to abolish American hegemony is through a new world war. He says that the purpose of the Russia-Ukraine war is to disintegrate NATO, make the EU independent, and rebuild the European security system. The Middle East War is aimed to further erode the US hegemony and achieve three-fold goals of Arab unity, the establishment of the Palestinian state, and a severe thrashing (痛殴) of Israel. The Middle East campaign is considered indispensable for breaking the US dollar hegemony, which Long asserts is tantamount to annihilating the enemy by disrupting its food supply lines. The way out for the US, according to Long is to kneel down, surrender, and negotiate compromises albeit in his assessment the "American imperialism is not used to shed tears until it sees the coffin". In the article written on 8 April 2023, Long not only predicts the end of US hegemony after the above three wars but also the disintegration of the US. Therefore, the essence of China's strategy in dealing with the US in Long Kaifeng view is "you fight yours and I fight mine" strategy.

28

China and the Taliban

While talks between the Afghan government and the Taliban have hit the dead end, the Taliban has been enjoying hospitality from Russia, Iran and China, thus legitimising the once deadly terrorist organisation. The Taliban's chief negotiator, Mullah Abdul Ghani Baradar was hosted in Tianjin on 28 July 2021 by none other than China's foreign minister and State Councillor, Wang Yi, just two days after the US Deputy Secretary of State, Wendy Sherman was hosted at the same venue. Though it is obvious that the Taliban is exploiting China's troubled relationship with the US, however, China too wishes to secure its interests in the AF-Pak region as the Taliban is poised to take over Afghanistan after the US withdrawal. The Chinese media has upheld that hosting the Taliban is consistent with China advocacy for 'Afghanistan-led and Afghan-owned' (阿人主导、阿人所有) peace process. Wang Yi, during his meeting with the Taliban in Tianjin pronounced them as "a very decisive (举足轻重) military and political force in Afghanistan" which is "expected to play an important role in the country's peace, reconciliation and reconstruction process." Why is China hosting the terror organisation?

One, the Chinese scholars believe that the hurried and "irresponsible withdrawal" (不负责任撤军) of the US from Afghanistan shows that the US has lost the two decade long war it initiated in Afghanistan. Lan Jianxue, director of the Asia-Pacific Institute of the China Institute of International Studies posits that "the US has completely abandoned the Afghan people, leaving only devastation and endless misery." Conversely, China has played the role of a "responsible major power and an important neighbour of Afghanistan, which has always "adhered to non-interference in Afghanistan's internal affairs," has been actively mediating between different political factions in Afghanistan, so as to strengthen and promote dialogue and contribute to Afghan peace and reconciliation process. Wang Yi's meeting with the Taliban has been stated by Lan as an outcome of China taking stock of the situation (审时度势), strengthening contacts with the Afghan government, the Afghan Taliban, and closely coordinating policy with neighboring countries such as Pakistan, Iran, and Central Asian republics. The Taliban on their part, has appreciated "China's fair and active role in the peace process" and pronounced China as a "trustworthy and good friend of the Afghan people." Lan, also says that the US withdrawal has "provided the Afghan people with an important opportunity to become the masters of their own country."

Two, it is owing to mutual security concerns that China hosted the Taliban. Hu Ge an analyst argues that the Taliban is lobbying for support of neighboring countries so as their prospective regime survives in Kabul. In other words, they want to "seek security" (寻求安全) from China, one of the most powerful neighbors of Afghanistan. In turn, China has also sought security for its restive Xinjinag and secured a guarantee from the Afghan Taliban that they "will never allow forces to use Afghan territory to threaten China's security." Obviously, China has the East Turkestan Islamic Movement (ETIM) in mind, which in tandem with the Taliban and foreign fighters has been operating in the Badakhshan region of Wakhan corridor since 2016. The Chinese media reports that in July 2020, they also participated in the Taliban's attacks on mining areas and towns near the Pakistani border. A recent bus attack in Pakistan in which 9 Chinese engineers were killed has also been attributed to the Tehrik-e-Taliban Pakistan (TTP) and the ETIM rebels. In tandem with Pakistan, China has urged the Afghan Taliban to make clean break from various terror outfits including the TTP and the ETIM. Wang Yi urged the Afghan Taliban to "hold high the banner of peace talks, set up peace goals, build a positive image (正面形象), and pursue an inclusive policy (包容政策)" even as the Afghan Taliban continues to perpetrate atrocities amounting to war crimes in the areas controlled by them or where they are advancing.

Three, the importance of Wakhan Corridor since 2015 has been replaced by the China Pakistan Economic Corridor (CPEC), the flagship of Xi Jinping's Belt and Road Initiative (BRI), the project of the century. China has committed to invest over US$ 70 billion in this corridor and desires to extend the same to Afghanistan. China building a road through Wakhan Corridor that will link Xinjiang to Afghanistan, and a road connecting Peshawar-Kabul-Dushanbe should be seen in this context. Once complete, the AF-Pak region and Central Asia will get connected to Xinjiang, and enable China to expand its investment in mining, energy and transport infrastructure on the one hand and export its products to the region on the other. No wonder, Taliban promised to protect Chinese investment in Afghanistan during their meeting with Wang Yi. Owing to security concerns, China has been cautious to invest in Afghanistan, its total investment in Afghanistan remains less than half a billion dollars. The promised investment of US$ 3 billion in the Mes Aynak copper mines has been stalled since the deal was signed in 2007. China has also secured a 25 year US$ 400 million bid to drill oil in Afghanistan.

Finally, as far as India is concerned, Lin Minwang, professor at the Institute of International Studies, Fudan University argues that since the US is unwilling to consign its "achievements" of decades in Afghanistan to flames, it has been actively seeking India to stand up and "takeover" (接盘). Since India has long stood on the opposite side of the Taliban in Afghanistan, it is unwilling to see the Taliban to regain power. This according to Lin, has formed the strategic basis of the US-India cooperation. He posits that the United States hopes that India plays a greater role in air support to the Afghan government forces, but it is still unclear how much role India is willing to play. He asserts that even if Afghan Taliban regains power, the two countries will not easily recognize its "legitimacy." On the question of Pakistan's apprehensions, scholars such as Wang Shida maintain that Pakistan's policy towards Afghanistan mainly stems from geopolitical and security considerations. It strives to ensure the establishment of a friendly or at least a neutral regime in Afghanistan, to prevent the expansion of India's influence and the continued tilt of the regional balance of power in favour of India, and to avoid having enemies on both its eastern and the western flanks (东西腹背受敌).

Considering that ethnic groups such as Tajik, Hazara, and Uzbek maintain contact with India to varying degrees, the Pashtuns can be described as Pakistan's "worst choice." In addition, Pakistan has also played an important role in the signing of a peace agreement between the United States and the Taliban. In the future, whether the Taliban focuses on consolidating their political status in Afghanistan or developing the economy after the formation of a government, they cannot do without Pakistan's support, asserts professor Lin. Therefore, maintaining friendly relations with Pakistan will be the top priority of the Taliban's regional policy.

29

China's 'Look the US in the Eye' Diplomacy

On 10 November 2023, Hua Chunying, the spokesperson of China's Ministry of Foreign Affairs announced that "At the invitation of US President Joe Biden, President Xi Jinping will be in San Francisco from 14 to 17 November for a China-US summit meeting and the 30th APEC Economic Leaders' Meeting. As could be discerned, the emphasis is on the summit meeting not the APEC. This is in sync with Chinese scholars arguing that it is the US officials who are streaming to China to seek China, not the other way around. It started with Secretary of State Antony Blinken in June, followed by Treasury Secretary Janet Yellen and the presidential climate envoy John Kerry in July, and the secretary of commerce Gina Raimondo in September. These visits according to Jin Canrong, professor of international relations at the Renmin University were "tactical" (战术性) rather than strategic (战略性) aimed to "ease off" (缓和) tensions and preventing the "spiralling down" (螺旋下降) of the China-US relations. The "easing off the tension" meetings, nonetheless, resulted in Wang Yi's US visit in late October, the precursor to President Xi Jinping's US visit.

According to the White House Readout of President Joe Biden's Meeting with President Xi Jinping, both sides expected to "manage competition responsibly to prevent it from veering into conflict." Some of the takeaways from the summit included the cooperation to combat global illicit drug manufacturing and trafficking, including synthetic drugs like fentanyl, the resumption of high-level military-to-military communication, addressing the risks of advanced AI systems through intergovernmental talks, and expansion of educational, student, youth, cultural, sports, and business etc. people-to-people exchanges.

The differences in the readout far outweigh the cooperation, which could be gleaned through the US' ironclad commitment to defending its Indo-Pacific allies, concerns regarding PRC's human rights abuses, including in Xinjiang, Tibet, and Hong Kong, opposition to any unilateral changes to the status quo in Taiwan, PRC's unfair trade policies, and preventing advanced US technologies from being used to undermine the US national security. Xi Jinping on the other hand was looking at US-China on an equal level when he said that "great power competition will not solve the problems China, the US, and the world face. This planet is big enough for both China and the US...", nevertheless also revealed his sensitivities as regards China's path, system and theory when he said China's doesn't engage in ideological confrontation with any country, and emphasized the importance of mutual respect, peaceful coexistence, and win-win cooperation – Xi's three points for building a new type of great power relationship.

The Chinese sensitivities are pointer to the structural contradictions between the US and China that sprawls into areas such as relative force structure, political system, civilisational and racial identity. Chinese scholars like Jin Canrong maintain that China-US relations has entered the protracted "game of the century" (世纪博弈) and the fundamental reason for this is that the US cannot digest the rise of China, for the US has the Darwinist mind-set and thinking that the US is capable of halting the rise of China. It is under such a thinking that China has formulated "Look the US in the Eye" diplomacy (平视外交) since early 2021.

We may recall CPC General Secretary Xi Jinping declaring on the sidelines of the "Two Sessions" in March 2021 that "China can now look the world in the eye." Soon after these remarks, on 19 March during the US-China meeting in Anchorage, Alaska, Yang Jiechi, Director of the Office of the Central Foreign Affairs Commission bluntly told the US that the "United States is not qualified (没有资格) to speak to China from a position of strength (居高临下). The Chinese do not accept such a trick (不吃这一套)." On 23 April 2021, Foreign Minister Wang Yi during a video exchange with the US Council on Foreign Relations reiterated that "Some in the United States claim that China does not respect the United States any more. As a matter of fact, it is China that values mutual respect and equality the most. When we stress "looking at each other on an equal level" (平视), we mean nothing but equality. It is neither looking down (俯视), or looking up (仰视). Stronger muscles and bigger fists should not be the decisive factor. There is no superior country in this world, and we do not accept that any country can dictate to others from a position of strength."

Yan Xuetong, one of the authorities on international relations in China, reciprocated the above formulations on 11 July 2021 in an interview when he said that China's diplomatic style in the New Era has changed to "look the world in the eyes diplomacy" and countries need to gradually adapt to it. He said the "look the world in the eyes diplomacy" has replaced the 'Bide your time and hide your capabilities" paradigm of the yesteryears. He posits that after 2017 there was no way for China to hide its national strength, but to take initiative and take centre stage to compete with the US and Western countries, especially when they positioned China as their biggest strategic competitor.

Anchorage outburst has been deemed as a necessary sermon to the US to change its "old habit" (老毛病). Huawei CFO Meng Wangzhou's release was also termed as a major victory for "look the US in the eye" diplomacy. The same has also been portrayed as making China discourse power better heard globally. For example, on 7 March 2023, Qin Gang former Foreign Minister of China said to the youths of China that "Our 5,000-year civilisation and our achievements in modernisation are the source of such confidence. I hope that young people will foster greater ambition, grit and determination through practice. I hope you will look the world in the eye (平视这个世界) and have dialogue with the world on an equal footing to share your unique perspectives, make your voices heard, and tell the world who you are."

Yan Xuetong like most of the Chinese scholars believes that the US has increasingly become a complex external variable affecting China's future development. The strategic game between China and the United States has increased in intensity and breadth. In view of this, China will continue to maintain strategic initiative, forge ahead, and unswervingly guide China-US relations to evolve in the direction of no conflict, no confrontation, mutual respect, and win-win cooperation, a part of the "new security concept" that evolved during the reform period.

The confidence to "look the US in the eyes" according to Yan, emanates from the development China witnessed in the last four decades.

He upholds that in terms of human development, the past 40 years have been the best period in the 4,000 years of Chinese history. Since 2008 financial crisis, China has contributed more than one-third to world economic growth. Ruan Zongze, executive vice president and researcher of the China Institutes of International Studies, echoes Yan's view and argues with this kind of economic strength "China will have an increasingly important voice in the global economy and the right to formulate global trade and investment rules. This has laid a more solid foundation for national rejuvenation and provided an important guarantee for China to lead (引领) the world's major changes and shape the external environment (塑造外部环境).

Ruan reciprocates Yan's argument by maintaining that China's attitude towards the world is inevitable due to the great changes of a century, and the great historical leap it has taken. He says this demonstrates the global significance of the Chinese Dream and provides the confidence for China's "look the US in the eye" diplomacy. Echoing what Yang Jiechi spelled out at the Anchorage meeting, he insists that the "American 'leadership' of the world is a fictional narrative (虚构叙事)." In fact, the US has never "led" the world, therefore, there is no question of the US "leading it again." The "hemispheric hegemonic order" (半球霸权秩序) according to Ruan, is limited to the US and its allies. Even if the entire population of Western countries is added together, it would be about 1 billion people. They are a minority in the world and are not qualified to "represent" the world at all. He believes, the American soul is sick (灵魂已病), and to "heal" it would not be easy. Therefore, rather than harping on the so-called "democracy and human rights" and to arbitrate on Hong Kong, Xinjiang, and Taiwan etc., affairs, the US must be worried about its own "civil war situation" (内战状态).

The last thing the US wants to see is China's peaceful and stable development, which could be discerned from Trump's "maximum pressure" (极限施压) to Biden's "containment through alliances," (联盟围堵), argues Ruan. In future too, the US is more likely to further interfere in China's internal affairs and engage in strategic blackmail (战略敲诈). Ruan posits that since the China-US relations have entered a stage of strategic stalemate (战略相持), therefore, equal treatment and mutual respect is the key to ameliorate the situation. Since the path, theory, system and culture is deemed important to realise the "Two Centenary Goals" and the great rejuvenation of the Chinese nation, any challenge to these would be fought resolutely until the final victory. The "Emperor's New Clothes" of the United States and the West should have been exposed long ago, says Ruan. It is in the backdrop of such strategic stalemate with the US that China has unfolded its "Look the US in the Eye" diplomacy on the one hand and initiated a powerful power discourse by rolling out concepts such as "Building of community with a shared future for mankind" and the "New Type of International Relations"– the two pillars of the Chinese diplomacy in the new era on the other.

30

Widening US-China Ideological Divide

On 9-10 December 2021, the US President Joe Biden hosted the first ever Summit for Democracy, which brought together leaders from government, civil society, and the private sector of more than a hundred countries. The summit aimed at promoting democratic values, fighting corruption, and standing up for human rights. According to the website of the US Department of State, the summit will "set forth an affirmative agenda for democratic renewal and to tackle the greatest threats faced by democracies." Undoubtedly, the Biden administration is wanting to put a united front with its allies against authoritarian regimes, primarily China so as to better deal with the threats from the emerging power, albeit many democratically elected governments have been left out, and those with a bad human right record have also been invited. In present context, democracy, as an ideology becomes important for domestic mobilisation for the US on the one hand and making a clear distinction between 'us' and 'them' internationally on the other. Raking up the issue of human rights, the US announced diplomatic boycott of Beijing Winter Olympics 2022, and other Anglo-Saxon countries like the UK, Australia and Canada followed the suit.

In response, China released a series of documents and warned that countries announcing boycott would "pay a price for their wrong moves." On 4 December 2021, China's State Council Information Office released 14393 words long White Paper entitled "China: Democracy That Works" that vehemently defends China's political institutions. The document refers to 'democracy' 201 times, and argues that China, rather than "duplicating Western models of democracy, has created a "new model of democracy" i.e. the whole-process people's democracy (全过程民主) that delivers and works. The White Paper defines the "whole process democracy" as the one that "integrates process-oriented democracy with results-oriented democracy, procedural democracy with substantive democracy, direct democracy with indirect democracy, and people's democracy with the will of the state." On 5 December 2021, the Ministry of Foreign Affairs website published a report titled The Sate of Democracy in the United States that rejected "One Person, One Vote" of the liberal democracies as the only democratic principle, and pronounced the US as a "dysfunctional democracy." It labelled the US democracy as corrupt, racist and the one that flares up "colour revolutions" around the world and undermines regional and national stability. Besides, between 2 and 8 December 2021, China organised a series of conferences debating democracy. It was during the "Dialogue on Democracy" on 2 December that Deputy Foreign Minister of MOFA, Le Yucheng argued that "China is a well-deserved democracy" (中国是当之无愧的民主国家) and that democracy is not something like "Feilaifeng" (the peak flown from afar, an Indian monk Huili named this peak in Hangzhou) and require no "preachers" (教师爷).

These reports and conferences generated a whole lot of debate inside China. One particular article by professor Wu Fei of Jinan University, entitled "Declaration of War! The United States invites more than 100 countries to encircle China, and the Chinese Ministry of Foreign Affairs issues a 'written challenge of war', 1 challenges 110", has been taken off the internet soon after it appeared on 7 December 2021. The article in a scathing attack characterizes the US as "a worthless person in imposing attire" (沐猴而冠), who is attempting to instigate "Taiwan independence" and argues that China "must let the US bear the corresponding price" for playing the Taiwan card. The Capitol riot, racism, tragic mishandling of the COVID-19 pandemic, widening wealth gap, purported "Freedom of speech" have been attributed to the "messy and chaotic practices of democracy" in the US by the Report issued on 5 December. While reiterating these 'chaotic practices', Professor Wu further classifies the US as "trafficker of democracy" (民主贩卖) who has rendered 10 million people homeless in Afghanistan, and flared up "colored revolutions" (颜色革命) across the Middle East, Latin America, North Africa and East Europe etc. regions.

The reports issued by China may be short of the "declaration of war", nonetheless, are pointer to the fact that the ideological chasm between the US and China is widening and the enthusiasm of the US for China's opening and reforms is long over, and that it has revisited issues related to human rights in places like Xinjiang, Tibet, Hong Kong, as well as those related to dissidence, prison labour, Tiananmen, and Falungong or religious freedom per se that was downplayed by the US and its allies in the reform era (1979-2012) in exchange of Chinese market. The US, under Trump administration had made good of ideological differences. A 2017 National Security Strategy declared that "a geopolitical competition between free and repressive visions of world order is taking place in the Indo-Pacific region;" the same was put more bluntly by Mike Pompeo, former US Secretary of State at The Richard Nixon Presidential Library and Museum speech entitled "Communist China and the Free World's Future" on 23 July 2020. China had reposed its faith on the Biden administration for resetting the US-China ties, however, the "Summit for Democracy" has dashed all such hopes. Biden may not seek a regime change in China, but will certainly compete with and undermine China's influence wherever possible.

The ideological contest also sprawls into the economic, technological and military fields. Even though China says that she adheres to the norms of the global economic system established by the liberal democracies, however, the US has come to believe that China not only doesn't comply with these including the pledges she made before joining the World Trade Organisation, but also undermine these by floating its own and strives to create its own standards. China's "Belt and Road Initiative", the "Communities of Shared Future for the Mankind," and related mechanisms are viewed as part and parcel of the Chinese governance model, which is "creating miracles in the achievement of rapid economic growth and long-term social stability" according to the above White Paper. In order to counter China's global influence, the US has deemed China a "revisionist" and "coercive power" which by way of relying on its "sharp power", "pierces, penetrates, or perforates the political and information environments in the targeted countries." In order to maintain its technological asymmetries with China, the US has made it clear that it will selectively decouple with China in hi-tech sector, develop 6G networks with allies like Japan and South Korea, and challenge China's BRI with "Build Back Better World." In the military field, the US has institutionalised a series of alliances, ranging from the "The Five Eyes", to "Quad" and "AUKUS" and has pledged to build a "free, open and rule based Indo-Pacific" with its allies and likeminded countries.

It appears that the US doesn't subscribe to the "three principles of mutual respect, peaceful coexistence and win-win cooperation" proposed by President Xi Jinping to Joe Biden during their virtual summit in November 2021. As regards mutual respect, Xi argued that "the two countries need to respect each other's social systems and development paths, respect each other's core interests and major concerns, and respect each other's right to development. They need to treat each other as equals..." the very premise of "Summits for Democracy" runs counter to "mutual respect" envisaged by China. As argued by eminent Chinese scholar Yan Xuetong, the US will never consider China fit for an equal footing in Asia Pacific as well as globally. If it does, its strategic relationship with some of its allies say Japan and South Korea will necessarily be 'downgraded.' Peaceful coexistence is interpreted as "no conflict and no confrontation" by China, however, here again issues such as South China Sea, Taiwan, Indo-Pacific, the Quad and AUKUS and China's conflict with US allies doesn't rule out the possibility of conflict and confrontation between the two. The third principle is problematic, if the first two are not realised. Therefore, if the interdependence between the US and Chinese economy is a reality, so is the ideological security dilemma. Although the dilemma was latent until now, but a visible shift in the balance of power in recent years has resulted in change of behavior in the US, which is nothing but all about the contest of influence in the larger framework of "strategic competition" between existing and emerging hegemon.

31

China and the Russia-Ukraine Crisis

In early February 2022, while the Russian troop build-up continued along the Ukrainian border, President Vladimir Putin found time to participate in the inaugural ceremony of the Winter Olympics, largely boycotted by the West diplomatically. Though the Russian and Chinese media rebuffed the western 'rhetoric' of an imminent invasion, Putin, in fact was seeking assurances from China as regards prospective punitive sanctions and its neutrality in event of the Russian assault. These were mirrored in a nearly 6000 words Joint Statement that according to Valdai, Alexey Maslov, director of the Moscow State University's Asia and Africa Institute "formalised bilateral alliance" in an interview to Tass. The nationalistic *Global Times* of China, called it "a new era of international relations not defined by the US." No wonder, the joint-statement "firmly supports each other's core interests, national sovereignty and territorial integrity" and "opposes external forces undermining the security and stability of the two countries." The two sides also signed 15 agreements including the much-talked about gas deal that says Russia will deliver 10 billion cubic meters of gas per year to China over a period of 25 years. It appears that not only was the invasion of Ukraine put on hold until the close of the Winter Olympics, but Beijing also passed information about the US seeking Chinese help to avoid Ukraine being invaded by Russia, according to a story filed by the *South China Morning Post*.

However, the Russian assault, which contrary to be limited to the breakaway Luhansk and Donetsk regions, sprawls into various cities of Ukraine including the capital Kyiv, has bewildered many, perhaps China too. China pronounced Russia's security concerns as "legitimate demands" (正当诉求), but, Foreign Minister Wang Yi, also said that "China always respects the sovereignty and territorial integrity of all countries." Rebuffing NATO expansion in Russia's backyard, Wang reiterated China's position that "the Cold War mentality should be completely abandoned, and a balanced, effective and sustainable European security mechanism should be finally formed through dialogue and negotiation." Two days later on 25 February, Wang put forth a five-point Chinese stand while talking to representatives from the UK, EU and France. The Chinese stand besides reiterating the above two points, called on the parties to "exercise restraint" (保持必要克制), that it supports all diplomatic efforts (外交努力), "direct dialogue and negotiations" (直接对话谈判), and opposes the UN authorising the use of force and sanctions (授权动武和制裁) under Chapter VII. On 1 March, during his talks with the Ukrainian foreign minister, Dmytro Kuleba, Wang Yi, mostly reiterated the Chinese position, but added that "regional security cannot be achieved by expanding military blocs" (地区安全不能以扩张军事集团来实现) and that both sides urgently need to deescalate situation on the ground. Undoubtedly, the Ukrainian crisis will further push Russia closer to China. The crisis seems to have thrown more challenges than opportunities to the Chinese diplomacy, and it would be interesting to watch how China navigates through these, especially at a time when its image has taken a beating around the globe.

At the outset, the Ukrainian crisis will take focus off China and the Indo-Pacific for some time. Needless to say, any conflict involving the US and its allies have immensely benefitted China, be it the US invasion of Iraq, Libya, Syria, and Afghanistan etc. countries. The breathing space China got in the last three decades or so has been instrumental in economic, technological and defense modernisation of China. It also provides China an opportunity to provide economic and military aid to its detractors' enemies, at the same time to play the role of a mediator in the conflict, as has been witnessed in the case of North Korea, Pakistan, Afghanistan and Iran etc. countries.

Second, Russian involvement in military conflicts, and the West slapping sanctions on Russia could further strengthen transactional Russia-China relationship, the same could well become China's burden. China could offer its Cross-Border Interbank Payment System (CISP) to

Russia in place of SWIFT, but will Chinese banks take the risk of inviting the US and EU sanctions? China may not be willing to take the risk of losing US and European markets. The Ukrainian crisis has united NATO members unprecedently since the end of the cold war, and China and Russia driving a wedge between the US and its allies that looked possible at one point in time, may be a remote possibility in wake of Russia's troubled relationship with Europe and the US. In case the war drags on, which looks possible, given the kind of information and weaponry the West has and continues to share with Ukraine, it will be Putin's nightmare and the war may take a different turn altogether, as could China's murky position, and its ability to take leverage from both the US and Russia.

Third, the reaction of the US, and its allies in the wake of the Russian assault, certainly has ruffled feathers in the power corridors of Zhongnanhai. "Today Ukraine, tomorrow Taiwan" became the most trending line in the last couple of days on both sides of the Taiwan strait. Since Russia adheres to the "One China Policy" and advocates Taiwan's unification with the Mainland, Taiwanese President Tsai ing-wen was quick to "condemn Russia's violation of Ukraine's sovereignty" and join the West to sanction Russia. While talking about the takeaways from the Ukrainian crisis, Zhu Lilun, Chairman of the Kuomintang, posits that "Only a solid national defense and determination of the whole nation to defend the country will always be the most important foundation for national security." While the US and its allies are likely to export the Ukrainian model of intervention and assistance, Taiwan further ramping up its defense preparedness looks certain. Moreover, if Ukraine being a distant core interest of the US has been getting full military and intelligence support from NATO members, importance of Taiwan to the US and its allies in Indo-Pacific will be very different from what the international community has witnessed in Ukraine. Moreover, Russia putting its nuclear deterrent force on high alert, and Belarus asking for the deployment of the same on its soil, will force Japan and other countries either to develop their own or ask for similar deployments.

Fourth, Ukraine is an important BRI partner of China and a gateway to Europe. Ukraine enjoys about US$ 16 billion in trade with China, which is one-tenth of China's trade with Russia. Besides, China has a very close military, space and technological cooperation with Ukraine. According to Yurii Poita, Head of the Asia-Pacific section at Centre for Army,

Conversion and Disarmament Studies (CACDS), Ukraine, "in defence sector, some of the most famous bilateral projects include the Ukrainian aircraft-carrier Varyag purchased by China in 1998, which was later upgraded and introduced into the PLA Navy under the name Liaoning; the acquisition of UGT 25000 gas turbine engines along with full technical documentation, which became the basis for QC 280 gas turbines, were delivered to the new Type 055 destroyers; amphibious Bison air-cushioned landing crafts, specifically built for China, which it requires for any landing operation on the islands in the East and South China Sea." Since the direction of Ukraine's foreign policy since 2014 has been EU and NATO centric, the same has created certain uneasiness in Ukraine-China relations owing to the latter's backing of Russia. In such a situation, "Ukraine did draw several 'red lines' in its cooperation with China, leaving the trade and investment sphere open, but not allowing China into sensitive sectors, including elements of critical infrastructure, cybersecurity, 5G networks, etc.," according to Yurii. There are reports that overseas Chinese in Ukraine are increasingly being despised for China's Russia policy, and also owing to certain irresponsible and predatory posts appearing on Chinese social media on Ukrainian people amidst the crisis.

Fifth, India too has been caught between a rock and a hard place. On 26 February, India joined China and the UAE in abstaining during a vote on a US sponsored UNSC resolution that deplored in the strongest terms Russia's aggression on Ukraine. Indian students who are leaving Ukraine and congregating at the borders, are facing the wrath of the Ukrainian army and police. India has been balancing its economic and political relations with the US, Russia and Ukraine. However, in the wake of the ongoing war, unfolding punitive sanctions, including the expulsion of Russia out of SWIFT, India's foreign policy is set for a litmus test. It has to be seen how India navigates these sanctions, and restructures its ties with the US, EU and Ukraine at a time when India desires to see itself as part of the new equilibrium in international order. Pakistan Prime Minister's presence in Moscow amidst Russian onslaught, does point to an emerging China-Russia-Pakistan nexus and India's vulnerabilities, but India perhaps will need to make hard choices given the emerging equations, especially when it comes to diversification of defense procurements.

Finally, it has to be seen how China bets on its "no limit" relationship with Russia, economic partnership and uneasy political relationship with Ukraine, its US$ 1.6 trillion-dollar market in the US and Europe, and how it orbits the US and EU sanctions on Russia. The Ukrainian crisis appears to have thrown more challenges to China than opportunities. These are likely to exacerbate if the conflict prolongs and Russia is weakened. Nevertheless, by way of redefining the messed up red lines by Russia, the US and EU could also redefine the nature of geopolitics, choices faced by all the stakeholders.

32

China's Position in Ukraine Crisis

The war in Ukraine has entered its seventh week and cities like Kharkiv and Mariupol are in ruins, yet there is no end to it in sight. Although, Sergei Rudskoi, head of the Russian General Staff's Main Operational Directorate, announced on 25 March that the "first stage of military operation" in Ukraine was complete and the next goal was the "complete liberation of Donbass," but he also said that the operation will continue as long as all goals are achieved. China, the "no limits" partner of Russia, has not only declined to condemn the Russian invasion, but has also amplified Russian narrative in its media. Why has China taken such a position?

Chinese scholars are of the view that the Ukrainian crisis has resulted from a number of civilisational and geopolitical reasons accumulated over the years, but the United States is the biggest culprit. The most direct cause of Russia-Ukraine conflict, according to Zhang Weiwei, professor of international relations at Fudan University, is the continuous eastward expansion of NATO led by the United States, ignoring Russia's legitimate security concerns. This view has also been echoed by China's official discourse on the issue, for example, China's foreign ministry spokesperson Zhao Lijian said during a press conference on 1 April in Beijing that "As the "main culprit" (始作俑者) and "biggest instigator"(最大推手) of the Ukraine crisis, the US has led NATO to engage in five rounds of eastward expansion in the last two decades after 1999. The number of NATO members increased from 16 to 30, and they have moved eastward more than 1,000 kilometres to somewhere near the Russian border, pushing Russia to the wall step by step." China's *Xinhua News*

Agency in a commentary on 2 April echoed similar position noting that "the US and NATO repeatedly challenged Russia's strategic bottom line (战略底线) and used Ukraine as a "tool" (抓手) to contain Russia, which naturally won't be acceptable to Russia. The war in Ukraine has resulted from the US "fanning the flames" (添柴加薪) for the sake of maintaining its global hegemony.

Though they are sympathetic towards the Ukrainian people, but squarely put the blame on President, Zelensky. Zhang Weiwei has blamed him for ruing his country and throwing people in the abyss of misery. Jin Canrong, professor and associate dean with the School of International Studies at Renmin University of China, calls it Ukraine playing the "小清新" (little fresh) and deems the leadership incompetent in governing the country, for it became a willing pawn of the US, rather than making its own foreign policy choices. For Russia, it was the choice between "to be or not to be"; if not now, may be after two years or so, Ukraine would be a part of NATO, according to Zhang Weiwei.

Ukraine crisis to China, is not a conflict of interests between Russia and Ukraine, but the US expansion of its hegemony. Since China sees US hegemony as the "trigger" (导火索) for wars and the biggest "source of turmoil" (动荡源) in the world, it ought to be opposed tooth and nail. Zhang Weiwei argues that in order to maintain hegemony, the US has adopted Halford Mackinder's "Heartland Theory" supported by Zbigniew Brzezinski, Polish origin national security adviser to President Jimmy Carter in place of George Kennan and Hennery Kissinger's warnings that Ukraine, rather than choosing sides between the East and the West should be a "bridge between them." Mackinder in the beginning of the 20th century had said that "Who rules East Europe commands the Heartland; who rules the Heartland commands the World-Island; and who rules the World-Island commands the world." Therefore, according to Zhang Weiwei, President Putin's aim of this "special military operation" in Ukraine is also to "subvert (颠覆) the "unipolar hegemonic international order" (单极霸权主义的国际秩序) of the US.

Since China's position on global governance resonates the Russian position, hence, China sees Russia as a "promoter" of fundamental global change. Ukraine's de-militarisation, de-nazification and neutralisation essentially achieves that goal and establishes Russia as an important pole in the new "post American era" (后美国时代). This conforms to China's advocacy of the "Rise of the East and decline of the West" (东升西降) paradigm, justification for the "Belt and Road Initiative" and "building community of shared future for the mankind." Economically too, whether Russia achieves all its goals in Ukraine or not, sanctions from the west, according to the Chinese scholars, will not cripple Russia. Moreover, these have been solely imposed by the West, not all the countries; in fact, there are many countries who do not support such sanctions, argue the scholars. Rather, these in the long run, will achieve another objective of weakening the petro-dollar, as more and more countries find ways out to evade dependence on the US dollar. Ideologically, it is also "a battle between democracy and autocracy, between liberty and repression, between a rules-based order and one governed by brute force" as pointed out by President Biden in Warsaw on 26 March. China, obviously finds it problematic. China has all along opposed the "colour revolutions" and decried them as a tool to interfere in internal affairs of other countries, subvert governments through "non-violent revolutions" in order to reinforce the US's global hegemony. From this perspective, China too finds itself by the side of Russia.

Finally, the scholars draw a few conclusions from the ongoing conflict. According to Jin Canrong, Ukraine in this conflict is the biggest loser, Russia will gain some and lose some. But for China, since the entire focus will be on Russia for a considerable period of time, this will ease up some "strategic pressure" (战略压力). China could mediate in the crisis, as has been asked by various countries, but it is totally upon China whether it deems the mediation appropriate or not. Two, China-Russia relations are bound to be more intimate, and if the West threatens China with sanctions, the most populous country with the largest consumer, investment and trading market will render them ineffective, posits Zhang Weiwei. Three, it has emerged that there are only three countries – China, the US and Russia having exhibited "strategic autonomy." The EU has lost it, Japan has none, and India is on shaky ground according to them. Four, the creation of an international platform to disseminate information is deemed crucial, one sided narrative originating from the war is too obvious for anyone to see. Nonetheless, Zhang Weiwei is also of the view that as long as strategic objectives are realised, who cares for the public opinion warfare (舆论战); of course, China must be prepared for it, he cautions. Finally, he also draws attention of China's "public intellectuals" (公知)

who have reposed their faith in the western model that they should not fall for the logic of that model, for once you fall for it, there would be no retreat. Therefore, even if Ukraine and Russia are able to ink a peace deal, it would be extremely difficult to execute it.

33

China's Policy Calibration Post the AXIS Act

On 27 April 2022, the US House of Representatives passed "The Assessing Xi's Interference and Subversion Act or the "AXIS Act" requiring the US State Department to submit ongoing reports to Congress on China's support for Russia's invasion of Ukraine, initially within 30 days of the enactment of the law and every 90 days thereafter. The abbreviation of the Act is surprisingly synonymous to the Axis powers (Germany, Italy and Japan) of the World War II. According to the Act, "the new Axis of evil threatens the United States and the rules-based international order." China's "no limits", "no forbidden areas" relationship with Russia pronounced weeks before Russia's invasion of Ukraine, 30-year China-Russia gas deal in Euros, China's abstentions from the United Nations resolutions that condemned the Russian invasion, and spreading disinformation whitewashing Russia's war crimes, are considered as "findings" and "sense" of the Congress; the report also includes any other material, technical, logistical and military Chinese support to Russia, and if found true the Congress recommends "swift and stringent consequences for China."

On 22 April, exactly five days before the passage of the AXIS Act, People's Bank of China held the party committee meeting to assess the current economic and financial situation in China. According to a brief press release, the meeting was of the view that while Chinese economy has "made a good start overall" (开局总体良好), but the uncertainty facing the current economic growth has further exacerbated owing to the Russia-

Ukraine conflict, domestic COVID-19 situation, and the disruptions of the supply chains. The committee emphasized on maintaining market and economic stability, and creating a conducive environment for the successful convening of the 20th National Congress of the Communist Party of China (CPC). The Financial Times, quoting the sources revealed in a report that in a meeting held on 22 April, officials from People's Bank of China, finance ministry, as well as executives from many local and international banks including the HSBC participated in the meeting. According to the report, Yi Huiman, chairman of the China Securities Regulatory Commission asked the participants "what could be done to protect the nation's overseas assets, especially its US$ 3.2 trillion in foreign reserves."

It is obvious that China is concerned about the safety of its assets in foreign countries, especially in the US, if China is subjected to "swift and stringent" sanctions as warned by the above AXIS Act that remains valid until the end of the war in Ukraine. Since the weight of the Chinese economy is more than eleven times of the Russian economy, the consequences are going to be disastrous. China is the largest trade partner of most of the countries in the world, trade alone, accounts for 34.18 per cent of the GDP, if disrupted, the entire industrial sector will suffer, rendering millions jobless. Unlike Russia, China's economy remains integrated with the world; of its US$ 3.5 trillion foreign reserves, almost 60 per cent are held in the US dollars. Though China has been buying good quantity of gold in recent years, but it is just a little over 3 per cent of the entire reserves. Therefore, is the structure of Chinese economy that makes it vulnerable to the kind of sanctions the US and its allies have imposed on Russia. Needless to say, the western economies will also bear the brunt and witness unprecedented disruptions of their supply chains. If this appears to be the case, then why on earth China should be asking the bankers how to protect its assets overseas? There could be two possible scenarios – China's support for Russian invasion of Ukraine, and China's possible invasion of Taiwan for realising the Chinese dream of national rejuvenation.

As regards the first scenario, a U.K. government report has alleged that "China launched cyber-attacks on Ukrainian military and nuclear targets shortly before the Russian invasion." Ukraine has also accused China that the Russians were using Dajiang Innovations (DJI) drones to navigate their missiles, and had asked the company to block all DJI products in Ukraine. Mykhailo Fedorov, Ukraine's deputy prime minister and minister of digital transformation, while attaching the two-page letter to the DJI CEO in a twitter on 12 March, asked the company to provide information as regards the "number of functioning DJI products in Ukraine, their ID, where and when they were purchased and activated, and whether there was a problem in activating a new DJI product in Ukraine?" obviously, China has denied all these allegations, but on 26 April, a day before the passage of the "AXIS Act" the company temporarily suspended business in Russia and Ukraine to ensure that its products were not used in combat. Huawei's situation is also somewhat similar; it has continued its operations in Russia even as Western companies suspended their operations one after another. Huawei has developed 5G network for Russia's biggest mobile phone operator, the MTS, but latest reports say that Huawei has stopped receiving new orders from Russia. Both Huawei and ZTE have come under scanner for selling the US technology to Iran and North Korea. As regards the second scenario, threat of a Chinese invasion of Taiwan is real according to the Taiwanese Foreign Minister, Joseph Wu in his recent interview to the CNN. He believed that Russia's invasion of Ukraine and China's threatening behaviour towards Taiwan share a number of similarities. He said that Taiwan was drawing lessons from Ukraine's successful resistance, including the importance of asymmetrical capabilities and civil defence, but also said that Taiwan also counts on support of the likeminded countries.

The "AXIS Act" undoubtedly is meant to subdue China, and intensify factional feud within the CPC. The Act is unprecedented as it has named Xi Jinping in person, and could be seen as an attempt to bolster his detractors to stop his third term. But, will this create the desired effects, seems very unlikely at this point. China has long realised the dangers of export oriented economy in an increasingly protectionist world, therefore, the restructuring has been going on for some years, and one witness that the proportion of trade has been gradually declining in the GDP. Simultaneously, China has been unfolding policies such as "unified domestic market" (统一大市场) to spur massive "internal circulation" (国内大循环) so as to make China less dependent on foreign countries. On the other hand, whether it is owing to the "AXIS Act" or the nature of Russia-Ukraine war, or domestic troubles amidst the pandemic, China, through its official media appears to have hinted at some policy calibration as regards Ukraine as well as the United States.

On 3 May, Cankao Xiaoxi published an article entitled "How Zelensky was governing his country from the bunker" which for the first time mentioned Russian "invasion" of Ukraine, massacre of Bucha, and Ukraine's resistance to Russia. The article was widely circulated on other official media outlets like Guanchawang, Sohu etc. The tone and tenor of Zhao Lijian, spokesperson of China's Ministry of Foreign Affairs during his press briefing on 29 April was unusually different when an AFP reporter quoted the Pew Research Center opinion poll that says 80 per cent of the Americans hold unfavorable views of China, and asked whether this can be attributed to some of China's remarks and actions in recent years? Zhao's reply was, "people of China and the United States have always had friendly feelings, and the friendship between the two peoples has always been the source and important foundation of the development of bilateral relations." He blamed "anti-China forces" (反华势力) for "wantonly provoking confrontation and division between China and the United States, and spreading a large number of political viruses, which seriously poisoned the public opinion atmosphere of the two countries." China certainly sees the pressure mounting at home and abroad, and perhaps sees the futility of "wolf warrior diplomacy" under present circumstances.

34

Chinese Media on Xi Jinping's Russia Visit

As the Chinese President, Xi Jinping was about to set on his state visit to Russia, the International Criminal Court (ICC) on 17 March 2023, issued a war crime arrest warrant for President Vladimir Putin. The day Xi landed in Russia, the US President, Joe Biden signed a bipartisan bill that directs the Office of the Director of National Intelligence to declassify intelligence related to China's Wuhan Institute of Virology, and the potential links between the research that was done in the institute and the outbreak of COVID-19. As regards the former, the Ministry of Foreign Affairs spokesperson, Wang Wenbin upheld that the ICC should avoid "politicization and double standards" (政治化和双重标准), adhere to an "objective and impartial stance" (客观公正立场) and "respect the jurisdictional immunity" (管辖豁免) that any head of state enjoys in accordance with international law. As regards the latter, Wang said, "the US bill seriously distorts the facts (严重歪曲事实), concocts false information (炮制虚假信息), hypes up the "laboratory leak theory" without any evidence, and smears and attacks China. China is strongly dissatisfied with this and firmly opposes it." Beside these, Chinese media has much more to say.

One, Xi's visit was well planned in advance and has been described as an "opening chapter of the new Chinese government's diplomacy" in an article entitled "Why is the Chinese leader visiting Russia?" published by the *People's Daily* and other media outlets in China on 18 March 2023. The article holds the US responsible for China's embrace of Russia and other global issues. It blames the US for "dual containment" (双遏制) of

China and Russia on the one hand, and creating a "wedge" (打楔子) between them on the other. It argues that in the wake of the Ukrainian crisis, the US is weakening Russia, and at the same time containing China by promoting the "Indo-Pacific version of NATO." The US desires to "crush" (压垮) both China and Russia at the same time, instead has pushed China and Russia closer to each other. It blames the US of "cognitive warfare" (认知战手法) with China that desires to reproduce the "Ukraine crisis" in China's vicinity, so as to induce China to fall into the "Thucydides Trap." China-Russia "Deepening the Comprehensive Strategic Partnership of Coordination for the New Era" signed during Xi Jinping's Moscow visit further cements the bilateral relationship.

Two, the US has been pronounced as a "paper tiger", "walking at night with gongs and drums" thus exposing its own "guilty conscience" (自身心虚). It declares, China will not be intimidated, for China's diplomacy doesn't suffer from osteomalacia, let alone be obsequious to the US intimidation. China's Russia relations, it says are based on non-alignment, non-confrontation, and non-targeting of third parties. The bilateral trade that exceeded $190 billion in 2022, an increase of 120 per cent over a decade, has been flagged as one of the astounding achievements of the close cooperation between China and Russia. During Xi's visit, another joint statement entitled "Pre-2030 Development Plan on Priorities in China-Russia Economic Cooperation" is certainly a breather for Russia that has been subjected to harsh sanctions by the West. Xi Jinping called on both sides to strengthen trade in traditional areas, such as energy, resources, and electromechanical products, enhance the resilience of industrial and supply chains, expand cooperation in such areas as information technology, the digital economy, agriculture and trade in services.

Three, China and Russia have been upheld as practitioners of "genuine multilateralism" (真正的多边主义) who are leading the developing countries to defend international fairness and justice, and maintain the international system with the United Nations at its core and the international order based on international law. By way of this, both supposedly have expanded their "friend circle" (朋友圈), which according to the above article has infringed upon the US "interests and cheese." It is precisely for this reason that the US continues to label China-Russia relations as an "axis of evil" (邪恶轴心) and an "authoritarian alliance" (威

权联盟) which according to the West is challenging the international order and instigating a new cold war. The article says that conversely, the US looks at Sino-Russian relations through the "filter of Cold War mentality" and "zero-sum game." It is the US that is keen in "building walls and creating barriers", "long-arm jurisdiction" and "decoupling and disrupting the supply chains."

Four, the article argues that from NATO to the G7, from the "Five Eyes Alliance" to the "Quad" and further to the "AUKUS", the US has built "small circles" to create an anti-China-Russia "hubs and spokes system" (辐轴体系) that will drag the world into the abyss of division and confrontation, nevertheless, the US still wishes to give the "mortally sick American democracy" (病入膏肓的美式民主) a shot in the arm, the outcome of which could be well imagined. Another article published by Xinhua on 20 March 2023, declares that it is time to say "four Nos" to the US: Don't make irresponsible remarks on normal exchanges between sovereign states; Do not compare Sino-Russian relations with the small circle of US allies; Don't undermine China's efforts to promote peace talks on the Ukraine issue; Stop using the Ukraine crisis as an excuse to assault and sanction China.

Finally, the visit has been portrayed as a "peace trip" (和平之旅). As for facilitating peace in Ukraine, China reiterates its 12-point peace plan it proposed on 24 February 2023. While the article makes mention of "China quietly facilitating a dialogue between Saudi Arabia and Iran in Beijing", however, argues that "the key to solving the Ukraine crisis is not in the hands of China, but in the hands of the US and the West." The article by Xinhua further posits that the Saudi-Iran deal has "made the US very envious and jealous, the US is very worried that the Ukraine issue could be resolved in a similar fashion." Though Xi Jinping in Moscow laid emphasis on the adhearance to the principles of the UN Charter and the international law, but refrained from asking Russia to withdraw from the occupied territories. The *People's Daily* article maintains that rather than cooling down the Ukraine crisis, the US has repeatedly used military aid to influence the direction of the war, and frequently spent tens of billions of dollars to lure Ukraine into a "bottomless pit" (无底洞).

Interestingly, while Russia gets entangled in the war, China has challenged Russia by renaming 9 Russian places including the famous

Vladivostok as Haishenwai, Nerchinsk as Nibuchu, Sakhalin as Quedao, Stanovoy Range as the Waixing'anlin in Chinese. The depletion of both the Russian and American resources in Ukraine certainly serves the Chinese interests, and like any other state China does what serves its national interests best.

35

Stratosphere Missile Attack: Punctured US-China Ties

On 4 February 2023, US President Joe Biden ordered the Pentagon to shoot down a massive Chinese airship over the US territorial waters, which according to Lloyd Austin, US Secretary of Defence "was being used by the PRC in an attempt to surveil strategic sites in the continental United States." The US had detected the balloon on 28 January, but the shooting was delayed until the balloon was over water off the coast of South Carolina to avoid any collateral damage.

Mao Ning, the spokesperson of the Ministry of Foreign Affairs accused the US of "overreaction" (反应过度) and "adamantly using force" (执意动用武力) on a civilian nature unmanned airship that entered the US airspace due to force majeure and didn't pose threat to any person or to the US security. She said that the US should have handled the incident properly in a calm (冷静), professional (专业), and without resorting to force (非武力). Interestingly, in 2019, Xinlang Junshi (Sina military news) filed a story of J-10C launching a Thunderbolt 10 missile to shoot down a foreign super high-altitude reconnaissance balloon. The writer says, the whole operation was "very exciting." Undoubtedly, the recent incident has further punctured the US-China relations, and Antony Blinken's scheduled visit to China became the first causality of this. Why should a "civilian" balloon cause such a furor in the US as well as in China? Or, is there more to this than meets the eye?

As the US-China rivalry intensifies, so does the strife between the democrats and republicans. Ann Wagner, a Missouri Republican maintained that "President Biden's decision to let the balloons travel the length and breadth of the United States of America was an unpardonable show of weakness on the world stage." In response, Democrat Chuck Schumer said relations with China were strained and that the Biden administration is looking at other actions that can be taken." Secretary Blinken cancelling his China visit could be regarded as part of this toughening approach. But more than this, a joint statement issued by Mike Gallagher and Raja Krishnamoorthi reveals the real American fear. The statement said, "...Indeed, this incident demonstrates that the CCP threat is not confined to distant shores – it is here at home and we must act to counter this threat." The Chinese of course has regarded such statements as "neurotic" (抑郁症). During his State of the Union address, Joe Biden almost yelled, "Name me a world leader who'd change places with Xi Jinping. Name me one!"

China, on the other hand, also adopted a tough approach. Besides Mao Ning's counterblast, China's Defence Minister, Wei Fenghe refused the US request for a secure phone call with Lloyd Austin. The spokesperson of China's Ministry of Defence had stated that "People's Liberation Army reserves the right to destroy US installations if there arose a similar situation." Enumerating the US violations of Chinese airspace, a report reminded the US that in January 2023 alone, the US dispatched a total of 64 large-scale reconnaissance planes into the South China Sea. At the same time, Chinese Vice Foreign Minister Xie Feng, in a demarche to the US embassy in China pointed out the serious damage (严重破坏) the incident has caused to Sino-US relations, and urged the US not to take further destructive actions (破坏动作)."

This is the fifth such balloon spotted over the US since 2017 and the first to be shot down. The sixth has been spotted over the airspace of Costa Rica. Have all these airships gone off course or are these part of China's worldwide fleet as claimed by the US? While sharing information with its allies, the US maintained that China was operating similar balloons over North and South America, South East Asia, East Asia and Europe. The crux of the matter is – why should China use an unmanned airship to surveillance the US military installations on the eve of Blinken's China visit?

There are all sorts of theories and arguments put forth by analysts. David Ignatius argued in *Washington Post* that there was possibility that "the Chinese military or hard-line elements within the leadership deliberately sought to sabotage the Blinken visit, the chief goal of which was to explore strategic stability measures and other guardrails that could limit the likelihood of unintended escalation over Taiwan or other issues of potential conflict." The "sabotage" logic has been firmly denied by Dr. Manoj Joshi on the NDTV debate citing the PLA incursions in the Indian territory of Ladakh during the state visits of Premier Li Keqiang and President Xi Jinping to India in 2013 and 2014 respectively.

The use of stratospheric airships for surveillance and metrological purposes lies in the fact that these move very slowly, can effectively monitor ground dynamics, and send information to various trans receivers at much cheaper price. According to Baidu Encyclopaedia, "the stratospheric information system or the High-Altitude Platform Stations (HAPS) generally refers to a quasi-stationary airship platform that carries a certain information payload, and cooperates with various ground communications and terminal equipment to form a system, abbreviated as SCS. The stratospheric platform is located between various communication satellites and ground relay communication stations. It is an uncultivated "virgin land" above the earth. Its development is of great significance to the future communication development." Essentially, besides airships and balloons, solar powered drones and high velocity vehicles could also be deployed in stratosphere for civilian and military purposes. Therefore, for all good or bad intentions, stratosphere is emerging as a new breeding ground for great power rivalry.

Deployment of such systems in stratosphere could certainly provide China an edge over the US. China may be acquiring various weapon systems five times faster than the US, however, to match US' military might weapon to weapon remains a distant dream. The best possible scenario therefore is to deplete present US military assets by launching HAPS over the territorial space of the US and its allies; probability of deploying these over Taiwan strait remains very high. In the words of a Chinese blogger, against a "worthless target" (最无价值目标) the US has to muster an F-22 Raptor, Boeing KC-135 Stratotanker, US Navy P-8A Poseidon, and the Lockheed HC-130 search and rescue aircraft. An AIM-9X Sidewinder missile alone is worth $400,000, while an F-22 costs more than $36,000 for an hour's sortie..., it is estimated that the cost of this operation is at least $500,000." Xinlang Junshi puts the cost at 1 million US dollars.

Finally, deployment and timings of such systems could also have been geared towards salvaging image of the Communist Party that has taken a beating in the face of dwindling economic growth, real estate bubble bust, anti-establishment protests in the form of "White Paper Revolution" and the latest workers protests in Wuhan. It will also fan nationalistic fervours in China and spearhead the domestic contradiction away toward a foreign enemy. As for the US, besides garnering bipartisan support for a stronger action against China on issues such as Hi-tech rivalry, Taiwan, South China Sea, Xinjiang and Tibet etc., the balloon gate will also add stratosphere rivalry to the long list of US-China protracted rivalry.

36

China's 'bottom line' and 'highest-limit' Thinking

Incidents of 'near collision' are not unheard of between the US and China, however, as the relationship touches new low, these are increasingly becoming frequent. On 26 May 2023, statement released by the US Indo-Pacific Command (USINDOPACOM) said that the People's Republic of China J-16 fighter pilot performed an unnecessarily aggressive manoeuvre during the intercept of a US Air Force RC-135 aircraft. "The PRC pilot flew directly in front of the nose of the RC-135, forcing the US aircraft to fly through its wake turbulence." In another statement released on 3 June 2023, the USINDOPACOM said that when the USS Chung-Hoon (DDG 93) and HMCS Montreal (FFH 336) were conducting a routine south to north Taiwan Strait transit, PLA(N) LUYANG III DDG 132 (PRC LY 132) "executed manoeuvres in an unsafe manner in the vicinity of Chung-Hoon. The PRC LY 132 overtook Chung-Hoon on their port side and crossed their bow at 150 yards." The worst collision in 2001 between the EP-3 and one of the J-8s, resulted in the death of a Chinese pilot, emergency landing and detention of the EP-3 along with its 24 crew members in Hainan.

One of the 'near collisions" happened the day US Secretary of Defence Lloyd Austin was making his speech at the Shangri-La Dialogue, an annual security summit organized by the International Institute of Strategic Studies, UK in tandem with the Singaporean government. In fact, the US had sought a bilateral meeting between the Lloyd Austin and Chinese Defence Minister Gen. Li Shangfu, but was spurned by China. China was indicating that how a sanctioned defence minister could engage in talks as if nothing had happened. Furthermore, both locked horns at the high-level security dialogue. On 3 June, Austin in his speech said, "The whole world has a stake in maintaining peace and stability in the Taiwan Strait. The security of commercial shipping lanes and global supply chains depends on it. And so does freedom of navigation worldwide. Make no mistake: conflict in the Taiwan Strait would be devastating." In a charged rebuttal on 4 June, General Li Shangfu said that "It is undeniable that a severe conflict or confrontation between China and the US will be an unbearable disaster for the world."

From the above posturing, it is clear that the US-China relations have further nose-dived and that both are playing a hard ball. Austin's pronouncement could be construed as a veiled warning to China, whereas Li Shangfu's reply takes the US-China conflict to a higher level that will bring unbearable disaster to the entire world. Undoubtedly, the simmering tension has forced China to focus more on its security that could be discerned from the meeting of the Central National Security Commission convened on 30 May. The meeting emphasized that the complexity and severity of the national security issues we are currently facing have increased significantly. The national security front must establish strategic self-confidence, strengthen confidence in victory, and fully see its own advantages and favourable conditions. We must adhere to bottom-line thinking (底线思维) and highest-limit thinking (极限思维), and be prepared to withstand the major test of high winds, choppy waters and even dangerous storms."

The bottom-line thinking and highest-limit thinking together with choppy waters demonstrates that Xi Jinping is preparing China for a protracted contest with the US and both the thoughts are likely to be tested in the South China Sea and Taiwan Strait. Increasingly high number of 'near collisions' is one of the manifestations. Li Shangfu's emphasis that "Taiwan is China's Taiwan, how to solve the Taiwan issue is the business of the Chinese people, and intervention of any external power is unacceptable. The DPP authorities who keep soliciting foreign support for Taiwan secession and the external forces who seek to contain China with Taiwan and interfere in China's internal affairs are the root causes of tensions in the Taiwan Strait and the largest trouble makers that are changing the status quo in the Strait. If anyone dares to separate Taiwan from China, the Chinese military will not hesitate for one second to take action. We fear no one and will resolutely safeguard national sovereignty and territorial integrity no matter at what cost."

Li Shangfu's speech at Shangri-la is not very different from the tone and tenor of speeches of other Chinese leaders. The speech echoes China's State Councillor and Foreign Minister, Qin Gang's speech at China Development Forum on 27 Mach 2023, and Premier Li Qiang's address at the Bo Ao Forum in Hainan on 30 March 2023. For example, Qin Gang had said that while humankind is confronted with unprecedented multiple crises and challenges, "some country, in order to maintain its hegemony and out of selfish interests, has been stoking tensions and confrontation along the ideological line, seeking decoupling, disrupting supply chains, erecting high fences around small yards, and even attempting to resurrect the Cold War and tear the world apart." This is nothing but reinforcement of Xi Jinping's advocacy of building a community of shared future, which since 2013 has been incorporated as one of the pillars of China's foreign policy.

Building community of shared future is China's long-term vision for transforming the global governance and making it compatible with China's own governance model. The concept upholds interconnectedness, mutual interests, progress and sustainable development of mankind as a whole. It argues in favour of dialogue of civilisations, common development and common security. From the Chinese perspective, it is an antidote to hegemonism, unilateralism, protectionism, block politics, and cold war mentality. Other discourses such as the Global Development Initiative (GDI), Global Security Initiative (GSI) and Global Civilisation Initiative (GCI) have been fed to the basic framework of the community of shared future. The New Type of International Relations is the second pillar having two distinctive flanks – major country diplomacy and China's relationship with the Belt and Road Initiative (BRI) countries. The Chinese Style Modernisation has been added to the list, thus making Chinese 'wisdom and model' very different from the American model. These initiatives are presented as important public goods provided by China for the benefit of humanity, as well as China's vision for the global development and governance.

37

Deepening Chasm between US and China

US Secretary of the State, Antony Blinken's much anticipated China visit that was stalled by an unmanned Chinese airship in the US airspace in February 2022, did take place on 18-19 June, 2023. Blinken is the highest-level US official to visit China since 2018. During the two-day visit, he met Chinese Foreign Minister Qin Gang, member of the politburo and director of the Foreign Affairs Office of the Communist Party of China Central Committee Wang Yi, and General Secretary of the CPC Xi Jinping. The US-China relation has been at the lowest ebb ever since the establishment of the relationship in 1979, and both have been wanting to steer the relations back on track as both are of the view that the relations need to be managed and stabilised.

From the optics of Blinken's China visit, the ever-widening chasm between the US and China was clear. What a contrast from the red-carpet reception accorded to much despised and sanctioned Mike Pompeo in 2018 and even the US billionaires like Elon Musk and Bill Gates who visited China in recent weeks. Even the head table Xi Jinping sat on gave the aura of the celestial empire receiving the tributary envoys from afar. And why not, when the meeting was sought by the American side. Not only the current visit, but Wang Yi's "informal contact" (非正式接触) with Blinken at side-lines of Munich Security Conference on 18 February 2023, and Qin Gang's telephonic conversation with Blinken on 14 June 2023 were all requested by the US according to a Sina.com article.

To a question as to "Why the US is so eager to resume exchanges with China?" Liu Weidong, a researcher at the American Institute of the

Chinese Academy of Social Sciences, posits that the Biden administration hopes to stabilize the current Sino-US relations. The year 2023 is a "window of opportunity" (窗口期) before the US goes to elections in 2024. The stable Sino-US relations provides a "favourable bargaining chip" (有利筹码) to Biden administration, as it can improve its image and status in the United States. Notwithstanding these reasons, Xi Jinping's thirty-five minutes long meeting with Blinken does indicate that both sides wish to put the relations back on the track. Some of the takeaways are that two sides agreed to maintain high-level exchanges, to encourage the expansion of cultural and educational exchanges, actively discuss the increase of passenger flights between China and the United States, and welcome more students, scholars, and business people to visit each other's countries. However, there was no agreement to restore military to military communication. From the briefing of Qin Gang, Wang Yi, and Xi Jinping's meetings with the US Secretary of State, and from Blinken's own Press briefings, it could be discerned that chasm is so deep that bridging it would be too daunting a task.

Though Xi Jinping struck a conciliatory tone when he said that the vast earth is capable of fully accommodating (完全容得下) the respective development and common prosperity of China and the United States, and assured Blinken that China will not challenge or replace the United States. However, he did tell Blinken that "Major-power competition does not conform to the trend of the times" that they need to find the "correct way to get along with each other" (正确相处之道). The final paragraph of the briefing gives the impression as if the US has digressed from the agenda set by the two heads of state in Bali, therefore, Blinken reiterating Biden's assurances to China that the US remains committed to returning to (重回) the agenda; does not seek a "new cold war", does not seek to change China's system, does not seek to oppose China by strengthening alliances, does not support "Taiwan independence", and has no intention to enter conflict with China, and looks forward to high-level exchanges with China.

As a matter of fact, these are some of the most contentious issues between the US and China, and Xi Jinping has been flagging them out time and again when talking about the "New Type of Major Power Relationship", one of the pillars of China's foreign policy in the New Era. In November 2021, Xi Jinping during a virtual summit with the US president Joe Biden proposed the "three principles of mutual respect, peaceful coexistence and win-win cooperation" as a framework for the New Type of Major Power Relationship, aimed at avoiding conflict and confrontation or the so-called Thucydides' Trap between the established and a rising power. As regards the mutual respect, Xi Jinping argued that "the two countries need to respect each other's social systems and development paths, respect each other's core interests and major concerns, and respect each other's right to development. They need to treat each other as equals..." This was perhaps one of the most candid explanations of the major power relationship to date, however, the US as ever, appears to look the other way, especially since president Donald Trump resumed office in 2017, and Biden administration has continued these policies, rather entrenched the competition with China in its strategic thinking. No wonder Qin Gang in his meeting with Blinken argued that China wishes to build a "stable, predictable (可预期) and constructive" relationship with the US.

Qin Gang on his part "solemnly" clarified the "core of China's core interests" (核心利益中的核心) – the Taiwan issue, and termed it as the most important issue and the most prominent risk (最突出的风险) between China and the US. Wang Yi was more blunt to ask Blinken to make a choice between dialogue or confrontation (对话还是对抗), cooperation or conflict (合作还是冲突). He said that the Sino-US relations reaching the lowest ebb is rooted in the US's "erroneous perception of China" (错误的对华认知). He underscored that Taiwan's unification with China is "unswerving historical mission" of the Communist Party of China, and China has no room for compromise (妥协退让的余地) on the issue. Scholars such as Zhang Weiwei have argued that Pelosi's Taiwan visit and Tsai Ing-wen's US visit has put the unification of Taiwan on the fast track. Wang Yi further urged the US side to stop hyping up the "China threat theory", lift illegal unilateral sanctions against China, stop suppressing China's technological development, and refrain from willfully interfering in China's internal affairs.

It could be discerned from Blinken's ten and a half hours' discussions with China's top leaders that the root cause for the deepening chasm between the US and China is related to trade, technology, territory and ideology. As regards the trade and technology, the US is not averse to doing trade with China. In fact, trade with China was all time high at $700 billion, however, as revealed by Blinken during his press briefing,

"China's unfair treatment of US companies was an issue. According to Blinken, the US was not decoupling from China, but "de-risking and diversifying" and protecting the US critical technologies, so that China doesn't use them against the US. It was in this context that he remarked, "We are clear-eyed about the challenges posed by the PRC." As for the territory, he reiterated that the longstanding US "one China" policy has not changed, however, he also stated that the US "remain opposed to any unilateral changes to the status quo by either side." Blinken revealed that human rights violations, including in Xinjiang, in Tibet, and Hong Kong were also raised with his counterparts. Finally, the ideological confrontation has also become inherent to the deepening chasm. The Chinese-style modernisation and the whole process democracy that Wang Yi talked about during his discussion, demonstrates the war of narratives that China has initiated against the US led discourses. Given the nature of the chasm on trade, technology, territory and ideology, from the US perspective, managing the ties would be a priority. From the Chinese perspective, challenging the US with "bottom line" and "highest limit" thinking would be a work in progress.

V

INDIA'S CHINA CHALLENGE

38

China's Land Border Law and India

On 23 October 2021, the 31st meeting of the Standing Committee of the 13th National People's Congress, passed a law entitled "Land Border Law of the People's Republic of China" (中华人民共和国陆地国界法) for the "protection and exploitation of the country's land border areas" that will come into effect from 1 January 2022. The 6200-character long Land Border Law (LBL) has 5 chapters and 62 articles. The LBL is applicable to the entire 22,457-kilometre land boundary of China bordering 14 countries. China has resolved its land boundary with 12 of its bordering states and Article 14 of the new law states that China "abides by treaties concerning land border affairs concluded or jointly participated (遵守同外国缔结或者共同参加) in with foreign countries. The only two countries with which China has not resolved its border are India and Bhutan having 3,488 and 477 kilometres of disputed boundary respectively. What could be the implications of such a law to India's disputed border with China?

At the outset, the passage of such a law in the backdrop of the prolonged border stand-off in the western sector since Galwan bloody clashes in June 2020, demonstrates that China is adamant about not restoring the pre-Galwan status quo. This was reiterated by the spokesperson for the Western Theater Command of the People's Liberation Army (PLA), Long Shaohua blatantly when he pointed out after the conclusion of the 13th round of the India-China corps commander level talks that "the Indian side still insisted on unreasonable and unrealistic demands, which added difficulties to the negotiations." Explaining it further, Lin Minwang, deputy director of the Centre for

South Asian Studies of Fudan University wrote in an op-ed that "restoration of the status quo ante of April 2020 is obviously unreasonable for China." The scholar maintains that the "confidence to make unreasonable demands" originates from India's security cooperation with the US, aimed at containment of China. As regards India's accusations of the PLA transgressing in Barahoti in Uttrakhand and near Tawang in Arunachal Pradesh, a PLA source has maintained that this was a "routine patrol" "unreasonably blocked by the Indian side." In the view of this understanding from China, it demonstrates that China is unwilling to withdraw from the rest of the friction areas in the western sector, and wants India to accept the changed status quo, and that if it is not acceptable to India, China will create more friction points in all sectors of the border. In this context Article 4 of the LBL could be exercised to the perceived boundary or LAC by China that stipulates that the "sovereignty and territorial integrity of the People's Republic of China is sacred and inviolable" (神圣不可侵犯) albeit the PRC has been reiterating it ever since its inception.

Two, Article 40, prohibits an organization or individual to build permanent structures near land borders without the approval of relevant competent authorities, however, Article 43 delegates the construction (建设), function (功能), and capacity building (能力建设) of border towns to the state. In recent years, after having successfully experimented with reclamation of islands in the South China Sea, China has followed a similar pattern by creating "border towns" in the perceived territory to bolster its territorial claims. Earlier on January 24, the Hong Kong-based *South China Morning Post*, filed a story stating that China built a village in the "conflict zone" of India-China boundary. Quoting a Chinese government source, it revealed that "China intends to build 624 border villages" in the disputed Himalayan areas as part of the poverty alleviation drive. No wonder, China allocated 200 billion RMB (US$ 20.5 billion) for infrastructure development in Tibet during the "13th Five-Year Plan" (2016-2020). The same has been increased to US$29.3 billion for the 14th Five-Year Plan (2021-2025). By the year 2020, 99 per cent of the villages in Tibet were connected to highways; the network in the region reached to 90,000 kilometres according to a commentary by Xinhua. The highways are also being connected to rail networks in the region. For example, the Lhasa-Shigatse line that was opened to traffic in 2014, has further been extended as Lhasa-Nyingchi Railway and Shigatse-Yadong line, the former is situated opposite Arunachal and the latter in the Doklam area. Earlier in July 2021, Xi Jiping made a rare visit to Nyingchi, and travelled back to Lhasa in a train. The construction of Sichuan-Tibet Railway has been going on feverishly. China believes that the opening of this line will alter China's disadvantageous position in Tibet, especially in the so called 'Southern Tibet'. China claims that once the line pass through Linzhi and Nanshan, logistics constraints as regards the areas won't be a concern in event of 'an incident'; China holds that areas such as Zayul 察隅, Motuo 墨脱, Cuona 错那, and Longzi 隆子 have been held by India. The establishment of the "border towns" perhaps could also be a response to Article 7 of the 2005 agreement on the political parameters and guiding principles for the settlement of India-China boundary, which stipulates that "In reaching a boundary settlement, the two sides shall safeguard due interests of their settled populations in the border areas."

Three, the LBL could also be seen as China's response to the abrogation of Article 370 by India. On 6 August 2019 when the President of India promulgated the abrogation, Hua Chunying, the spokeswomen of the Ministry of Foreign Affairs (MOFA) told in a press briefing that "China has always opposed the Indian side's transfer of Chinese territory in the western sector of the Sino-Indian border into the administrative jurisdiction of India." "...Recently, the Indian side has continued to damage China's territorial sovereignty by unilaterally modifying the domestic law. This practice is unacceptable and will not have any effect..." No wonder, the Ministry of External Affairs of India, has also reacted to China's LBL in somewhat similar fashion. The statement read out that "China's unilateral decision to bring about a legislation which can have implication on our existing bilateral arrangements on border management as well as on the boundary question is of concern to us... We also expect that China will avoid undertaking action under the pretext of this law which could unilaterally alter the situation in the India-China border areas."

Four, in order to facilitate the connectivity goals of the Belt and Road Initiative (BRI), China has been building five major economic corridors along the BRI for a new type of regional development model. These corridors are being increasingly connected with China's connectivity projects within the bordering provinces. Since China's trade with the BRI countries accounts for more than 50 per cent of China's GDP, to secure the exit and entry points, establishment of dry ports and marts has been accorded high priority and will be regulated by the LBL. For example, Article 6 allocates responsibilities to manage various facets of border affairs to relevant departments such as MOFA, the Public Security Department of the State Council, the General Administration of Customs, the National Immigration Management Department etc. Article 7 entrusts relevant military agencies to organize, guide, and coordinate the defence control of land borders. The task to secure border from armed aggression, terrorist activities, transgressions has been delegated to the PLA and People's Armed Police Force. There are various other provisions such as promoting economy, tourism, culture, sports, disaster relief and ecological environment with bordering countries.

Finally, the LBL doesn't change the status of the border on the ground, as has been the case with abrogation of the Article 370. We may recall that in 2013 various claimant nations in the disputed South China Sea (SCS) passed legislations claiming certain island in their perceived territorial waters. In February that year Philippines Senate and House of Representatives passed Baseline Bill and declared its ownership over Scarborough (Huangyan in Chinese) island and some others in Spratly. In June, Vietnam also passed a Maritime Law declaring indisputable sovereignty over Paracel and Spratly islands, but none altered the prevailing status quo on the ground. As enshrined in the Article 15 of the LBL, it is hoped that China will adhere to the principles of equality, mutual trust, and friendly consultation, while resolving its land border with its neighbours through negotiations, therefore, actions, not words in the LBL will be watched for to understand the intentions of China.

39

PLA's New Book on 1962 India-China War

Recently, starting from 7 January 2022, observersnews.com has been featuring excerpts from a newly published book entitled 《中印边境自卫反击作战一百问》(*One Hundred Questions on Counterattack in Self Defense along the China-India Border*) in a special feature dedicated to mark the 60th anniversary of the China-India border war. The book is written by Zhang Xiaokang, younger daughter of Zhang Guohua, the general who led People's Liberation Army's (PLA) assault on Tibet in 1950-51, headed the committee that negotiated the 17-point agreement on Tibet with China, and was the field commander of the PLA's attack in the Eastern Sector during the 1962 India-China war. With nationalistic fervours on the rise in China, and the prolonged military confrontation in the Western Sector of India China boundary, the publication is yet another war cry for the PLA after last year's war movie, *The Battle at Lake Changjin* (Chosin Reservoir) 《长津湖》and this year's *The Battle at Lake Changjin II* 《水门桥》on the Korean War, in which China sustained heavy losses and three companies of the PLA 'volunteers' froze to death. In contrast, the 1962 war with India has been described as "a complete victory" and often cited as a "lesson" taught to India. As regards the choice of using "counterattack in self-defense", in true Confucian tradition of "rectification of names" the decision was taken on 3 December 1962, according to the article.

Going by the three excerpts that have appeared in Chinese media, the book is mostly on the lines of official and unofficial histories on India-China war such as《中印边境自卫反击战争史》 (*History of China's counter attack in self-defence along the Sino-Indian border*), 《中印大战

纪实 *1962*》 (*Records of the 1962 Sino-Indian War*), 《喜马拉雅山的雪》 (*Snow of the Himalayas*) published in the 1990s. According to the first article published on 7 January 2022, in order to commemorate the 60th anniversary of the counterattack in self-defence on the Sino-Indian border, Zhang Xiaokang organized war history researchers to compile this book on the basis of first-hand information and interviews with the veterans who had participated in the war. It says that though a considerable time has passed, but the war has not been forgotten with the passage of time. In China, the article says that "generations of soldiers and military enthusiasts have always held a strong interest in the counterattack operation" of the 1962, and have wondered how was it possible for the PLA "to annihilate more than seven brigades of the Indian army's most elite forces in just a few days", and some other questions such as why did the PLA "retreat unilaterally on the day of victory", why did the PLA "release Indian prisoners of war and return their weapons and equipment" and many more are asked and answered perhaps on the lines of existing literature. The article has attempted to understand the nitty-gritty of the war from three facets, namely "direction of the operation and command structure", "stages of the operation and troop deployment", and "outcome of the operation and strategic significance."

The "counterattack" operation according to the first article, was carried out under the unified command of Chairman Mao and the Central Military Commission along the two strategic directions of the eastern (1100 kilometres) and western (600 kilometres) fronts. The frontline command post of the Tibet Military Region was located at Ma Magou, Cuona County of the Tibet Autonomous Region (TAR) headed by Zhang Guohua. The post was coordinating with Lhasa, the base command centre of the Tibet Military Region headed by Tan Guansan. The frontline command was located at Banggang, north of Tawang. It also gives details of other members associated with the operations at different levels. In the Western Sector, the command centre of the Xinjiang Military Region was at Kangxiwa headed by He Jiachan. Combat operation along the western front was divided into four defence areas namely Tiantian, Heweitan, Kongkashankou and Ali defence areas.

The operations are divided into two stages, i.e. from 20 October 1962 and 18 November 1962, and the closure dates are different along both the sectors. The directions of the combat in Eastern Sector were primarily in

Kejielang (Khinzemane) and Tawang areas under 419 Unit (equivalent to 1 infantry division), and auxiliary operations under Chamdo Linzhi and Shannan military divisions. The direction of the operations in the western front was under the unified command of the 3rd Battalion of the 10th Infantry Regiment of the 4th Army Division, the 3rd Battalion of the 11th Infantry Regiment, the 3rd Cavalry Regiment, and the 2nd Infantry Regiment. The troop deployment, according to the article was successful in annihilating each of the four battalions of the 114th Indian Infantry Brigade, and ejecting them from the 37 strongholds in the "occupied territories." In the second stage, the main battle campaigns were, Xishankou-Bandila (Bomdilla) and Walong and some other smaller campaigns carried out by the Nyingchi Military Division in places such as Mechuka and Rimi, Jin, and Bolang, etc. areas, thus restoring the "traditional customary line." In the Western Sector, remaining six strongholds of the Indian army were also destroyed subsequently.

As regards fatalities, these remain same as declared by the earlier official accounts of the war. Indian fatalities and captured have been given as 4,885 and 3,968 respectively, whereas the PLA fatalities and wounded have been put at 722 and 1697 respectively. Battles of Kejielang and Xishankou-Bandila are considered "big victories at a small price" (以小的代价夺取了大的胜利), accounting for 79 per cent of annihilation rate of the Indian forces. The killing of Brigadier Hoshiar Singh and capture of Brigadier John Dalvi, also figures prominently in the narration. Brigadier Dalvi's dramatic capture has been narrated in the third article published on 21 January 2022, a few paragraphs from his *Himalayan Blunder* have also been reproduced. Dalvi is quoted saying upon his capture that "you eliminated a brigade within 24 hours, which is rare in the world."

The above-mentioned statistics have been considered as authentic, however, if corroborated with the PLA's narration in other war histories, they are contradictory. Consider the following passage about the PLA campaign in the Western Sector from the *Snow of the Himalayas: Sino-Indian War Records* (1991) by Sun Xiao, a PLA officer: "...From the very beginning of the war, the firepower of the Indian army was extremely fierce. After two hours of fierce fighting, though the Chinese army occupied Galwan Valley, but the price it paid was too heavy. 874 Chinese soldiers fell on the icy snow of this river valley. It was not until the beginning of the1980s that the bodies of more than 800 soldiers were brought back from the frozen snow." As regards the killing of Brigadiar Hoshiar Singh, the official account of the 1962 war by S.N. Prasad (1992) says that he was ambushed by the Chinese on 27 November, a few days after declaring the ceasefire (p.194).

As regards the outcome and significance of the 1962 war, the article says: Militarily, it was a "complete victory" that "negated the illegal McMahon Line", forced the traditional customary line, enhanced national prestige of China, and peace along the India-China border was established for the next 60 years. Politically, it "dealt a heavy blow to the regional hegemonism and expansionism of Nehru's government", forced India to abandon the obstinacy that "the Sino-Indian border issue is non-negotiable" (中印边界问题不谈判) and engage in peaceful negotiations of border issue "in accordance with China's proposition" (按照中国的主张). Diplomatically, it "completely exposed the pursuit of power politics" (奉行强权政治) by the Indian government, tore the veil of Nehru's 'non-alignment' (撕掉了尼赫鲁"不结盟"的面纱), and shattered his illusion about being the 'leader of an alliance' (打破了其当"盟主"的梦幻). Besides, the PLA established "huge psychological advantage (巨大心理优势) over the Indian army, and "seized and maintained the initiative" (夺取和保持…主动权) on the Sino-Indian border. It also won China "high praise from peace-loving countries and people around the world, as well as a strong response from international public opinion."

The essay refutes that it was "China's India War" as pronounced by Bertil Lintner in his book, and hence the theory of Chinese invasion of India. It also refutes PLA's voluntary withdrawal owing to weak logistical support. It doesn't throw light on the three-year man made famine in China and the power struggle within the Communist Party, as people like Liu Shaoqi and Peng Dehuai were pointing fingers of accusations at Mao for the manmade calamity that killed millions of Chinese people, nevertheless, the article does say that Deng Xiaoping wanted to buy time in the face of Mao's order, for he was concerned about the food situation in Tibet. However, Mao had already ordered to "wipe out" the Indian forces from Kejielang on 8 October, for Tibet was treated as a "sacred territory" belonging to China. The second article of 14 January 2022, reveals that the leadership had taken into consideration the possibility of China suffering setbacks in the war, and in case it becomes a reality, the PLA "will not blame heaven and earth but their own incompetence", nonetheless, there will be the day, when they will snatch it back.

With China consolidating its position and infrastructure in the disputed border areas by way of building border villages and naming a few more places inside Arunachal recently, India is also likely to hasten the pace of border infrastructure. This together with China's policy of "competition continuum" along the disputed areas is bound to create more friction points and exacerbate the already delicate situation. China's worsening relations with the United States, economic slowdown, domestic political compulsions, may result in greater challenges for India, and India in turn may have to respond to a hundred questions indeed!

40

India and China: How Not to Build Trust

While responding to questions after delivering a lecture on "India's Vision of the Indo-Pacific" at Chulalongkorn University in Bangkok on 18 August 2022, India's External Affairs Minister (EAM), S. Jaishankar emphasised that the "Asian Century would not happen if the two neighbours could not join hands." He reiterated these remarks on 29 August at the launch of Asia Society Policy Institute in New Delhi. According to him, the "pre-requisite for an Asian Century is India and China coming together. Their inability to do so will undermine it." Jaishankar's remarks received wide publicity in China. Chinese Foreign Ministry spokesman, Wang Wenbin said at a regular press conference on the 19th that "China and India have the wisdom and ability to realize "mutual accomplishments" (实现相互成就) instead of "mutual depletion" (彼此消耗). Nonetheless, there is a huge difference between the rhetoric and the ground reality. Let's examine the following:

While the Chinese government and its media lauded Jaishankar's vision of the Asian Century, however, the media was quick to blame India for what had happened at the border in June 2020 and thereafter the state of bilateral relations. The *Huanqiu Shibao* argued in a commentary that it was "India's deliberate provocation" (蓄意挑衅) that led to the conflict. It further said that the spokesperson of the Chinese Ministry of Foreign Affairs has repeatedly emphasized that the "right and wrong of the situation on the Sino-Indian border is very clear" (是非曲直是十分清楚), and that the "responsibility does not lie on the Chinese side" (责任不在中方).

This obviously was in response to what Jaishankar has said in Chulalongkorn University that "the [India-China] relationship is going through an extremely difficult phase after what China did at the border." Now, the answer to question about the "right and wrong" of the situation along the border could be found in questions such as: who mobilised the troops first; who changed the status quo in certain points along the LAC; and who is reluctant to restore the status quo that existed before April 2020? If China didn't change the status quo, what was the need to withdraw from Galwan Valley, Gogra Heights, and from Finger 3 to the east of Finger 8 in the Pangong Tso. Also, why should then both be talking about disengagement and de-escalation in 16 rounds of tedious talks at the Corps Commander level? It is the new modus vivendi, often disseminated through the proposition that India must put the border issue at an "appropriate place" (适当位置) that India finds problematic and unacceptable, especially when over hundred thousand soldiers are engaged in a prolonged stand-off.

Away from the Himalayas, India and China engaged in another diplomatic spat in the Indian Ocean on the question of Chinese satellite tracking vessel Yuan Wang 5 docking at Sri Lankan port of Hambantota on 16 August. India's harsh response could have been avoided had the Chinese ambassador to Sri Lanka, Qi Zhenghong not linked Nancy Pelosi's Taiwan visit and "One China Policy" with the docking of the ship, thus proving a point that "China and Sri Lanka having altogether resisted the rude and unreasonable interference from third parties." The Chinese envoy further said that "External obstruction based on the so called "security concerns" but without any evidence from certain forces is de facto a thorough interference into Sri Lanka's sovereignty and independence." He also made mention of China's "century of humiliation", but forgot that 99-years lease of Hambantota would not be construed as an act of safeguarding the territorial integrity by the Sri Lankans.

In a strongly worded twitter thread, the Indian mission in Sri Lanka lashed out at the Chinese envoy by saying that "His view of Sri Lanka's northern neighbour may be coloured by how his own country behaves. India, we assure him, is very different. His imputing a geopolitical context to the visit of a purported scientific research vessel is a giveaway. Opaqueness and debt driven agendas are now a major challenge, especially for smaller nations. Recent developments are a caution. Sri

Lanka needs support, not unwanted pressure or unnecessary controversies to serve another country's agenda."

Chinese scholars have admitted that "India's broader geopolitical ambitions have to an extent been held in check by its rivalry with China and Pakistan", fundamentally the containment of India by China as clearly spelled by Ye Hailin in his contributory chapter written in Chinese entitled "Development and Challenges of China-Pakistan Relations", for an edited volume by Zhang Yunling titled China and its Neighboring Countries: Building New Partnerships. Conversely, when India engages the regional and resident powers in the Indo-Pacific, has been pronounced as containment of China. So much so, most of the Chinese intellectual discourse revolves around the same theme. For example, China Going Global Think Tank (CGGT) posits that under the influence of geopolitics of the "Indo-Pacific Strategy" and the "Indo-Pacific Economic Framework" of the United States, India has increasingly viewed India-China relations from the perspective of "competitors and even adversaries" (竞争者甚至对抗者). It is this approach of India, which according to the think-tank is responsible for "putting China-India relations into an 'extremely difficult' stage. It further says that "If China and India want to "truly set aside the estrangement" (真正放下隔阂) and "boost their sanity" (健全双方思维), the onus is on India.

Irrespective of such divergences and deep rooted mistrust, there are other multilateral forums such as Shanghai Cooperation Organisation (SCO) and BRICS etc., where India and China are collaborating, even sending troops to Vostok 22 joint military manoeuvres between the SCO nations starting from August 30. Meanwhile, Pakistan is expected to send its armed contingent for counter-terror drill in India in October. Since last year, both have been dispatching troops for such exercises, even as the military stand-off between India and China continues. Last year, India, China and Pakistan also took part in the Zapad drills in Russia. Here again, China believes, India's opposition to the BRICS expansion, was due to India's "sitting on the fence diplomacy" (骑墙外交) and not wanting to "offend" (得罪) the US. Another reason, a commentary in 163.com gave was that "India cannot compete for influence with China and Russia (无法跟中俄争夺影响力) within the BRICS" because of its weaker comprehensive national power. India's entry into the SCO with Russian support and China countervailing it with Pakistan is no different a case.

Given such a state of affairs between India and China, building trust would be a herculean task. It is a paradigm where China looks down upon India, and India doesn't think big of China, which ought to change for good if they wish to realise the Asian century.

41

China on the Yangtse Face-off

On 13 December, while addressing the Parliament about the face-off between Indian and Chinese troops in the Eastern Sector on 9 December 2022, Defence Minister Rajnath Singh said that the "PLA tried to transgress the Line of Actual Control (LAC) in Yangtse area of Tawang Sector and unilaterally change the status quo." The face-off according to the statement led to a physical scuffle, in which both sides suffered injuries. The transgression was thwarted and the Chinese side has been asked to refrain from such actions and maintain peace and tranquillity along the border.

The issue was also discussed in a flag meeting on 11 December in accordance with the existing mechanisms. When asked, Chinese foreign ministry spokesperson Wang Wenbin said, "the China-India border areas are generally stable", albeit Colonel Long Shaohua, spokesperson for the Western Theatre Command of the PLA in a press release said that during a "routine patrol" on the Chinese side of the LAC in Dongzhang area, the PLA troops "encountered obstruction from the Indian troops, who illegally crossed the LAC". The Chinese also demanded that "the Indian side should strictly discipline and control its front-line troops and work with the Chinese side to maintain peace and tranquillity in the border areas".

From the above statements of the respective governments, it is the blame game as usual. If the video making rounds on the social media is indeed of 9 December 2022, the PLA has certainly climbed up to the Indian position and challenged them. This has been admitted by the Chinese that the PLA "took initiative to dismantle military strongholds of the Indian army" (主动出击拆除印军工事). In various other videos, not necessarily of the Yangste area, the PLA soldiers have been shown dismantling similar stone walls, and being dissuaded or challenged by the Indian side. This is a major confrontation since the June 2020 Galwan clash that saw fatalities on both sides. Therefore, why such provocations time and again?

Liu Zongyi, a senior fellow and secretary general of the South Asia and China Centre, Shanghai Institutes for International Studies (SIIS) like other Chinese write ups has blamed India for encroaching the area in the 1990s that resulted in an 82 days long face-off between the two armies in 1999 at a place called Maila pass, not far from the 9 December confrontation. According to Liu, India further encroached Dongzhang Waterfall in 2001 and grasslands in the vicinity in 2003. What Liu is arguing is that the Indian army crossed the McMahon Line, yet China avoided "head-on collision" (迎头相撞) in 1999 "for the sake of maintaining stability in the area".

However, another article by an anonymous Chinese reporter contradicts the above thinking and claims that the Indian army took control of the area in 1968, and since then has built stone walls and other structures on the ridge line that marks the LAC. It boasts that "in the past two years, the PLA has gradually launched counterattacks and removed the sentry posts and strongholds erected by the Indian army" in the area. On 9 December, it wasn't any different. "About 250 to 300 (larger than 2021) PLA troops went prepared (经过准备) to the mountain pass to demolish illegal structures, but encountered a large Indian patrol team". The article also declares that Dongzhang in Yangtse area cannot be the last gateway of China to Arunachal, but 150 kilometers south of this place should be China's border with India as depicted in the Chinese maps. "Therefore, there is still a long way to go to recover the territory of the entire southern Tibet region." Tang Bohu, a journalist with Fenghuang wang (Phoenix net) reiterates the above position and advocates that only by taking "tough and actual control" (强硬地实控) launching "aggressive public opinion" (舆论出击) can China shatter India's illusion.

It is precisely owing to the Chinese stand on the McMahon Line in the Eastern Sector that China desires to change the status quo as it is doing in the Western Sector. China has long abandoned the swap deal for the resolution of the border, rather it believes that the power has shifted in its favour, therefore, has no compulsions to maintain the kind of understanding it had reached with India on the border during the reform era. There is a certain thinking in China that believes that India can ill afford to engage with China in both the low intensity and an all-out conflict, therefore, the so-called salami slicing is the best approach.

Given this posturing of China, and India's readiness to challenge the same, we will continue to witness similar face-offs along the entire India-China border. The conflict in Yangste area is not new, a little farther away from 9 December face-off location, at Tulung pass, India lost a few soldiers in an exchange of fire at the border in 1975. The pattern of the face-offs, right from 1999 to 2021 and 2022 shows that as both India and China revamp their infrastructure along the LAC, such stand-offs are bound to happen. Added to this the worsening relations between China and the US, and close partnership between India and the US in the Indo-Pacific has made China to believe that both India and the US are in hands and glove to contain its rise. In fact, Chinese scholars have made statements that "in place of Pakistan, now China has become the biggest catharsis for Indian nationalist sentiments."

42

China's Strategy and Thinking on the Succession of Dalai Lama

The Tibetans believe that the issue of incarnation of the Dalai Lama would be decided by the Dalai Lama himself. However, the People's Republic of China (PRC), which sent the People's Liberation Army to wrest control of Tibet in 1950, insists that the ultimate authority to designate a Dalai Lama lies only with it. The Dalai Lama on his part has been emanating varied signals as regards his reincarnation. He has been saying that the issue of reincarnation would be decided by his believers; that there would be no Dalai Lama after his death; or rather a beautiful maiden may be his reincarnation, or his reincarnation would be outside China, and even outside the planet. Notwithstanding the Dalai Lama's thinking, the Tibetan people, in all probabilities will have two Dalai Lamas – one designated by their spiritual and temporal leader and the other by the PRC. This brief study looks into China's strategy and thinking on the succession of Dalai Lama.

1. The Dalai Lama on Reincarnation

The 14th Dalai Lama (2011) has made a formal written declaration concerning his reincarnation on 24 September 2011. The declaration concludes by saying:

The author is grateful to the Institute for Peace and Development Studies, Sweden and ORCA, New Delhi for agreeing to reprint the article in this volume.

> When I am about ninety I will consult the high Lamas of the Tibetan Buddhist traditions, the Tibetan public, and other concerned people who follow Tibetan Buddhism, and re-evaluate whether the institution of the Dalai Lama should continue or not.... I shall leave clear written instructions about this. Bear in mind that, apart from the reincarnation recognized through such legitimate methods, no recognition or acceptance should be given to a candidate chosen for political ends by anyone, including those in the People's Republic of China.

On 18 March 2019, the *Reuters* published an exclusive interview of the Dalai Lama in which the Dalai yet again addressed the issue:

> In future, in case you see two Dalai Lamas come, one from here, in free country, one chosen by Chinese, then nobody will trust, nobody will respect (the one chosen by China). So that's an additional problem for the Chinese! It's possible, it can happen.

These arguments put forth by the Dalai Lama demonstrate apprehensions of the Tibetan people as to what will happen to this important institution of Tibetan Buddhism under the PRC. No wonder, various Tibetan organizations have been raising China's interference in the Dalai Lama's succession. The International Campaign for Tibet (2022), testified at the hearing of the US Commission on International Religious Freedom on 14 December 2022 about the PRC's "policy of altering the very identity of Tibetan Buddhism to make it subservient to the Chinese Communist Party." Ever since the passage of the Tibetan Policy and Support Act of 2020, the US has made it official that "the Chinese Government should have no role in the succession process of the Dalai Lama" (Ned Price 2021).

2. The Chinese Response

On 19 March, Geng Shuang (2019), the spokesperson of China's Ministry of Foreign Affairs responded to the Dalai Lama's interview to the *Reuters* in the following words:

> Reincarnation of living Buddha's, as a unique institution of inheritance in Tibetan Buddhism, comes with a set range of rituals and conventions. The Chinese government implements the policy of freedom of religious belief. The reincarnation system is respected and protected by such legal instruments as Regulations on Religious Affairs and Measures on the Management of the Reincarnation of Living Buddha's. The institution of reincarnation of the Dalai Lama has been in existence for several hundred

years. The 14th Dalai Lama himself was found and recognized following religious rituals and historical conventions and his enthronement was approved by the then central government. Therefore, reincarnation of living Buddha's including the Dalai Lama must comply with Chinese laws and regulations and follow religious rituals and historical conventions.

Geng Shuang's reply could be regarded as a Chinese thinking and counter argument to the Dalai Lama's arguments on his reincarnation as well as the US stand on the issue. It emphasizes on two things. One, the incarnation of the Dalai Lama must follow the *rituals and historical conventions*. And two, it would be decided by such *legal instruments* as "Regulations on Religious Affairs and Measures on the Management of the Reincarnation of Living Buddha's" formulated by the PRC, which the Dalai Lama has castigated in his statement on the reincarnation in 2011.

2.1 The Rituals and Historical Conventions

As regards the rituals and conventions, while explaining China's position, a document posted on the National People's Congress (NPC 2009) of the PRC, argues that the very title of the Dalai Lama was "granted by the central government of China's dynasties", thus trying to establish the fact that Dalai Lama's authority in Tibet has been sanctioned by China. Historical records point to the fact that it was owing to the Gelupa (Yellow Hat) influence in Mongols that in 1576 they invited Sonam-gyatso, the third Dalai Lama to Qinghai, where the ruler Altan Khan conferred on him the title of "The Overseer of the Buddhist Faith, Vajra-dhara Dalai Lama", a title which was posthumously given to the first two Dalai Lamas and adopted by all his successors. The title at this stage, according to Yang Dongquan (2008), former director of China's national archives, "was only a personal honorific title, without any political and legal significance", the legitimacy, however, was granted to the third Dalai Lama once the Ming emperor, Wanli conferred on Dalai the title of "Vajradhara"(朵儿只唱 Dorjechang) in 1587 by way of issuing an imperial order and a letter of credence.

It was from hereafter that the Chinese emperors followed the tradition of conferring titles to Dalai Lamas, especially the Manchus (1644-1911). In 1653, Qing emperor Shunzhi conferred the fifth Dalai Lama, Ngawang Lobsang Gyatso (1617-1682), the title of "Most benevolent, living Buddha, universal ruler of the Buddhist faith, Vajradhiara, Dalai Lama of the

Western Paradise" (西天大善自在佛所领天下释教普通瓦赤喇怛喇达赖喇嘛). Besides, the emperor also gave the lama a golden letter of credence (金册) and a seal (金印) bearing inscription written in Manchurian, Tibetan and Chinese (Zhang 2014). The sixth and the seventh Dalai Lamas received titles from Kangxi. In the wake of Gurkha invasion of Tibet between 1791 and 1792, emperor Qianlong dispatched 170,000 strong force and drove out the invaders and established the often quoted "29-Article Ordinance for More Effective Governance of Tibet." The ordinance stipulated that the Ambans or the Qing imperial resident commissioner in Tibet will enjoy the same status as the Dalai and the Panchen; the reincarnation of the Dalai Lama, the Panchen and various Hotogtu Rinpoche must follow the procedure of drawing lots from the golden urn under the supervision of the Ambans and the same must be reported to the imperial court for approval; a new uniform currency bearing title of the emperor was issued; traders were required to carry a passport; all communication with neighboring states was to be conducted through Ambans. The rule of golden urn was followed for the selection of successive Dalai Lama's except the ninth, thirteenth and the fourteenth. In case of the 14th Dalai Lama, the then nationalist government under Jiang Jieshi (Chiang Kai-shek) issued an order which read (NPC 2009):

> The Qinghai soul boy Lhamo Toinzhub, with unusual wisdom and extraordinarily intelligent signs, has been found as the reincarnation of the 13th Dalai Lama and should be allowed to ascend his throne as the 14th Dalai Lama without going through the lot-drawing ceremony.

Though the present Dalai Lama agrees to the golden urn practice, but also states that a majority of the Dalai Lamas have not followed this tradition, and if it was followed, it was due to the priest-patron relationship between Tibet and the Manchu dynasty. Once the dynasty came to an end so ended the relationship. According to the Dalai's statement on reincarnation, by the time the reincarnation of the 14th Dalai Lama took place in 1939, "the Priest-Patron relationship between Tibet and China had already come to an end." As regards the nationalist government's assertion that they allowed the reincarnation without drawing lots, the Dalai says in his statement that it was a sheer lie that has been exposed by Ngabo Ngawang Jigme, the most trusted lieutenant of the Chinese in Tibet.

2.2 Legal instruments

As regards the 'legal instruments', the "Regulations on Religious Affairs and Measures on the Management of the Reincarnation of Living Buddha's" were issued by the State Administration for Religious Affairs of the People's Republic of China on 18 July 2007 and went into effect from 1 September 2007. These provide the legal basis for China rejecting any incarnation announced outside Tibet. In all, there are 14 articles in these 'Regulations' however, article 2 remains most crucial as it stipulates:

> Reincarnating living Buddha's should respect and protect the principles of the unification of the state, protecting the unity of the minorities, protecting religious concord and social harmony, and protecting the normal order of Tibetan Buddhism. Reincarnating living Buddha's should respect the religious rituals and historically established systems of Tibetan Buddhism, but may not re-establish feudal privileges which have already been abolished. Reincarnating living Buddha's shall not be interfered with or be under the dominion of any foreign organization or individual.

It could be discerned that the "legal instruments" reiterate Tibet as an inalienable part of China and that any attempts to split Tibet from China will not be tolerated. These also attach importance to historically established systems and debars any foreign individual or organization from the reincarnation of the Dalai or other lamas. It is for these reasons that China has all along criticized and spurned the Dalai Lama's Middle Way approach. In 2008, when mass protests broke out in Tibet over persecutions of the Tibetans, Qin Gang, the then spokesperson of Ministry of Foreign Affairs alleged in one of his press conferences that on the one hand the Dalai preaches the so called "middle way and "nonviolence", on the other hand, he is giving free hand to the radical organization such as "Tibetan Youth Congress" to engage in sabotage, rioting and bloodshed. The aim of both these methods adopted by the Dalai Lama is to seek Tibetan independence (*Renmin Ribao*, 18 March 2008). Reiterating Qin Gang's remarks, An Caidan (Qiu et.al 2008), a researcher from China's Tibetology Research Centre in Beijing said that the myth of Dalai's Middle Way approach is exposed in the following five points:

1. The Dalai clique maintains that "historically and culturally, Tibet is an independent country, not part of China."
2. The Dalai Lama insists that the Chinese army and military

installations should be withdrawn from Tibet, and that the status of Tibet be deliberated in an international forum and Tibet be declared as a "zone of peace" and a "buffer."

3. That Tibet be allowed to maintain diplomatic relations with other countries or international organizations.
4. The Dalai Lama insists on including 2.4 million square kilometers of Tibetan inhabited areas in Qinghai, Gansu, Sichuan and Yunnan provinces in the so called "Greater Tibet" enjoying "genuine/meaningful autonomy"; that is to say he wants to overthrow the socialist system and regional autonomy of all these areas and wrest control of "greater Tibet" solely in his own hands.
5. Finally, he maintains that all non-Chinese be thrown out from the so called "Greater Tibet."

Therefore, if a government allows one of its regions to establish diplomatic relations with other countries or international organizations and withdraws its armed forces from its own territory, could it be called a sovereign nation? In the words of Qiu et. al. (2008), the real motive of "genuine autonomy" could be best described as "three-step symphony" (三步曲) to secure Tibetan independence:

1. To secure his return to Tibet through negotiations, for the Dalai clique has failed to achieve any success irrespective of engaging in independence activities for decades from outside China. In order to "directly and more effectively" command the pro-independence activities, it is important to return home first.
2. Second step is to gain political power through "genuine autonomy."
3. And finally realise "Tibetan independence" through a "referendum."

No wonder, China has rejected the Dalai Lama's proposals or the demand for 'genuine autonomy' and described it as a ploy to seek independence, semi independence or even independence in disguised form, for according to China the charter of the Tibetan in exile promulgated in 1991 maintains that efforts shall be made to transform a future Tibet into a Federal Democratic Self-Governing Republic and a zone of peace throughout her three regions, and the Dalai Lama as the head of such a future entity. Furthermore, the Tibetan government in exile, in China's view, has continued to expand in its size and scale and hence the scope of its activities. For example, in September 2006, the "government in exile" set up seven ministries such as the "Ministry of the Interior", "Ministry of Foreign Affairs and Public Information," "Ministry of Religion and Culture", "Ministry of Education", "Ministry of Finance", "Ministry of Health" and "Ministry of Security" etc., and the Dalai clique has continued to sing the so-called "Tibet's national anthem" and hoist the so called "Tibetan national flag", a clear sign of defiance and seeking independence (Qiu et. al 2008).

It is owing to above thinking of China that the so called "visiting groups" (参观团) dispatched by the Dalai Lama to China post reforms and opening up have been treated as an opportunity provided to the Dalai Lama so as to "correct mistakes" (改正错误) and mend fences with China. Between 1979 and 1993, three such groups visited Tibet, and between 2002 and 2010, ten more visits took place. White Paper (2015) argues that "instead of accepting the goodwill and precious opportunities provided by the central government, the 14th Dalai Lama insisted on "Tibet's independence", intensified separatist and sabotage activities (分裂破坏活动), and lost the opportunity to reconcile with the central government." It also maintains that the "Tibet Government in Exile" is an illegal entity and there cannot be any dialogue with it on the status and system in Tibet. If at all, the contacts with the Dalai Lama's representatives is "about personal future (个人前途) of the Dalai Lama, and at most the future of some people around him."

3. Strategizing for the Future

In the new era under Xi Jinping, the three core demands, i.e. the Dalai Lama "accepting Tibet an inseparable part of China, abandoning 'Tibet independence', and stopping activities to split the motherland" have been reiterated and the Dalai Lama has been advised to "discard any illusion, face reality squarely, correct mistakes, and choose an objective and rational path." Rather, the White Paper (2021), talks about tremendous achievements Tibet has made since its "peaceful liberation." The 1951 Tibet's GDP of RMB129 million has been compared to that of RMB190 billion of the year 2020. In the new era, Tibet declared to have eradicated poverty.

Notwithstanding the development and prosperity in Tibet, China remains wary of the sensitivities surrounding the Tibet issue and influence of the Dalai Lama in the Tibetans as well as the international community.

China has admitted that its passive and knee jerk reaction to the discourses emanating from the Tibetan émigrés and the West has put it on the back foot. Scholars like Wang Jiaquan (2022) quoted in a report released by the International Tibetan Network (2022) have argued that there is need for course correction as the "post Dalai Lama era" would be an era of strategic opportunity for China.

Wang's short essay translated into English and made available on the Network argues that since China's criticism of the Dalai Clique has not been accepted by the West, but once the "idol vanishes" the clique would be greatly splintered and the resort of the Tibetan independence forces to violence, the "Middle Way" approach of the Dalai Lama could be questioned and even abandoned. With the burgeoning international economic and political clout of China, China's passivity on Tibet is bound to change, but the weight Tibet issue carries internationally may not diminish. He suggests a national strategy that moves away from demonizing the Dalai Lama, stop pronouncing Tibetan culture as backward, and recommends building of a strong discourse inside and outside Tibet through the 11th Panchen, even molding of the 15th incarnation's image. Given China's battered image in the backdrop of the stringent dynamic zero COVID strategy and its sliding economic growth trajectory, unfolding discourses on the reincarnation of the Dalai Lama from China, Tibetan émigrés and the democratic world will continue to generate interest in academic as well as geopolitical circles.

References

Dalai Lama. "Reincarnation". His Holiness, the 14th Dalai Lama of Tibet. 24 September 2011. https://www.dalailama.com/the-dalai-lama/biography-and-daily-life/reincarnation (accessed on 3 January 2023).

Geng Shuang. "Foreign Ministry Spokesperson Geng Shuang's Regular Press Conference on March 19, 2019." https://www.fmprc.gov.cn/mfa_eng/xwfw_665399/s2510_665401/2511_665403/t1646704.shtml

International Campaign for Tibet. "Dalai Lama succession interference raised at religious freedom hearing." 14 December 2022. https://savetibet.org/dalai-lama-succession-interference-raised-at-religious-freedom-hearing/ (accessed on 2 January 2023).

International Tibet Network. "Tibet, the Dalai Lama and the geopolitics of reincarnation" https://tibetnetwork.org/free1/wp-content/plugins/pdf-poster/pdfjs/web/viewer.html?file=https://tibetnetwork.org/free1/wp-content/uploads/2022/10/ITN_Reincarnation-Report_Mid_OnlineReading.pdf&download=true&print=vera&openfile=false (accessed on 3 January 2023)

Ned Price. "Department Press Briefing". 9 March 2021, https://www.state.gov/briefings/department-press-briefing-march-9-2021/ (accessed on 2 January 2023).

NPC. "Origin of the title of 'Dalai Lama' and its related backgrounder." 18 March 2009. http://www.npc.gov.cn/zgrdw/englishnpc/Special_NPC_Delegation/2009-03/18/content_1493972_3.htm (accessed, 8 December 2022)

Qiu, Lihua and Tang, Zhaoming.《达赖集团 "中间道路" 的真正用意就是要 "西藏独立"》 "The real motive of Dalai Clique's "Middle Path" is to seek "Tibet's independence." *Renmin Ribao* (29 March 2008).

Renmin Ribao《外交部发言人秦刚举行例行记者会》 "Foreign Ministry Spokesperson Qin Gang's Press Conference," 18 March 2008.

Reuters. "Dalai Lama contemplates Chinese gambit after his death." *The Reuters*, 18 March 2019, https://jp.reuters.com/article/us-china-tibet-dalai-lama-exclusive-idUSKCN1QZ1NS (accessed on 12 December 2022).

Wang Jiaquan. "Escaping a predicament: thoughts on the opportunities and considerations for communicating on Tibet in the "post-Dalai era" https://tibetnetwork.org/free1/wp-content/uploads/2022/08/Escaping-a-predicament_-thoughts-on-the-opportunities-and-considerations-for-communicating-on-Tibet-in-the-post-Dalai-era.pdf (accessed on 3 January 2023)

White Paper.《西藏发展道路的历史选择》白皮书 (全文) (Full Text of the White Paper on (Historical Choice of Tibet's Development Path) The State Council Information Office of PRC, 15 April 2015. http://www.scio.gov.cn/ztk/dtzt/2015/32720/32741/Document/1415491/1415491.htm (December 7 2022).

White Paper. 《西藏和平解放与繁荣发展》 (Peaceful liberation of Tibet and prosperous development). May 21 2021. http://www.tibetol.cn/html/zhuanlan/3/ (accessed on 3 January 2023)

Yang Dongquan. 2008. 《档案证明历世达赖喇嘛都是经中央政府认定、册封》 (Archives prove that successive generations of the Dalai Lamas have been confirmed and conferred the titles by the central government) www.gov.cn 2008 年 04 月 26 日 http://www.gov.cn/jrzg/2008-04/26/content_955279.htm (accessed 8 December 2022)

Zhang, Yun. 2014.《清朝西藏治理中的若干问题》 (Issues related to the Governance of Tibet during the Qing Dynasty). *Shixue Jikan*, 5 December 2014. http://www.tibet.cn/zxyj/xjdt/201412/t20141205_2141099.htm (accessed 7 December 2022).

43

Frayed India-China Relations

On 22 February 2023, India and China held the 26th meeting of the Working Mechanism for Consultation & Coordination on India-China Border Affairs (WMCC) in Beijing, the first in-person meeting since the 14th meeting in 2019. Eleven such meetings have been held since the Galwan bloody clashes, but all on online. The official statement released by the two sides varied in contents. The Ministry of External Affairs noted that "the two sides reviewed the situation along the LAC in the Western Sector of the India-China border areas and discussed proposals for disengagement in the remaining areas...." The four point Chinese statement emphasized on "both sides agreed to actively implement the important consensus (重要共识) reached by the leaders of the two countries to further stabilize the border situation… consolidate the results of the negotiations (巩固谈判成果)... move forward on the basis of the consensus previously reached, accelerate the resolution of issues related to the Western Sector of the Sino-Indian border and reach a mutually acceptable solution at an early date...discussed other measures to ease the situation and to return the border to normalised control phase (常态化管控阶段)… maintain close communication through diplomatic and military channels and hold the 18th round of military commander-level talks as soon as possible."

It is obvious from both the statements that the border in the Western Sector is far from the "normalised control phase". Does it include disengagement in the remaining areas such as Depsang and Chardingnala or just the disengagement of the troops who remained deployed in a prolonged standoff since 2020? Whatever may be the interpretation, the in-person meeting is a welcome step, especially in the present global and bilateral context. When the entire world is fixated at ending the war in Ukraine, Modi-Xi solution, as argued by Raja Mohan could offer a silver lining. More importantly, later this year, India would be hosting the G20 and Shanghai Cooperation Organisation (SCO) summits. As a leading global economy, and as one of the founders of the SCO, can Xi Jinping afford to miss the summits? Will India be comfortable in hosting him, if the prolonged standoff is not resolved? According to Liu Zongyi, China's support for concluding the successful summits in Delhi is crucial. The very thinking that one is indispensable for the success of the summit is problematic. According to Xunzi (BC 316-235) "the law of nature has its own way, it doesn't exist because Yao is a benevolent ruler or perish because Jie is a tyrant." The fact of the matter is can India and China reset their relations?

One may argue that the kind of equilibrium and understanding between India and China that was built on the premise that both were at the same level of development during the cold war, and hence need to give full play to their complementarities and potentialities has visibly been lost; the Galwan standoff was the last nail in the coffin. Qian Feng, a researcher at the National Institute for Strategic Studies, Tsinghua University is quick to remind that "China's comprehensive national strength has far surpassed that of India for at least 15 years." This may be the case, nonetheless, there is a need to seek a new equilibrium and understanding, and both need to rebalance their relations, the faster the better is for both the sides and the regional peace. To rebalance the frayed ties, both India and China need to look at the factors that stabilised the relationship. There are many however, the following could be regarded as the most important.

One, the stable security environment that guaranteed peace and tranquillity along the India-China border is in tatters. Currently, the security issues, especially the border standoff has taken precedence over other issues, and has impacted negatively on the bilateral ties. This could be gauged from the fact that as of now 16 corps commander level meetings and 26 WMCC meetings have taken place between India and China to ameliorate the security environment. According to a story filed by *The Hindu* based on a research paper tabled at the annual Director Generals of Police Conference organised by the Intelligence Bureau, India may have lost access to 26 out of the 65 patrolling points that mark the Line of Actual Control (LAC) in Ladakh.

The fact demonstrates that the status quo ante India is seeking is impossible. Will India and China move beyond the border and reset their ties before the G20 summit later this year? Will both the sides withdraw their forces from the frontline? Will China agree to the status quo ante and India the new status quo on the ground? At this point in time, it appears that both sides are not ready; Lan Jianxue, Director and Associate Research Fellow, Institute of Asia-Pacific Studies, China Institute of International Studies argues that "in the foreseeable future, the relationship between the two countries will continue to be disrupted by negative factors such as the border dispute, Tibet issue, and provocations by third countries." These issues will continue to persist in all possible scenarios, but it is not impossible to find a middle ground.

Two, trade was a stabilizing force between the two countries during the equilibrium phase. However, today it is ironical that when the bilateral trade has broken all records of the previous years, each other's markets have been perceived as risky and unfriendly. According to Qian Feng, India's has echoed calls for decoupling from China and wishes to surpass China by following a three-stage strategy. In the first stage, replace "Made in China" by "Make in India", in the second stage replace the "Chinese capital" with "Indian capital", and finally replace "US-West + China" industrial cooperation model with that of "US-West + India" model. While speaking on $100 billion plus trade deficit with China, External Affair Minister, S. Jaishankar said it was a "big concern" and posited that the India Inc. must share responsibility for the same. The trade volume of $135 billion demonstrates that there are massive complementarities between the two countries and both must create an amicable trade and investment environment that is sustainable and mutually beneficial so as a long-term partnership is established.

Three, the high-level visits and people-to-people ties that once stood witness to the brisk exchanges between India and China are at their lowest ebb presently. The first ever India-China High Level Mechanism on Cultural and People-to-People Exchanges inaugurated on 21 December 2018 is dead and needs to be revived. After all, it was through the circulatory movement of ideas, people, and technologies that India's cultural capital was disseminated to China and rest of the world.

Unfortunately, in the backdrop of the frayed relations, an important bilateral project – Translation of 25 Chinese classic, modern and contemporary works into Hindi, an undertaking of the Ministry of External Affairs has been put in the backburner. The two sides need come out of the self-isolation shadow of the pandemic and give full play to people-to-people exchanges.

Finally, there is already too much negativity about India and China in their respective media, the high-level visits will certainly add some positivity to the tattered ties and set these back on the track. In this connection, the visit of Qin Gang, China's Foreign Minister to India is an important one, and perhaps lay the ground for Jaishankar's China visit and ultimately Xi Jinping's India visit later this year.

44

Xi's Absence from G 20 and India-China Relations

Barely 5 days before the G20 summit in Delhi, China's foreign ministry spokesperson, Mao Ning announced during a regular press briefing on 4 September that "Premier of the State Council Li Qiang will attend the 18th G20 Summit to be held in New Delhi, India on September 9 and 10." There were apprehensions about Xi Jinping's attendance from the very beginning, but Xi Jinping skipping the key meeting of BRICS Business Forum, China issuing a controversial "standard map" on 28 August that irked India, Japan, even Russia and many southeast Asian countries, and diametrically opposite versions of Modi-Xi brief meeting at the side-lines of BRICS Summit in Johannesburg demonstrated that Xi's chances of attending the G20 were slim. Early in May, when Xi hosted the first China-Central Asia Summit a few weeks before the SCO Summit hosted by India, it also signalled that China desired to set up a separate kitchen, the summit was held online. What are the reasons and what does his absence tell about the state of India-China relations?

Internally, as the Chinese economy shows deflationary trends owing to the diminishing returns on investment, shrinking consumption and export figures – the three pillars of China's growth trajectory, requires that Xi Jinping stays home to salvage the economy. Two, the purge of the top commanders' of the PLA's Rocket force (PLARF) and mysterious death of PLARF deputy commander, Wu Guohua reveals a high degree of trust deficit between the top leadership of the party and the PLA top echelon. It is speculated that Wei Fenghe, former commander of the PLARF and the defence minister are also on the radar. Three, Xi's absence also indicates that China prefers small groups that allow China to have more say, such as the BRICS and SCO, which are considered reflecting "true multilateralism" as opposed to most of the groupings dominated by the West. Finally, the widening chasm with the US and its allies would certainly make Xi Jinping uncomfortable and isolated during the summit, but his absence also polarises the world along the ideological lines.

More importantly, it is the state of India-China bilateral relations and the way China perceives that India has been setting its own agenda at the G20 has also forced Xi Jinping to stay back. I wish to draw readers' attention to two recent articles – one written by Lan Jianxue, Director of the Asia-Pacific Institute of the China Institute of International Studies in the in-house *International Studies* (3), 2023, and another by Xu Qin, researcher at the Chinese Institute of Contemporary International Relations (CICIR) that reveal the Chinese thinking on India and the approaches China has adopted recently.

In the words of Qin, "From India's perspective, in the context of intensifying global divisions, taking over the G20 presidency and successfully hosting the summit will provide it with a rare opportunity to shape the global agenda, *demonstrate international leadership* and its *ambitions as a great power*. However, India's behaviour of "bringing in its own goods" (夹带私货 literally carrying contrabands) in terms of selecting locations of the meetings and agenda setting has also exposed India's "petty-mindedness" (小心思) under a "big layout" (大布局) and added more discordant factors (不和谐因素) to the G20 such as differences and competition." Shedding light on "carrying contrabands", Xu says that "India violated international practice (违背国际惯例) by holding relevant meetings in disputed territories, thus forcibly inserting (强行塞入) territorial disputes into the G20 agenda. "In March this year, the Indian Ministry of Science and Technology hosted a G20 meeting in the so-called "Arunachal Pradesh" (Southern Tibet)... In May, India held a G20 tourism working group meeting in Srinagar, the capital of Indian-controlled Kashmir…India wants to *gain international attention* by holding the G20 meeting in the disputed area, and in disguise, it can raise international support for the *"legitimacy" of its territorial claims*." Xu argues that beside creating a diplomatic and public opinion furore, India got its priorities wrong (喧宾夺主), undermined the cooperative atmosphere of the

G20 meeting, and hindered the meeting from achieving substantive results."

Lan's article strikes a chord with Xu, and is more elaborate in expounding the Chinese thinking on the state of India-China relations. He argues, "In order to highlight India as a 'leading force' (领导性力量) in reshaping the international order, the Modi government holds high the banner of 'rules-based, transparent, and reform-oriented multilateralism', but its enthusiasm for small multilateral mechanisms in which China plays an important role has obviously waned." Lan posits that India has been trumpeting the position of the US and the West on platforms such as the SCO, BRICS, East Asia, and G20 summits, and trying to prevent "multilateral mechanisms from becoming a booster for the rise of China as a great power." Worse, India in the words of Lan, has been conniving with the West in projecting itself as an "ideal choice" (理想选择) for "dislodging China from its position in the global supply chain." Since Galwan, the scholar says, India has further adjusted its strategy and policies towards China, "resorting to retaliatory and confrontational decoupling" across the spectrum, be it politics, economy, military, diplomacy, etc., exacerbating the dangerous trend of "diminishing cooperation effects" (合作效应递减), intensifying the game of competition (竞争博弈加剧) and continuing the drift and deformation (持续漂移变形) of Sino-Indian relations.

In the field of trade and investment, notwithstanding the burgeoning trade figures that stood at US$84.49 during the first eight months of the 2023, the grievances are numerous. Lan argues that India has resorted to "digital suppression" (数字打压) of China by blocking hundreds of Chinese apps, deliberately delayed the approval process for mobile phone parts of Chinese brands such as Xiaomi and OPPO, and confiscating huge assets of Chinese companies such as Xiaomi. India has restricted Chinese investment and purchase of Chinese equipment such as solar cell equipment, the import of Chinese-made power generation, transmission and distribution equipment. The scholar also cites that India has used the so-called "rules of origin" (原产地规则) to obstruct Chinese goods and services. Furthermore, India has deliberately blocked people-to-people and cultural exchanges between the two countries and waged a "public opinion war" (舆论战) against China; suppression of Chinese media and investigation of the Confucius Institutes in India have been cited as some examples. India has also been accused of manipulating (操弄) China's core issues such as Tibet and Taiwan, has been sowing discord with China's neighbours such as Nepal, Bhutan, and Sri Lanka etc., countries, and has tried to discredit China's "Belt and Road Initiative." Xu on the other hand maintains that in the garb of debt restructuring, India used the issue to attack China, and frequently cooperated with the United States and the West in hyping the "debt trap" theory. The establishment of the India – Middle East – Europe Economic Corridor (IMEC) by the governments of the Kingdom of Saudi Arabia, the European Union, the Republic of India, the United Arab Emirates (UAE), the French Republic, the Federal Republic of Germany, the Italian Republic, and the United States of America during the sidelines of the G20 summit reinforces the fear of China.

The above-mentioned actions of India according to Lan are intended to force China to make concessions on the border issue and restore the status quo ante as defined by India, but will inevitably have an "unassessable backlash (难以评估的反噬效应) on India's own interests and the long-term development of China-India relations." Worsening China-US relations has also been factored in the deterioration of India-China relations. Lan posits that the "full-scale suppression and containment" of China by the US, has been taken as "a period of strategic opportunity" (战略机遇期) by India. India and the United States are coordinating to promote the "de-sinicization" (去中国化) at the economic and technological level. In the future too, the United States will continue to "suppress and contain China" in an all-round way, and India will further "cater to the relevant actions" of the United States (迎合美国相关动作), maintains the scholar.

Multilateral cooperation was once the cornerstone of Sino-Indian relations, however, in recent years, India has deliberately highlighted its differences with China on regional and global governance and sustainable development, intending to push China out of the "global South" camp, argues Lan. This thinking is also echoed by Xu. Citing the online conference of "Voices of the Global South" convened by India in January 2023 to discuss issues of concern to developing countries such as climate change, debt, food and energy security, Modi telling the countries that "Your voice is India's voice, and your priorities are India's priorities," reflected "India's determination to use its G20 presidency to serve as a spokesperson for the Global South." No wonder, China fears that concepts like *vasudhaiva kutumbakam*, one of the core values of the Indian civilization will further dilute the influence of China's own foreign policy pillar – "Building a community of shared future for the mankind" and "people centric approach" in the global south. After "thoughtful consideration" (颇见心思), India chose not to invite China, Brazil and other major developing countries to participate in the conference, which reflects India's intention to dominate the conference agenda according to Xu.

Finally, Lan asserts that in the coming times, "China will go through a process of "rediscovering India" (重新发现印度). He suggests that it is necessary to abandon the stereotype approaches towards India, and make corresponding adjustments to India's strategic thinking and policies for a longer period of time. He suggests Kissinger's "co-evolution" (共同演进) model for cooperation between India and China, so as the "Thucydides trap" is avoided, albeit, the scholar says that India-China relations are on a different footing comparing US-China ties. He recommends that both the countries need to maintain strategic communication, and prevent miscalculations and misfires. If this is the thinking of Chinese policy formulators on India, India "must be ready to withstand high winds, choppy waters and even dangerous storms" to use Xi Jinping's phraseology.

45

China and the India-Middle East-Europe Economic Corridor

The announcement of the ambitious India-Middle East-Europe Economic Corridor (IMEC) on the sidelines of the G20 Summit in Delhi was the biggest takeaway from the congregation, no wonder Chinese president chose to stay away from the summit. The IMEC was jointly announced by the leaders of the US, India, Saudi Arabia, the United Arab Emirates, France, Germany, Italy and the European Union on 9 September. According to the MoU posted by the White House on its website, "the IMEC will be comprised of two separate corridors, the east corridor connecting India to the Arabian Gulf and the northern corridor connecting the Arabian Gulf to Europe. It will include a railway that, upon completion, will provide a reliable and cost-effective cross-border ship-to-rail transit network to supplement existing maritime and road transport routes – enabling goods and services to transit to, from, and between India, the UAE, Saudi Arabia, Jordan, Israel, and Europe."

The IMEC aims to achieve a "transformative integration of Asia, Europe and the Middle East" through a network of laying cable for electricity and digital connectivity, as well as pipelines for clean hydrogen export, thus "secure regional supply chains, increase trade accessibility, improve trade facilitation, and support an increased emphasis on environmental social, and government impacts." Prime Minister Narendra Modi hailed the corridor as the one that "promises to be a beacon of cooperation, innovation, and shared progress charting a journey of shared aspirations and dreams." European Commission President Von der Leyen, described it as "much more than just a railway or a cable", she said "It is a green and digital bridge across continents and civilisations." Israeli Prime Minister Benjamin Netanyahu described it as the "largest cooperation project in our history" that will "change the face of the Middle East, Israel, and will affect the entire world". In the words of Raja Mohan, "India has finally found a formula to connect to both Arabia and Europa" as the IMEC "breaks Pakistan's veto over India's overland connectivity to the West."

China, though supported the establishment of the IMEC, but also said that the same should not be used as a "geopolitical tool." Nevertheless, the Chinese media has pronounced it as the one that will "counter" China's "Belt and Road Initiative." The issue of funding has been highlighted by most of the writings. An article in the Guancha.cn says that the White House memo is silent on listing "funding sources" (资金来源) for the project. Orientaldaily.com on the other hand says that "in addition to countering China's "Belt and Road" Initiative, it is also an attempt by the United States to reach a broader diplomatic agreement in the Middle East, including getting Saudi Arabia to recognize Israel and reaching a Middle East reconciliation." Another article in 163.com calls the IMEC as an "unfettered imagination" (畅想) that is designed to "compete" with China's BRI. The article further says, "Judging from the map [of IMEC], this has indeed blocked China's advancement from Central Asia to the south. But the problem is that Saudi Arabia and the United Arab Emirates are already BRICS countries, and they are still working hard to become members of the Shanghai Cooperation Organization. Then there is Iran and Egypt... without Iran's participation, the prosperity and problems of the Middle East would be a "mirage" (海市蜃楼) in the desert."

Another issue is that the signatories to the IMEC do not have an "industrial manufacturing" block, which according to the article seems problematic as it is related to a country's land and labor policy, human capital, government system and efficiency. Currently, in the entire world only China can meet the existing production and processing capacity worth six trillion US dollars. For the emerging economies, the large-scale transfer of production capacity led by the United States is not only bad for them, on the contrary, it will also destroy their industrial systems in one move. No wonder, the 163.com article calls the IMEC as a "fragmentary" (残缺) "illusion" (幻想). Furthermore, China believes that the project is "politically exclusive" (政治排他性). Wang Jin, associate professor at the Institute of Middle East Studies at Northwestern University aired such views in an interview to the Huanqiu Shibao. "The countries participating in the project are all having good relations with the United States, including some European countries and the US "allies" in the Middle East. The ideological and geopolitical factors are too obvious to be ignored." Wang Xiaoyu, an associate researcher at the Middle East Studies Center of Fudan University, identifies "three roadblocks" (三道坎) for the project – achieving consensus, funding, and the China-Arab community with a shared future for the new era.

Undoubtedly, China's economic engagement with Africa and Arab world far exceeds any other major country. In 2022, China's trade with Africa reached US$ 282 billion. China has heavily invested in Africa's energy resources, infrastructure development, telecommunications and mining sectors. Today, over a million Chinese have settled in Africa, a US$ 4.5 billion Djibouti-Addis Ababa and Mombasa-Nairobi railway is one of the milestone projects China has executed. Even more ambitious Electrified Standard Gauge Railway between Mombasa and Nairobi that would cost US$ 13.8 billion is on the table. As regards the Arab-China engagement, a mechanism of "1+2+3" has been proposed by Xi Jinping since 2014, where '1' refers to cooperation in energy as the core, '2' for 'two wings' – infrastructure and trade and investment, and '3' stands for using three advanced technologies – nuclear energy, space satellites and new energy as breakthrough levers in an effort to raise the level of pragmatic Sino-Arab cooperation. China sees its cooperation with the Arab and Africa as an example of South-South cooperation over the past decade, China-Arab trade has grown by US$ 100 billion, with the total volume exceeding US$ 300 billion.

It could be discerned that China's BRI footprints in Asia, Europe, Africa and Latin America have forced the United States and its allies to counter the BRI with their own projects. Some of the initiatives such as the Asia-Africa Growth Corridor (AFGC) (2017), Indo-Pacific Infrastructure Forum (2018), Build Back Better World (B3W) (2021), EU's Global Gateway strategy (2022) etc., have been launched to counter China's influence. These have been projected as part of a 'liberal and value-based order' that intends to bring in "transparency" and "high quality" to the projects. However, some of these such as AFGC have remained nonstarter for the want of investment. As regards the B3W, the US argues that "it will collectively catalyse hundreds of billions of dollars of infrastructure investment for low and middle-income countries in the coming years." EU's Global Gateway strategy looks more promising, wanting to mobilise up to 300 billion euros of investment over the period 2021-2027. Though China could as well be a beneficiary of the IMEC, however, it remains to be seen how fast the corridor would be able to overcome the "three roadblocks" identified by the Chinese scholar.

VI
THE ‘BELT AND ROAD’ INITIATIVE

46

China's Kazakh Challenge

In an explosion of popular discontent, triggered by the hike of price in liquefied petroleum gas (LPG) against the government in a number of cities in Kazakhstan starting from 3 January 2021, President Kassym-Jomart Tokayev, a career diplomat handpicked by former president Nursultan Nazarbayev was forced to declare a nationwide state of emergency on 5th, invoke security provisions of the Collective Security Treaty Organisation (CSTO) and invite Russian forces on 7th for his political survival as the mobs went berserk and damaged many government buildings. With the presence of Russian troops, the order was restored by 7 January, but after the loss of 164 lives and several thousand injured and imprisoned. In a CSTO virtual summit on 10 January, Tokayev claimed that it was a coup d'état from within by the "terrorists and thugs" backed by hostile foreign forces. China as a major economic player in Kazakhstan, watched the development nervously and sent a "verbal message" on 7th that supported security crackdown and denounced intervention by foreign forces for provoking unrest and instigating "colour revolutions" in Kazakhstan. Why is China concerned about developments in Kazakhstan?

At the outset, it demonstrates an uneasiness in the relationship of convenience between China and Russia. Russia is very much aware of economic inroads China has made in the Central Asian Republics (CARs). In the last 30 years, China has replaced Russia as one of the most important economic players in the region. According to China's Diplomacy in the New Era website, China's trade at the beginning of the establishment of diplomatic relations with the CARs, was only US$ 460 million, which in

2020 reached US$ 38.6 billion, and is expected to exceed US$ 40 billion in 2021. It could be gleaned that the increase is 100 times compared with the beginning of the establishment of diplomatic relations. As of now, China is the largest trading partner of Uzbekistan, Kyrgyzstan and Turkmenistan, the second largest trading partner of Kazakhstan and the third largest trading partner of Tajikistan. China has maintained a trade surplus with the CARs; in 2019, it was US$ 5.78 billion according Liu Huaqin in a paper entitled "Current Situation and Prospects of Economic and Trade Cooperation between China and Central Asian Countries." The drivers behind this growth have been energy exports and other natural resources from the region including those from Russia.

Second, Russia is competing with Kazakhstan and Turkmenistan for a share in China's huge energy market. China has built A, B and C lines of the Central Asian natural gas pipeline, the Sino-Kazakhstan crude oil pipeline, the Sino-Russian crude oil pipeline, and the Sino-Myanmar oil and gas pipeline for its energy security. According to a report in the *Global Times*, by March 2020, China-Central Asia natural gas pipeline delivered 304.6 billion cubic meters of natural gas to China. Kazakhstan and Turkmenistan have been at the centre of this diversification strategy. The first investment China National Petroleum Corporation (CNPC) made in Kazakhstan was in 1997 when it purchased a 60.34 per cent stake in AktobeMunaiGas. The CNPC AktobeMunaiGas (CNPC AMG) now owns five oilfields, two gas fields and one oil exploration block in Kazakhstan. Since then, CNPC has signed six more deals. Since all the A, B, and C pipelines runs through Kazakhstan, the disruption may affect China's energy supplies. Therefore, the line D of the China-Central Asia Gas Pipeline, which is still under construction, will not pass through Kazakhstan and will enter China via Wuqia County in Xinjiang. Since Russia fears China taking undue advantage of its economic leverages in Kazakhstan and other CARs, therefore, by way of the Eurasian Economic Union that envisages to establish a unified market like the European Union, will give it a say in controlling and setting prices of the oil and gas trade between China and the CARs.

Third, China's Belt and Road Initiative projects in Kazakhstan could also be perceived by Russia as security risks. Russia continues to use Soviet era Baikonur space station in Kazakhstan; one of Russia's missile test sites, Kapustin Yar is partially located in Kazakhstan; besides Russia is also engaged in oil exploration and uranium mining in Kazakhstan.

China too has been engaged in uranium mining in Kazakhstan; in summer of 2021, China's CGNPC acquired for US$ 435 million a 49 per cent stake in a Kazatomprom. This is important as China wishes to quadruple its current nuclear power generation by 2035 in the face of its zero-carbon emission declared for 2060. China's strategic depth in Kazakhstan could be gauged by the kind of investment it has undertaken in Kazakhstan by way of its Belt and Road Initiative. Quoting Chinese Embassy in Kazakhstan, *South China Morning Post* reported amidst protests in Kazakhstan that between 2005-20, China invested US$ 19.2 billion in the country and 56 China-backed projects worth nearly US$ 24.5 billion are due to finish by the year 2023. Therefore, Russia's willingness to use military force to defend its position in its backyard is understandable not only from the perspective of "colour revolution" where both China and Russia has unanimity of thought, but also from China's inroads in the region.

Finally, the most feared thing by China is perhaps the "colour revolution" and mass protests in countries adjoining Xinjiang, especially Kazakhstan where 224,713 Uighurs are believed to reside, largest outside Xinjiang. An equally large number of Kazakhs numbering 326,000 reside inside Xinjiang. As of now Kazakhstan's position on Xinjiang has been somewhat ambiguous, however, there have been anti-China protests by Uighurs and Kazakhs inside Kazakhstan intermittently as were witnessed in September 2021. Therefore, China is sensitive to disturbances in CARs like Kazakhstan, Kirghizstan and Tajikistan bordering Xinjiang. It is apprehensive of the domino effect these will have in tandem with the so-called forces of "three evils" i.e. terrorism, separatism, and religious extremism. From the history of general public outbursts in the CARs, it becomes clear that the binary of rural urban divide, usurpation of power and wealth by the authoritarian rulers and their families, exploitation of national resources by outsiders, and the problematic leadership transition has been the root cause of such protests. Some of these reasons were responsible for the very collapse of the Soviet Union, which undoubtedly have been looked into by the leadership in China. Added to these, the pandemic fatigue, rocketing inflation and unemployment figures have exacerbated the situation. Though, the demonstrations have been put down, however, as long as inherent structural issues are not addressed, similar outbursts cannot be ruled out in future.

47

A Decade of Belt and Road Initiative

During the opening ceremony of the third Belt and Road Forum on 18 October 2023, President Xi Jinping remarked that "the original intention" (初心) of the "Belt and Road" Initiative (BRI) was to "take lessons from the ancient Silk Road" and over the past 10 years, he said "we have adhered to our original aspirations and worked hand in hand to promote the "Belt and Road" international cooperation from scratch, which has since vigorously developed and achieved fruitful results." The BRI cooperation has entered the "meticulous details" (工笔画) stage from the "general freehand brushwork" (大写意), and has expanded from "hard connectivity (硬联通) to soft connectivity (软联通)." "What we have practiced is interconnectivity, mutual benefit and reciprocity, and what we have pursued is common development and win-win cooperation. We do not engage in ideological confrontation, geopolitical games, or group political confrontations. We oppose unilateral sanctions, economic coercion, and decoupling and disruption of supply chains."

The BRI along with many other initiatives pronounced as the global public goods is major flagship of China for international cooperation, primarily connecting the global south. Establishment of a Silk Road Fund with US$ 54.40 billion, Development Bank of China, Export-Import Bank of China, Asia Infrastructure Investment Bank (AIIB) and the BRICS New Development Bank (NDB) where China has major stakes have been pronounced as financial institutions supporting the initiative. Xi Jinping revealed that during the Entrepreneurs Conference held on the sidelines of this summit forum, projects worth US$ 97.2 billion were signed. The

China Development Bank and the Export-Import Bank of China have pledged to set up a financing window of 350 billion yuan, and add 80 billion yuan of new funds to the Silk Road Fund to support the projects."

A stock of the BRI in the last ten years tells us that the initiative has moved from five major goals – promoting policy coordination, facilitating connectivity, uninterrupted trade, financial integration and people-to-people exchanges – to a high quality and green development what Xi Jinping prefers to call soft connectivity mostly in the field of green and digital economy. According to the BRI portal, in 2022, the "friend circle" of the BRI countries has extended to 150 countries and 32 international organisations. China's total export and import with the BRI countries reached US$ 1.82 trillion, registering 20 per cent growth over 2021. In the same year, contracted value of projects reached US$ 98.19 billion. According to a report published by Christoph Nedopil Wang of Shanghai-based Green Finance and Development Centre (GFDC), since 2013, China's cumulative BRI engagement amounts to US$ 932 billion, about US$ 561 billion in construction contracts, and US$ 371 billion in non-financial investments. Oil and gas investments constituted about 80 per cent of Chinese overseas energy investments and 66 per cent of Chinese construction contracts. During the third forum, Xi Jinping revealed that in the next five years (2024-2028), China's import and export volume of trade in goods and services is expected to exceed US$ 32 trillion and US$ 5 trillion respectively.

Ten major projects completed or under completion have been listed as – development of Greece's main port, Piraeus; US$ 300 million investment in Serbia's state-owned Zelezara Smederevo steel plant; The China-Belarus Industrial Park; water supply project in Senegal; US$ 6 billion Lao–China Hi-speed Railway; construction of central business district (CBD) of Egypt's new administrative capital; China Europe Railway Express that operated 15,162 trains in the first 11 months of the 2022 passing through 24 countries and 204 cities; construction of $1.4 billion Colombo Port City; The Orange Line Metro Train (OLMT) built under the framework of the China-Pakistan Economic Corridor (CPEC) in Lahore; and $4.7 billion Santa Cruz Hydroelectric Project in Argentina. Other major projects that have been completed are construction of the Jakarta-Bandung High-speed Railway, the Gwadar Port and Djibouti-Addis Ababa and Mombasa-Nairobi railways.

Undoubtedly, these massive projects have contributed to the local development and provided employment opportunities to thousands of people. However, these have also raised various concerns, some genuine and some geared towards demonising China. For example, in Piraeus, China holds 67 per cent of the shares and could determine the fate of the port. Heavy investment and borrowings has made it difficult for smaller countries to service their debt. Laos' public debt has reached 88 per cent of its gross domestic product. The case of Colombo Port City is no different, China has been given 43 per cent of stakes and a 99-year lease. In Argentina, the environmentalist fear that China-funded dam could disrupt key Argentine glaciers and biodiversity.

Conversely, Chinese scholars have refuted the "debt trap" theory of the West. Quoting the RAND Corp research report on the BRI, Liang Haiming, Director of Hainan University BRI Research Institute argued during the third BRI Forum in Beijing that the "BRI railway projects have led to a 2.8 per cent increase in exports for participating countries." He further posited that "studies have shown that BRI transportation infrastructure projects, have reduced logistics time by 1.2 per cent to 2.5 per cent in surveyed countries, lowered global trade costs by 1.1 per cent to 2.2 per cent, and contributed to a global income increase of 0.7 per cent to 2.9 per cent. These findings provide solid proof of the positive economic effects of Chinese investments in BRI projects. Citing figures calculated by the Indonesians, he said, "the first High-Speed Railway in Indonesia is expected to generate over $23 billion in revenue over the next 40 years." Therefore, that BRI has brought opportunities and mutual growth to participating economies, not the debt traps, argues Liang. Nevertheless, there has always been a trade-off between the development and ecological protection, and since China is willing to undertake such development projects, developing countries seems to find them as "game changers" for their development.

Notwithstanding the challenges and concerns, China has demonstrated the will and purpose to invest and complete these projects across the continents. China's BRI footprints in Asia, Europe, Africa and Latin America has forced the United States and its allies to counter the BRI with their own projects. Some of the initiatives such as the Asia-Africa Growth Corridor (AFGC) (2017), Indo-Pacific Infrastructure Forum (2018), Build Back Better World (B3W) (2021), EU's Global Gateway strategy (2022) and the recent India Middle East Economic Corridor (IMEC) have been launched to counter China's influence. These have been projected as part of a 'liberal and value-based order' that intends to bring in "transparency" and "high quality" to the projects. However, some of these such as AFGC have remained nonstarter for the want of investment. As regards the B3W, the US argues that "it will collectively catalyse hundreds of billions of dollars of infrastructure investment for low- and middle-income countries in the coming years." EU's Global Gateway strategy looks more promising, wanting to mobilise up to EUR 300 billion of investment over the period 2021-2027. Given China's massive investments in the BRI projects, the commitment from developed world appears too little too late.

Moreover, China's economic integration with Asia, Africa, Central Asia, Europe and America far exceeds that of the US and its allies, China is better placed to strategize its investment, especially in developing countries, for Chinese enterprises according to prof. Chen Shouzhen of Xiamen University "not only occupy a dominant position in labour-intensive industries such as food, textile, leather, footwear, wood, and paper, but also occupy an important position in capital-intensive industries such as electronics, electrical, chemical, metal, machinery, and transportation." This is what China calls having developed massive production capacities which no other country can match at this point in time. The new BRI projects have become "small and beautiful" (小而美) which are integrated to new technologies such as e-commerce, big data, cloud computing and artificial intelligence to enhance efficiency and efficacy. Meanwhile, we will see China accelerating the construction of free trade pilot zones, cross-border and economic cooperation zones etc. along the Belt and Road countries for promoting regional economic integration. Xi Jinping has rolled out an eight-point action plan for strengthening the BRI cooperation. These are – promoting a three-dimensional interconnectivity network, an open world economy, practical cooperation, green development, scientific and technological innovation, people-to-people exchanges, a path of integrity, and perfecting the BRI international cooperation mechanism.

Finally, notwithstanding China turning to the "small and beautiful" approach, the BRI is here to stay. For the simple reasons that the BRI is one of the flanks of China's "New Type of International Relations" paradigm, and the latter one of the two pillars of China's foreign policy.

The other pillar is "to build a community with a shared future for humanity." New ideas such as Global Development Initiative (GDI), Global Security Initiative (GDI), Global Civilisation Initiative etc., have been added to this larger framework. Above all, these all converges to only one idea – The Chinese Dream of national rejuvenation.

48

Destruction and Construction in China: A 'Millennium Plan' for Xiong'an New Area

During the Second World War, when the US planned the bombardment of Japan, it sought the help of a Chinese architect from Tsinghua University, as to which were the areas that should be protected and spared destruction. The architect was none other than Liang Sicheng 'the father of modern Chinese architecture' and the son of one of the tallest intellectuals of the 20th century China, Liang Qichao. Junior Liang not only set aside Kyoto, Nara and Osaka but also marked precisely the location of the ancient architectural wonders in these cities and requested the US to spare these. Liang Sicheng succeeded in protecting these cities but could not protect Beijing from destruction in the wake of communist victory in 1949.

After the founding of the People's Republic of China, Liang Sicheng was appointed as Deputy Director of the Beijing Metropolitan Planning Commission. Liang proposed that the ancient city be kept intact in totality and that the administrative centre may be constructed on the western suburbs of Beijing. He proposed that Beijing must be a political and cultural center opposed to the industrial center. However, his proposal was rebuffed by the then Beijing mayor, Peng Zhen, for Peng described them as the 'symbols of feudalism' which must be toppled. He told Liang that it was Chairman Mao's desire to see chimneys all around from the Tiananmen rostrum.

Thus, started the colossal destruction of old Beijing: in 1953 Left Anmen was flattened, in 1954 Qingshou twin pagodas were pulled down, in 1956 Zhonghuamen was destroyed, in 1957 Yongdingmen, Guangqumen, Chaoyangmen etc. towers were leveled. The fury of destruction continued in mid and late 1960s that witnessed the destruction of Dongzhimen, Xuanwumen, Chongwenmen, Andingmen, Fuchengmen, Xizhimen etc., places which were reduced to mere names of many metro stations along line 2 in Beijing. Imagine the grandeur of Beijing had these structures been spared by the leaders of New China who wanted to convert Beijing into another Kremlin for mass gatherings!

If these were the ambitions of the first-generation communist leaders in China, the ambitions of the fifth-generation leadership are equally grandiose but diametrically different. Xi Jinping, perhaps has seen the logic in Liang Sicheng's vision. On 1 April 2017, the Central Committee of the Communist Party of China and the State Council decided to establish Xiong'an New Area in Hebei province. It wasn't an April fool, but a serious and even more ambitious developmental plan that would exceed the scale of Shenzhen Special Economic Zone and the Shanghai Pudong New Area, according to the State Council. The *Xinhua News Agency* termed it as 'Millennium plan and a mega event of national significance.' It was reported that Xi Jinping chose the area after visiting Anxin in February 2017.

If Deng Xiaoping envisioned the development of Shenzhen and Pudong, and if Hu Jintao and Wen Jiabao designed the development of Beijing-Tianjin plan, Xi Jinping after envisioning the Yangtze River Delta and Guangdong-Hong Kong-Macao Greater Bay Area, his plan for Xiong'an is as grandiose as his 'China Dream' of 'great rejuvenation of the Chinese nation.' Shenzhen Special Economic Zone was built in 196 square kilometer land, Pudong in 1210 square kilometers, and Xiong'an is being built in 2000 square kilometer land. It will span the counties of Xiongxian, Rongcheng and Anxin, which are at the center of the triangular area formed by Beijing, Tianjin and Hebei's provincial capital Shijiazhuang. According to the initial reports, some 87 industries from Beijing, most of the educational institutions, hospitals, schools and administrative divisions would be relocated to Xiong'an.

Essentially, Xiong'an would serve as the sub-capital of China. The decision marks China's efforts to solve problems facing mega cities, like education, health, traffic, pollution, and heavy smog. Besides, South-North water diversion that affects over 400 million people would also incur huge financial burden, and since the diversion is against the law of nature, it may have huge implications in future. Xiong'an on the contrary would be a green and ecological project that will see the economic integration of Beijing-Tianjin and Hebei. There is another viewpoint that since successful reforms have bred various interest groups in Beijing, in order to break their monopoly, it would be desirable to build a new capital. Still others argue that since the model of establishing municipalities directly under the central control has not worked out well, the establishment of sub capital will provide a new direction to the reforms.

Ever since the announcement of the Xiong'an New Area, massive structures have been built in a vast land mass. Beijing Daxing International Airport, known as the 'Starfish' is the world's largest single-building airport terminal built in an area of 700,000 square meter. It was opened to operations in 2019. Xiong'an Railway Station, described as the largest train station in Asia has been built in an area of 130,000 square meter and was completed in 2020. An intercity railway line linking Beijing Daxing International Airport and Xiong'an Railway Station commenced operation in September 2019. Meanwhile, the main road building and paving work for the Jing-xiong Expressway linking Xiong'an to the outside world and the region's Rongyi highway network are proceeding on schedule. It would be a green and intelligent city having next-generation infrastructure such as city-wide intelligent sensing systems, next-generation telecommunication networks, urban cloud and big data platforms, urban computing capacity, and city brains etc.

When the plan was announced, real estate magnates flocked the area, catapulting the existing per square meter rates manifolds. The officials from Xiong and Anxin counties were forced to put property ban in the area. However, in the aftermath of the COVID-19 and real estate bubble bust in China, people are hesitant to relocate to Xiong'an. There are fears that it may result in the building of another mega ghost city or a 'rotten tail project' as has been the case with many real estate projects across China. Though the SOEs, colleges and hospitals administered by central government in Beijing have been ordered to relocate to Xiong'an since

2021, but very few have actually moved or at the most have just registered their offices. On 10 May 2023, Xi Jinping inspected the progress of what he called the "future city". He was accompanied by Premier Li Qiang, Cai Qi, director of the General Office of the CPC Central Committee, and Vice Premier Ding Xuexiang, indicating that the party-state is serious in completing the project.

49

China and the Arab World

The announcement of the ambitious India-Middle East-Europe Economic Corridor (IMEC) on the sidelines of the G20 Summit in Delhi created a lot of excitement and anxieties in and around the subcontinent. An article in 163.com calls the IMEC as an "unfettered imagination" (畅想) that is designed to "compete" with China's BRI. Jin Canrong, professor at the School of International Relations, Renmin University posits that "if they can really accomplish this, it will not be inconsistent with the purpose of the "Belt and Road" initiative. However, it is difficult to say whether it can be achieved. How the United States, some European countries and India will implement it, how to ensure funds, and whether they have sufficient infrastructure capacity to execute it are all problems." Wang Xiaoyu, an associate researcher at the Middle East Studies Center of Fudan University, identifies "three roadblocks" (三道坎) for the project – achieving consensus, funding, and the China-Arab community of a shared future for the new era. Implying that China-Arab relations are on a solid footng and the establishment of the IMEC will not have much impact on it.

Indeed, as the American economic engagement diminishes in the region, the Arab world has emerged as a new a strategic pillar of multilateral engagement for China. China sees its cooperation with the Arabs as an example of South-South cooperation and also a part of building communities of shared future. In 2014 during his keynote address at the opening ceremony of the Sixth Ministerial Conference of the China-Arab States Cooperation Forum in Beijing, Xi Jinping proposed the establishment of a "1+2+3" cooperation mechanism, where '1' refers to cooperation in energy as the core, '2' to "two wings" – infrastructure and the trade and investment, and '3' refers to using three advanced technologies – nuclear energy, space satellites and new energy as breakthrough levers. In December 2022, Xi Jinping visited Saudi Arabia to participate in the first ever China-Arab States Summit and the first China-GCC Summit. In his keynote address during the China-Arab States Summit on 9 December, Xi Jinping remarked that "as strategic partners, China and Arab states should carry forward the spirit of China-Arab friendship, strengthen solidarity and cooperation, and foster a closer China-Arab community with a shared future."

Xi Jinping disclosed that the "two sides have established 17 cooperation mechanisms under the framework of the China-Arab States Cooperation Forum. Since he took office, bilateral trade registered a jump of US$ 100 billion, reaching a total of US$ 300 billion; China's direct investment in Arab states was up by 2.6 times, reaching US$ 23 billion; over 200 Belt and Road projects were carried out, benefiting nearly two billion people of the two sides." China aims to expand its trade with Arab states to 430 billion dollars by 2027. China has been engaging the Arabs bilaterally as well as multilaterally through mechanisms such as the Arab League, the GCC, and the Organisation of Islamic Cooperation. Some of the dialogue mechanisms China has established include the China-Arab States Political Parties Dialogue, the China-Arab States Energy Cooperation Conference, the China-Arab Cities Forum, the China-Arab Solidarity Conference the China-Arab Beidou Cooperation Forum, the China-Arab States Women's Forum, the China-Arab Health Cooperation, the China-Arab Agricultural Cooperation Forum, the China-Arab University Chancellors Forum, China-Arab Expo, the China Middle East Security Forum, and the list goes on to include film, television, technology transfer, water resources etc., areas.

These mechanisms are guided by the China-Arab States Summit with purpose of promoting comprehensive China-Arab cooperation covering areas of political, trade, defence, energy and cultural cooperation. Some of the issues where there is unanimity are strategic autonomy of the Arab states, opposition to linking terrorism with certain religion and politicisation of human rights issues and weaponisation of sanctions, and the currency swaps. There are consultations on issues such as Palestine,

Syria, Yemen, Libya, Somalia, Lebanon, and the Ukraine crisis etc. Chinese brokered peace deal between Saudi Arabia and Iran is seen as the one that has "changed the geopolitical structure and situation, and is expected to provide opportunities for cooling down and resolving other burning issues in the Middle East" according to analysts like Zou Zhibo, Deputy Director of the Institute of World Economics and Politics, Chinese Academy of Social Sciences. Zou also touts Saudi-Iranian reconciliation model as a "new model of great power mediation" for solving other complex issues around the world. The community of a shared future for mankind and the Global Security Initiative advocated by Xi Jinping according to the scholar have aided such an outcome.

The Arab League has emerged as China's largest supplier of crude oil and the largest trade partner. China is in collaboration with the Arabs in building new infrastructure in the spheres of new energy, cyberspace, big data, AI and E-commerce. The establishment of technology transfer and joint training centres in the Arab states for the peaceful use of nuclear energy, and introducing China's BeiDou Navigation Satellite System to the Arab states are important elements of such collaboration. Besides, China-Arab cultural ties are also on an upward trajectory. By the end of 2022, there were 20 Confucius Institutes in Arab countries. Both sides have built a China-Arab Digital Library Website and are engaged in mutual translation of classic, modern and contemporary works. China has pledged that it will invite 100 young scientists from the Arab world to China for scientific research exchanges, 3,000 teenagers for China-Arab cultural exchanges, and 10,000 Arab talents for professional training in poverty alleviation, health and green development.

Furthermore, the BRI is aimed at building capacities and robust trade and security ties. According to the "eight major initiatives" proposed by Xi Jinping during the China-Arab States Summit, China will provide the Arab states assistance projects worth 5 billion yuan (about $719 million) in development cooperation, and include 30 projects from the Arab world in the Global Development Initiative project pool. Both sides are also strengthening cooperation in the area of global governance; the building of a China-Arab community with shared future that talks about promoting security through common development and dialogue has been pitched against the major power rivalry. No wonder, in the expansion of the BRICS in South Africa, four (Saudi Arabia, Iran, United Arab Emirates and Egypt) of the six countries are from the Arab world. As could be seen, the BRI in the Arab world encompasses everything under heaven. The Arabs according to Ebrahim Hashem, are already in the post-West and post-US era, "demonstrating strategic autonomy" by adhering to the "policy of multi-alignment", participating in initiative such as the BRICS, IMEC and BRI at the same time.

VI
CHINA AND THE INDO-PACIFIC

50

China Reacts to the Indo-Pacific Economic Framework

In order to assert the US's role in providing both security and public goods in the Indo-Pacific region, the US launched Indo-Pacific Economic Framework (IPEF), a new trade deal in Tokyo on 23 May 2022 with 12 Indo-Pacific nations, namely Australia, Brunei, India, Indonesia, Japan, South Korea, Malaysia, New Zealand, the Philippines, Singapore, Thailand, and Vietnam. President Biden was joined by the Japanese Prime Minister Kishida Fumio and the Indian Prime Minister Narendra Modi in-person, while other countries joined by video call. The region representing 60 per cent of world population and 40 per cent of global GDP is considered as a fulcrum of future geopolitics and geo-economics. Though not many details of the framework has been revealed, however, a White House Statement issued on 23 May has listed four pillars as connected, resilient, clean and fair economy, largely on the lines of what President Biden had stated during the 16th East Asia Summit, last year. The launch could be considered a response to China led Regional Comprehensive Economic Partnership (RCEP) and possibly a replacement to the Comprehensive and Progressive Trans-Pacific Partnership (CPTPP).

Obviously, the elephant in the room, is a resurgent and assertive China that has trounced the US as a major trade partner of most of the countries in the region since 2013. With enhanced defence capabilities and technological advancement, China has announced the arrival of a new hegemon in Asia that is not shy of challenging the US in the region and beyond. The launch of the IPEF in Tokyo, a day before the scheduled summit of the Quad nations, has invited the wrath of China's diplomatic establishment as well as its strategic community, for China believes that the security and economic alliances the US are building in the region are aimed at diminishing China's influence.

China's State Councillor and Foreign Minister Wang Yi, in a press briefing with the Pakistani Foreign Minister, Bilawal Bhutto stated on 22 May that the "US 'Indo-Pacific Strategy' is doomed to fail." According to Wang, the so-called "strategy" not only wants to erase (抹去) the name of "Asia-Pacific" and the effective regional cooperation structure (有效的区域合作架构), but also the peaceful development and momentum (平发展成果和势头) created by the joint efforts of countries in the region for decades. He further said that the "Indo-Pacific Strategy" concocted (炮制出来的) by the US under the banner of "freedom and openness" is to gang up and create small circles (拉帮结伙搞 '小圈子') to encircle/contain China (围堵中国) and desiring the Asia-Pacific countries to be the "pawns" (马前卒) of US hegemony. Wang concluded by saying that the so-called "Indo-Pacific strategy" is essentially a strategy for creating divisions (制造分裂), confrontation (煽动对抗), and destroying peace (破坏和平). He blamed the US for creating economic decoupling, technological blockade, supply chain disruption, and geopolitical confrontation. Wang Wenbin, spokesperson of the Ministry of Foreign Affairs, resonated Wang Yi's remarks in a press briefing on 25 May and added that the "framework" is an attempt to establish the US led trade rules, restructure the industrial supply chain system, and "decouple" regional countries from the Chinese economy. *China Daily,* the official English daily pronounced the IPEF as a "cynical manipulative tool" which it said was "more political than economic, more unilateral than multilateral, and more exclusive than inclusive."

The response of the academic and strategic community is no different from the official crriticism. Liu Zongyi, of the Center for China and South Asia Studies at the Shanghai Institute for International Studies, argues that the main reason for the IPEF is that the "Indo-Pacific" strategy falls short of a strong economic pillar. Since the US remains out of the CPTPP headed by Japan, and the Regional Comprehensive Economic Partnership (RCEP) led by China aimed at building "a truly open, inclusive, equitable and high-quality Trans-Pacific Free Trade Area, the US has come out with its own trade deal, or has "set up a separate kitchen" (另起炉灶) if we use

Wang Yi's analogy. Striking a similar tone with Wang Yi, Liu says that the United States not only do not wants to provide Asian countries with more market access, but it also wants to undermine Asia's booming economic integration process. Liu argues that although the world has witnessed the emergence of three economic pillars – China, the US and Germany-France, however the Asian economic plate is centered around China, which is relatively more "Asian" and less "Pacific", therefore, the US is apprehensive of being "pushed out" ("排挤") of Asia. Liu posits that as China makes rapid progress in technological innovation, and creates an industrial and supply chain that is independent of the US, the US is wanting to re-establish its core position in the global supply chains, and to turn other countries in the Asia-Pacific region into its "economic colonies" (经济殖民地). According to him, there are not many countries in the region willing to board the US train, except for the "second-class citizens" (二等公民) in the international system and global industrial chain ruled by the United States such as Japan, South Korea, Singapore, Australia, New Zealand and some other countries.

Zhao Minghao, a researcher at the Institute of International Studies at Fudan University, opines that the IPEF is essentially a tool to compete with China. He sees two "inherent deficiencies" in the framework. One, the US will not open its market to other member states; and two, the IPEF has been advanced through executive orders signed by the Biden administration, without congressional approval. In case there is a change of government, the framework faces the risk of getting derailed, as was witnessed in the case of the TPP. Whether the IPEF will have any impact on China-ASEAN partnership, Zhao believes, it will not have much impact, as China is the largest trade partner of the ASEAN with a trade volume of US$ 878.2 billion in the year 2021, registering a year-on-year increase of 28.1 per cent. Xu Liping, a researcher at the Institute of Asia-Pacific and Global Strategy of the Chinese Academy of Social Sciences, echoes Liu's viewpoint that the containment of China is likely to backfire in the end. However, he cautions that China cannot take the IPEF lightly, for the very motive remains to "establish a key supply chain system independent of China"; especially the one centered on semiconductors, will create more "strangleholds" (卡脖子) for China.

As regards India, Liu in another article entitled "India smells another "godsend opportunity" (天赐良机) to contain China" argues that India's participation in the IPEF is to counter the "Belt and Road" initiative of China. He posits that the "debt trap" narrative is rather part of India's information war (信息战) against China. India hopes that Asia's industrial and supply chains are relocated to India, thereby enabling it to replace China's position in the global supply chains. Nevertheless, maintains that India's entry in the IPEF at its present stage of economic development will effectively delay the shaping of the IPEF. There are others like Hu Wenli of the China Youth Daily, who believe that India is not willing to blatantly provoke confrontation in the "Indo-Pacific region", and there is also a question mark about how much actual benefits the IPEF can bring to India.

51

Three Decades of India's Eastward Engagement: China's Perceptions and Responses

This issue brief looks into China's perceptions and responses to India's Act East Policy. It argues that China sees India's Act East Policy in three phases – the first two correspond to a period when both managed to establish an equilibrium and understanding, and when India desired to strike a balance between the US and China. The third phase corresponds to the ascendance of Prime Minister Modi to the Indian political scene – the time when the equilibrium was lost owing to the power shift favoring China, and China's malevolent relations with India following frequent standoffs resulting in the Doklam and Galwan conflicts. India realigning its Act East Policy and sub-regional and multilateral mechanisms like BIMSTEC, SAGAR, IORA, and Quad, etc., have been pronounced as part and parcel of India's Act East Policy serving the unstated goals of India's Indo-Pacific strategy. Since China views the Indo-Pacific strategy essentially as containment of China by the US and its allies, India's broader geopolitical ambitions have to an extent been held in check by its rivalry with China and Pakistan, according to the Chinese scholarship. It is for this reason, they believe that India's strategic vision is governed by its thinking on South Asia and the Indian Ocean. Nonetheless, they are apprehensive that the Indo-Pacific strategy does give it levers to intervene in the South China Sea, diminish ASEAN centrality, and oppose China's connectivity projects.

China sees India's Look/Act East Policy (AEP), sometimes also pronounced as "March Eastward Policy" (东进政策) in three stages – strategic layout (1991-2002), strategic expansion (2002-2013), and strategic partnership with the US, Japan and Australia (2013-till date). Reasons for India's eastward engagement during the first phase are cited as – India's economic crisis, pressure of globalisation and China's gradual economic integration with Southeast Asia.[1] Some of the accomplishments have been enumerated as: India becoming a sectoral partner of the ASEAN in 1992 and full dialogue partner in 1995; India joining the ASEAN Regional Forum in 1996; formation of Bay of Bengal Initiative for Multi-Sectoral Technical and Economic Cooperation (BIMSTEC) in 1998; India initiating the "Mekong-Ganges River Cooperation Project" with five ASEAN countries (Vietnam, Laos, Cambodia, Myanmar and Thailand); and India's joint naval exercises with Indonesia, Malaysia and Singapore near the Andaman Islands; and MILAN, the annual naval exercises of the Bay of Bengal navies in 1995.

During the second phase, security cooperation, especially naval exercises with countries such as Vietnam, Indonesia and Singapore along with increased arms exports to these countries have been cited.[2] Dialogue mechanisms like ASEAN+1 in 2002 and ASEAN+4 in 2004, India participating in the East Asia Summit as a founding member, and the India-ASEAN FTA of 2009 have been listed as some other achievements, enabling India to secure a place in the ASEAN-led Asia-Pacific multilateral framework.

It is the third phase that China finds problematic and has reacted sharply to. The formation of a "strategic arch" in the Indo-Pacific with Japan, the US and Australia as "three poles" since 2014 on the one hand, and mechanisms such as "Security and Growth for All in the Region" (SAGAR), the BIMSTEC, and the Indian Ocean Rim Alliance (IORA) on the other, have been pronounced as serving the objectives of the Indo-Pacific strategy of the US. According to Wang,[3] India has been "setting the agenda" of these groupings aimed at shaping its leadership and expanding its influence in the Indian Ocean region, thus attempting to create a "unified Indian Ocean identity" and "Indian Ocean Region Community."

Strategic Goals and Limitations

China believes that the intent behind India's engagement in the Indo-Pacific is owing to a number of factors. The foremost goal, is to make India a "great power", for "seeking great power status" (寻求大国地位) and extending influence beyond the Indian Ocean has been the priority of the Indian leadership right from Nehru to Modi.[4] Therefore, India's "March Eastward Strategy" that aims at forging close economic and defense partnership with the ASEAN, US and its allies has been seen in this context. Unique geo-economic conditions "will inject vitality into the rapid development of the Indian economy", India's close economic ties with the East and South Asia will be conducive to build the "Indo-Pacific Economic Corridor" (印太经济走廊) as envisaged by the Quad countries.[5] The same has materialized in the form of the Indo-Pacific Economic Forum and has invited lot of criticism from the Chinese leadership and scholars alike.[6] India realigning its Act East Policy and sub-regional and multilateral mechanisms like BIMSTEC, SAGAR, IORA, and Quad, etc., are said to be serving the unstated goals of India's Indo-Pacific strategy. Therefore, Ning views India "dwarfing" (矮化) the AEP and making it subservient to the Indo-Pacific strategy,[7] which according to Chinese scholars will make it difficult for India to achieve substantial progress in its relations with ASEAN. India's engagement with ASEAN has also been seen through the prism of a "multipolar regional order" (多极化地区秩序) aimed at reshaping the international order by India. It is India's advocacy for multipolarity where China sees an opportunity to engage India in mechanisms such as BRICS, SCO and AIIB, often bracketed within the "concept of "True multilateralism" (真正的多边主义) pitched against the "selective" (有选择的多边主义), "small circle" (小圈子*多边主义*) or "pseudo-multilateralism" (伪*多边主义*) of the US,[8] a reference to the Quad and AUKUS.

Nevertheless, China holds the view that "India is still relatively weak in terms of economic and political power" and argues that India's broader geopolitical ambitions have to an extent been held in check by its rivalry with Pakistan and China.[9] China is quick to refer to the massive China-ASEAN trade (US$ 878.2 billion in 2021) against India's US$ 78 billion with ASEAN. Chinese scholars argue that it is owing to "India's limited financial capacity" and "complex multinational construction procedures" that projects such as the India-Myanmar-Thailand Trilateral Highway, the Bangladesh, Bhutan, India and Nepal (BBIN) project, "Project Mausam"

SAGAR, BIMSTEC, Kaladan Multi-Modal Transit Transport Project, are progressing rather slowly. According to them, India and ASEAN "seriously lack endogenous motivation for economic and trade cooperation" notwithstanding the FTA both have signed. Internal and external drivers in terms of opening up, business environment, labor force have been compared. Rising tariffs, "self-reliance" and "Swadeshi" have been regarded as anti-free trade, and also cited as reasons for India not signing the ASEAN-led RCEP.[10]

China's India Dilemma and Responses

China is cognizant about "an emerging India becoming a "strong competitor of China" in the Indo-Pacific and apprehensive that India may become a drag in developing Sino-ASEAN relations in future. Therefore, it has been questioning as to "what interests India has to defend in the region." From this perspective, though the Chinese scholars accept the presence of Indic culture in Southeast Asia, they are, however, quick to posit that the region has been within the orbit of Sinosphere. It is for this reason that China perceives India as an Indian Ocean power rather than an Asia-Pacific power, and hence an "external power" (外部势力) in East Asia. China and Malaysia preferring to use "10+3" (ASEAN + China, Japan and the ROK) as a vehicle to shape the region into a desired economic community, and exclude the US and India in the region has similar undertones.[11]

There is a general belief in China that India's AEP has widened in scope; it is no longer limited to ASEAN but encompasses the entire East Asia to start with, and now the entire Indo-Pacific. Chinese scholars view that the widening security boundary of India's AEP "provides an opportunity for India to intervene in Asia-Pacific affairs; act as a "balancer" (平衡者); engage in "strategic balancing" (战略制衡) of China by way of India-Japan-US-Australia strategic arc, and weaken China's influence in the Asia-Pacific.[12] Therefore, China has denounced the Indo-Pacific strategy as a containment theory aimed at diminishing China's geopolitical and economic influence.

Even though China has all along harped that India is very low in the Chinese foreign policy calculus, however, India's policy of multi-alignment, especially in the Indo-Pacific, has belied that thinking. Chinese scholars have recognized the fact that the US no longer treats India from a "US' regional policy framework of South Asia" but from a "global perspective", dubbing it as a "natural strategic partner", the "net security provider in the Indian Ocean", the "bulwark of democracy", the "strategic offshore counterweight", etc., and has clearly supported India as a permanent member of the UN Security Council." It is perhaps owing to this cognition that the Chinese scholarship talks about "cognitive asymmetry" (认知不对称) between China and India, generally held responsible for not pushing India-China relations in a "positive direction".[13]

China holds the view that since India's AEP is in "cahoots with" US' "rebalancing to Asia" or the Indo-Pacific strategy, it has resulted in a situation where the US and India are unitedly balancing (联合制衡) or countering China. This along with its "small circles" like AUKUS, the Quad, Five Eyes Alliance and G7 are "attempting to reconstruct the network of alliances and partners of the United States in the Asia-Pacific region." However, they also believe that owing to the US policy of "saying one thing and doing another" (表里不一), it is unlikely that the ASEAN is pulled over to the US.[14] As regards India, Bao believes that India in recent years has been deviating from the principle of "ASEAN centrality" and accelerating its shift to the "Indo-Pacific Strategy" of the United States; however, he posits that ASEAN countries are looking for "real money" (真金白银) not "empty promises" (空头许诺). Sun Xihui in a commentary argues that the US committing US$ 150 million during the recent US-ASEAN Special Summit 2022 is "almost negligible."[15]

Furthermore, China believes that India's AEP "will allow India to intervene (插手) in the South China Sea issue, which will have an impact on some of China's core interests. This apprehension of China arises out of the fact that China has a very troubled relationship with ASEAN countries owing to the South China Sea issue. No wonder, the "ASEAN 'Indo-Pacific' Outlook" (2019) and "ASEAN-India Joint Statement on Cooperation on the ASEAN Outlook on the Indo-Pacific for Peace, Stability, and Prosperity in the Region" (2021) all have emphasized on the 1982 UN Convention on the Law of the Sea (UNCLOS) and open, inclusive and rules-based regional architecture. China is apprehensive that India, by strengthening political, economic and diplomatic relations with Asia-Pacific countries, will make it easy for India to "warm up" (抱团取暖) to other countries on the South China Sea issue and put its weight behind them. China believes that this will further add unfavorable factors to the settlement of the South China Sea issue. India's recent US$ 375 million anti-ship BrahMos missile deal with the Philippines[16] and India's close defense cooperation with Vietnam is likely to be cited by China as one of the examples. India's intervention in disputes by one way or another, is to enhance its so-called "presence" (存在) in the region "out of strategic consideration" and its "global power ambitions," posits Zhao.[17]

Conclusion

The writings of the Chinese scholarship reveal that their understanding of India's LEP/AEP and engagement in the Indo-Pacific has undergone a fundamental change. From an Indian perspective, this could be attributed to a power shift with the rise of China and widening asymmetries with India, its belligerence along Line of Actual Control and the Indo-Pacific. As a result, the kind of equilibrium and understanding that existed between India and China has been lost, and the ambiguity and the nature of India being a "swing state" between the US and China has been addressed.[18] At present, it is obvious from the assertions of the Chinese scholars that whether it is India's Act East policy, sub-regional mechanisms or Quad, one and all have been considered active tools of US' Indo-Pacific strategy aimed at containing China and diminishing its influence in the Indo-Pacific.

Nevertheless, China still holds the view that irrespective of "grand strategic goals" in the "Indo-Pacific" region, India's strategic vision is governed by its thinking on South Asia and the Indian Ocean, for the want of economic heft as well as its adversarial relations with both China and Pakistan. This, however, is not to say that India is not seeking to play a strategic role in the Indo-Pacific region, it certainly is, but India has not yet "publicly stated" its strategic goals in the Asia-Pacific region, according to the Chinese. Though the Chinese scholars acknowledge the fact that the Southeast Asian countries are positively inclined towards India's engagement in the Asia-Pacific region, most of them have not expressed their support for India's role as a "net security provider" in the Western Pacific. They also admit the fact that at present the "informal alliance" or the "strategic consensus" between US-India and its allies is purely due the China factor, and that if India desires China to "recognize its role in the Asia-Pacific region, then India must cede a certain role in the Indian Ocean region to China".[19] Will India become an Indo-Pacific power? It will depend upon India's economic, technological, military drivers along with soft power, diplomatic and leadership skills, argues Shi.[20]

NOTES

1. Zhao Hong, "India's changing relations with ASEAN: From China's perspective," *Journal of East Asian Affairs* 20, no. 2 (Fall/Winter 2006): 141-170.
2. Ning Shengnan, 《"印太"视角下印度与东盟关系研究》(India-ASEAN Relations from the "Indo-Pacific" Perspective), 《印度洋经济体研究》Indian Ocean Economies Study, 2021, https://www.ciis.org.cn/yjcg/xslw/202105/t20210510_7926.html.
3. Lina Wang, 《印度莫迪政府 "印太" 战略评估》(An assessment of Modi government's "Indo-Pacific" strategy). *Journal of Contemporary Asia Pacific Studies* 3 (2018): 90-114.
4. Zeng Kai, 《浅析印度"东向行动政策"新发展》(A brief analysis of the new development of India's "Look/Act East Policy") 《智富时代》(Wisdom and Wealth Times, 2017 (1) https://m.fx361.com/news/2017/0310/1101400.html; Shi Xuewei, 《印度 "印太" 战略: 逻辑、目标与趋向》(India's "Indo-Pacific" Strategy: Logic, Goals and Trends). *Pacific Journal* 27, no. 9 (2019): 23-34.
5. Shi Xuewei, 《印度 "印太" 战略: 逻辑、目标与趋向》(India's "Indo-Pacific" Strategy: Logic, Goals and Trends). *Pacific Journal* 27, no. 9 (2019): 23-34.
6. B. R. Deepak, "Indo-Pacific Economic Framework riles China," *Sunday Guardian*, 28 May 2022, https://www.sundayguardianlive.com/opinion/indo-pacific-economic-framework-riles-china.
7. Ning Shengnan, n.2.
8. Wang Yi, 《践行真正多边主义的四点主张》(Four propositions on practicing true multilateralism) MOFA, 7 July 2021, https://www.fmprc.gov.cn/wjbzhd/202105/t20210507_9137265.shtml.
9. Zhao Hong, n. 1; Shi Xuewei, n. 5.
10. Li Li, 《印度对印太外交的考虑及其局限》(India's Considerations and Limitations of Indo-Pacific Diplomacy), *China and International Relations*, 2021 (2): 50-62; Ning Shengnan, n. 2.
11. Li Li, 《印度东进战略与印太外交》(India's Act East Strategy and Indo-Pacific Diplomacy) *Contemporary International* Relations, 2018 (1): 37-45; Zhao Hong, n. 1; Zhao Gancheng, 《从"东向"到"东向行动"——印度莫迪政府的外交抱负及其限度》(From "Look East" to "Act East" Policy: Diplomatic Ambitions of the Modi Government and its Limits), *Contemporary World*, 2016 (1): 56-59.
12. Li Li, n. 11.
13. Ning Shengnan, n. 2; Zeng Kai, n. 4.
14. Bao Zhipeng, 《亚太不是大国博弈的"棋盘"》(Asia-Pacific is not a "chessboard" for the game of great powers), *Beijing Daily*, 22 April 2022, https://m.ciis.org.cn/sspl/202204/t20220422_8526.html.
15. Sun Xihui, "Biden wants to strengthen ties with ASEAN but US investment in region suggests otherwise," *Global Times*, 17 May 2022. https://www.globaltimes.cn/page/202205/1265828.shtml.

16. "Philippines to buy BrahMos missile system from India for $375 million," *Indian Express*, 28 January 2022, https://indianexpress.com/article/india/philippines-india-brahmos-missile-system-7745669/.
17. Zhao Gancheng, n. 11.
18. B.R. Deepak, "India and China: Perceptions of images and the lost equillibrium," *China and the World* 4, no. 2 (2021), https://doi.org/10.1142/S259172932150005X.
19. Li Li, n. 10.
20. Shi Xuewei, n. 5.

52

Abe's Assassination Excites Schadenfreude in "Little Pinks" of China

On 8 July 2022, the assassination of the Shinzo Abe, longest serving Japanese Prime Minister shocked the entire world. Condolences poured in from around the world, as the world mourned the tragic death of Abe. Even Russian President, Vladimir Putin, who has been increasingly treated as a social pariah in the wake of Russia's "special military operation" in Ukraine, and has been subjected to harsh sanctions by Japan, was quick to send his condolences to the mother and to the wife of the late Shinzo Abe. President Putin called him "an exceptional statesman" and a "wonderful man" who did a lot for good neighbourly relations between Russia and Japan. National flags around the world flew half mast, and many countries including India declared a day of national mourning. This was certainly owing to his personal bonding with global leaders, his statesmanship, Abenomics – that brought Japan out of deflation, and his vision for Japan, the region and beyond.

Surprisingly, President Xi Jinping and his wife Peng Liyuan, offered their condolences only on 9 July 2022, however, by now Abe's assassination had already ignited unprecedented schadenfreude in the hearts of the "Little Pinks" (小粉紅) and "Old Pinks" (老粉紅), mostly jingoistic nationalists in China. Chinese social media was flooded with messages cheering the assassination and pronouncing the assassin as a "hero." Some called it a "party time", some lamented that no "fireworks were allowed" and yet others opined that would have been better had the "serving prime minister" been shot together with the Korean. Soon the shops and restaurants started to flash photographs with red banners in the backgrounds rejoicing Abe's tragic demise and offering discount on the occasion. "Celebrate Abe's return to the West, milk tea buy one get one free, celebrations will continue for three days, rejoice with the world "read one of the banners. Another was even accompanied with its Japanese translation –Yesterday, it was the 7 July incident, today Abe bade good bye, in order to celebrate Abe's demise, buy one dozen of beers and get one dozen free." The most atrocious of all was a group of Chinese drinking around a round table with a banner in the background reading, "Warmly celebrate the glorious assassination of Japanese devil Shinzo Abe." Yet those who sympathized with Abe, invited the wrath of the "Little Pinks", amongst these were the hawkish *Global Times* former editor, Hu Xi Jin and Renmin University professor, Jin Canrong who happened to share Hu's thread. Conversely, Malaysian singer Fish Leong's (梁静茹) song "unfortunately it's not you" (可惜不是你) was taken off the internet when netizen started dropping messages underneath the song. Why has Abe's assassination excited schadenfreude in China?

Though the "Little and Old Pinks" in China have demonstrated similar traits during India's pandemic deaths last year, but in Japan's case the national hatred is more complex and deeper. At the outset, Japan has a certain role in China's "century of humiliation" besides the Western nations. Qing China was totally decimated by Japan in the First Sino-Japanese War (1894-95) that tilted the balance of power in Asia favoring Japan for the first time. China was forced to accept the independence of Korea, pay an indemnity of 200 million silver taels and cede the Liaodong Peninsula, Taiwan and Penghu Islands to Japan. Though the Senkaku or Diaoyu Islands were not mentioned by the treaty, but Ryukyu had long terminated its tributary relations with China in 1874, and in 1879 these were formally annexed and renamed as Okinawa Prefecture by Japan. China argues that the Cairo Declaration of December 1943 and the Potsdam Proclamation of July 1945 explicitly states that Japan should restore to China all the territories it had stolen or taken by violence and greed. Having had a foothold in Liaodong Peninsula, Japan later created the Manchuguo or the State of Manchuria in China's northeast in 1932, in which most of the deputy ministers were Japanese. Shinzo Abe's maternal grandfather, Nobusuke Kishi was one of them and served as the Deputy Minister of Industrial Development. After Japan's all out invasion of aggression of China on 7 July 1937, Kishi was instrumental in using slave labour in Manchukuo for propping up Japan's industrial production to fulfil the war goals. Kishi also served in the wartime cabinet of Prime Minister Hideki Tojo, and has been listed by China as a "Class-A war criminal." His paternal grandfather Kan Abe was also a member of the House of Representative, but opposed Tojo's militarism.

Nobusuke Kishi abhorred communism, visited Taiwan in official capacity in 1957 and later in 1969, and approved of Chiang Kai-shek recovering mainland. His government pronounced China as an aggressor and was against restoring China's permanent membership in the United Nations. Japan's Taiwan complex continues to haunt Sino-Japanese relations. An ardent supporter of Taiwan, Shinzo Abe has openly supported Taiwan against the Mainland threat. In December 2021, Abe hinted at a possible Japanese military role in Taiwan contingency. Abe had said during a virtual appearance at a Taiwan think tank that "A Taiwan emergency is a Japanese emergency, and therefore an emergency for the Japan-US alliance." "People in Beijing, President Xi Jinping in particular, should never have a misunderstanding in recognizing this." China had reacted sharply on these comments, and had recounted the war crimes of Abe family in China. The *Global Times* remarked in one of its commentaries that "One of the real problems within the family that concerns every Chinese is that they all have an above-mentioned filthy finger stretched into the Taiwan Straits, which, in a serious narrative, is an outrageous attempt to relive its militarist dream."

China has also been riled by the Indo-Pacific construct, materialisation of which is also credited to Shinzo Abe. Abe had first mentioned it during his Speech to the Indian parliamentarians in 2007, and since then, spin offs of the strategy such as the Quad, AUKUS, and Indo-Pacific Economic Framework (IPEF) have come into being. China sees them as "small circles" (小圈子), with an attempt to reconstruct the network of alliances and partners of the United States in the Asia-Pacific region for containing China. Obviously, China is concerned as more and more countries, now the European Union too, are increasingly using freedom of navigation and overflight along with a free, open and inclusive Indo-Pacific to defy China's coercive policies in the region. Abe could be regarded as the promoter and champion of the global economic order. When President Trump withdrew from the Trans-Pacific Partnership (TPP) in 2017, Abe convinced 10 other TPP member states to stay on the course and won their support for a Comprehensive and Progressive Agreement for Trans-Pacific Partnership (CPTPP), the new avatar of the TPP. In 2015, he announced US$ 110 billion in aid for "high-quality" infrastructure development in Asia over the next five years. Other measures like Asia-Africa Growth Corridor and IPEF etc., frameworks that emphasize transparency and high quality are believed to be pitched against China's Belt and Road Initiative (BRI). In a recently concluded G7 summit, the block also committed to raise US$ 600 billion in private and public funds over five years to finance infrastructure in developing countries and counter China's BRI.

Finally, in the face of China's rise and its burgeoning hard power, Abe wished to change the Japanese pacifist constitution, especially the Article 9 that not only forbids the use of force as a means to settle international disputes, but also bars Japan from maintaining an army. Since 2014, Japan has lifted the ban on collective self-defence, particularly in a bid to strengthen its cooperation with the US, and defend allies under attack irrespective of on the Japanese or overseas territories. The Taiwan contingency mentioned above could be interpreted in this context and pave way for Japan's entry into the South-China Sea and Taiwan Strait etc. conflicts. Abe's legacy, the way he steered diplomatic, economic and security interests of Japan and allies in the region and beyond, and built alliances to realise his vision, is sure to be furthered by the present Japanese administration. As rightly put forth by Prime Minister Narendra Modi, "His [Abe's] life may have been cut short tragically, but his legacy will endure forever."

53

The Fourth Taiwan Strait Crisis: Much Ado about Everything

One of the outcomes of the First Sino-Japanese War (1894-95) was that Taiwan and Penghu Islands were ceded to Japan by the Qing China; these were returned to the Republic of China (ROC) in October 1945 only after Japan's defeat in the World War II. However, the ROC was overthrown by the Communist Party of China in a four year long civil war (1946-1949) resulting in the establishment of the People's Republic of China (PRC) and retreat of the ROC to Taiwan, and hence the notion "Two Chinas" and both pledging to unify the other. Mao's PRC attempted to take Quemoy and Matsu islands controlled by the ROC in December 1954, what is also known as the "First Taiwan Strait Crisis," but in vain, resulting in pushing the US and the ROC signing a defence treaty. In October 1958, the PRC shelled the islands once again, creating the "Second Taiwan Strait Crisis", but was forced to retreat when the US sent forces in defence of Taiwan. The ROC continued to represent China in the United Nations until it was "expelled" and the seat restored to the PRC in 1972 in the backdrop of the US-China rapprochement aimed at containing the Soviet Union.

In 1979 when the US established formal diplomatic relations with the PRC, the US also signed the Taiwan Relations Act that mandates the US to supply defence articles for Taiwan's self-defence capability. The communiques the US signed with the PRC in 1972 and 1982 "acknowledges" the Chinese position that there is but "One China and Taiwan is part of China." This is also the origin of US's policy of ambiguity on Taiwan, nonetheless, US-China relations flourished in the field of economy, technology and defence, except briefly post 1989 Tiananmen crackdown when the US suspended military sales to China and imposed sanctions. Relations further deteriorated when pro-independence leader Lee Teng-hui won elections in Taiwan and the US granted him visa to visit his alma mater, the Cornell University. Between 1995-1996, the PRC conducted a series of military exercises and fired missiles in the Taiwan Strait and surrounding Taiwan, precipitating the "Third Taiwan Strait Crisis." The US in a display of force sent its aircraft careers forcing China to back down. By now, China's market was too big to be ignored, and the US normalised its trade relations with China in the year 2000, which set a stage for China's accession to the WTO.

These were the years, when China-Taiwan exchanges were also cemented, the "Three Nos" (no contact, no negotiation, no compromise) of the Chiang Kai-shek era paved way to "New Three Nos" (no independence, no unification and no use of force) aimed at maintaining the status quo while deepening economic and people-to-people ties with the PRC. No wonder, today over 2 million Taiwanese work and live in China. In Shanghai and its surrounding areas alone, more than 400,000 Taiwanese businessmen and their families stay. Conversely, nearly 339,000 Chinese spouses reside in Taiwan, accounting for close to 65 per cent of the 533,000 new immigrants from Mainland over the past decade. Taiwan's exports to mainland increased from $85 billion in 2011 to $125.9 in 2021, accounting for 42.3 per cent of total Taiwanese exports. Last year, Taiwanese approved FDI into the Mainland was $5.86 billion. However, in recent time, in the face of realignment of forces post-COVID and Russia's invasion of Ukraine, Taiwan is diversifying its trade and investment from Mainland to other regions, but decoupling won't be easy. Furthermore, the PRC having bridged its economic and technological gaps including military capabilities with the US, believes it has no compulsion to behave the way it did in the last two decades, forcing the US to pronounce China as a revisionist and coercive power.

Added to this, the autocracies verses democracies narrative orchestrated by the US has vindicated China's fears of its containment. The Indo-Pacific strategy, the Quad, AUKUS and Five Eyes Alliance have made China believe that the US and its allies have formed "small cliques" to encircle and diminish its rise and influence, and that Taiwan all along has been used as a card. China has also come to believe that the US has gradually shed its ambiguity on Taiwan, as was demonstrated by Joe Biden‘s remarks during a joint news conference with the Japanese Prime Minister Fumio Kishida in May 2022. It is in this background that the US Speaker of the House, Nancy Pelosi's Taiwan visit should be viewed, albeit there are other elements such as domestic compulsions and her own anti-China traits too.

Pelosi's visit sparked instant outrage from China once the Financial Times published the story on the 19 July. The spokesperson of the Taiwan Affairs Office of the State Council, Zhu Fenglian urged (敦促) some people in the US Congress to "stop condoning and supporting the "Taiwan independence" forces, and stop all acts of playing with the fire (停止任何玩火行径)". Zhu firmly opposed any form of official exchange (任何形式的官方往来) between the US and Taiwan, and above all Pelosi's "sneaky visit" (窜访) to Taiwan. This set the tone for China's fierce opposition and psychological escalation. Wang Wenbin, the spokesperson of Ministry of Foreign Affairs (MOFA) cautioning that "we will do what we say" (我们说到做到); Tan Kefei, a spokesperson of China's Ministry of National Defence warning that the "Chinese military will by no means sit idly by" (中国军队绝不会坐视不管); and Zhao Lijian, the spokesperson of MOFA reiterating the warning that "if the US insists on going its own way (一意孤行), and "challenges China's bottom line" (挑战中方底线), it will be resolutely countered." These warnings culminated into Xi Jinping bluntly telling President Joe Biden in a phone call on 28 July that "those who play with fire, will perish with it (玩火必自焚). In order to deter Pelosi's visit, China announced live ammunition training missions (实弹射击训练任务) near the Pingtan islands off Fujian on 29th July.

On 31 July, Pelosi confirmed that she was "leading a Congressional delegation to the Indo-Pacific to reaffirm America's unshakeable commitment to our allies & friends in the region." Taiwan certainly was one of the "friends" though she didn't mention it in her itinerary for obvious reasons. As anticipated, she did land on 2 August, stayed overnight and met President Tsai on 3 July before her onward journey to South Korea. China fumed with anger and announced another round of live military drills between 3 and 7 August in the surrounding waters of Taiwan; two of the six areas China marked for these drills were well within the twelve nautical miles of Taiwanese territorial waters. Five of the eleven missiles it fired reportedly landed in Japan's exclusive economic zone and four were fired over the Taiwan's outer space, a warning to both Japan and Taiwan not to breach China's "bottom lines". Though the fighter jets have been crossing the Median Line, but the battle ships are still off the limits, an indication that a serious conflict is ruled out.

Nevertheless, it could be gleaned from the "Fourth Taiwan Strait Crisis" that, China has immensely enhanced its defense capabilities. Today, China's air, naval and missile power has grown by leaps and bounds; it has broken through the "first island chain" and has challenged the "second island chain." On 31 July, the *Global Times* posted a video featuring the launch of a "DF-17" hypersonic missile, termed as the "aircraft carrier killer", a warning to the US that China has anti-access/area denial capabilities, and that it will not hesitate to use force if required to defend its core interests. The missile was publicly displayed at the National Day military parade on 1 October 2019 in Beijing. It is in this context that Shen Yi, director of Research Institution for Global Cyberspace Governance at Fudan University, has argued that the US must "avoid misunderstanding China's strategic capability to defend its core interests" and that gone is the "era of extremely asymmetrical power balance between China and the United States."

For President Xi Jinping, Taiwan's unification is part of the "great rejuvenation of the Chinese nation" project. Xi's third term is closely linked to the unification agenda. Therefore, in the face of China's stringent "dynamic zero" COVID policy, slower economic growth, real estate and mortgage crisis, show of force will rally good public support for a strong leader before the Beidaihe meeting and subsequently the 20th Party Congress. Taiwan, Japan and India are rallying points for Chinese leaders to divert attention from the domestic troubles. Recently, when social media suddenly discovered a "Chinese Yasukuni shrine" inside the Xuanzang Temple in Nanjing, where memorial tablets of Japanese war criminals [Matsui Iwane, Hisao Tani, Takeshi Noda and Gunkichi Tanaka] were displayed for worship, sparked a public outcry at a time when Japan debated to amend its pacifist constitution. Notwithstanding the "Hu Xijinisation" of China, Xi Jinping can ill afford to let the situation go out of control before the 20th Party Congress, therefore, a military conflict at this juncture is a big no. Had it been the case, China would have started military exercises in the surrounding waters of Taiwan on 3rd not 4th of

August. What China is likely to respond with in coming days is to render the Median Line ineffective by air and sea intrusion and assert its sovereignty; fire missiles in the surrounding waters, demonstrate its capabilities to blockade Taiwan, launch cyber-attacks, pass the unification law as was done in the case of Hong Kong security law, and impose economic sanctions to cripple Taiwan. China did resort to some of these in the wake of Pelosi's visit, more will depend on posturing from both the sides, especially after Xi's "re-election" later this year.

As for the US, it is clear that Pelosi's Taiwan visit has been politicised owing to the upcoming mid-term elections. She was incited and challenged by the republicans; former Secretary of the State, Mike Pompeo telling her "Nancy I will come with you" and former President Donald Trump slamming her making the "China mess" even worse. As for President Biden, though he didn't make moves to stop her, but did tell the public that the military "thinks it's not a good time right now" for her travel. In such a situation, had she cancelled her visit, it would have been a loss of face for her as well as the Biden administration. The US would have been levelled as a "paper tiger" and its international prestige further dented. However, since Pelosi defied all odds, breached China's "bottom line", she managed to rally the American opinion in support of her visit, called China's bluff, but also exposed Taiwan and the region for greater turbulence.

As for Taiwan, it has been caught between a rock and a hard place. While there is a bipartisan support for Pelosi's Taiwan visit, however, there are also voices who have opposed the visit. Chen Hui-wen, a Taiwanese journalist while hosting a UFO Network programme, requested Nancy Pelosi that "You (Pelosi) are on a graduation trip (毕业旅行), and we (Taiwanese) will bear the cost of Taiwan Strait crisis for you? Are you worth it?" The silence of President Tsai Ing-wen and her administration was understandable as Taiwan couldn't have afforded to offend Washington and anger Mainland at the same time, nevertheless, Tsai Ing-wen, chose Washington over China. Though Pelosi said that the "US will not abandon Taiwan", but would be tested when the PLA will use force to liberate Taiwan in future. Undoubtedly, Pelosi's visit is a precursor to a dangerous conflict in the Taiwan Strait.

Index